A Chain of Theological Principles
By John Arrowsmith

A Chain of Theological Principles
By John Arrowsmith

Edited and updated by C. Matthew McMahon and Therese B. McMahon
Transcribed by C. Matthew McMahon and Wayne Sparkman

Some language and grammar has been updated from the original manuscript. Any change in wording or punctuation has not changed the intent or meaning of the original author(s), and has been made to aid the modern reader.

Published by Puritan Publications
A Ministry of A Puritan's Mind
4101 Coral Tree Circle #214
Coconut Creek, FL 33073
www.puritanshop.com
www.apuritansmind.com
www.puritanpublications.com

This First Modernized Hardback Edition, 2012
Electronic Edition, 2012
Manufactured in the United States of America

ISBN: 978-1-938721-51-9
eISBN: 978-1-938721-50-2

TABLE OF CONTENTS

[Original Title Page]

ARMILLA CATECHETICA
A CHAIN OF PRINCIPLES;
OR,
AN ORDERLY CONCATENATION
of
Theological Aphorisms and Exercitations
IN WHICH
THE CHIEF HEADS OF CHRISTIAN RELIGION ARE
ASSERTED AND IMPROVED.

BY JOHN ARROWSMITH, D. D.
Late master both of *St. John's* and Trinity College successively,
and professor of divinity in the University of Cambridge.

To which is prefixed, an account of the life of the author,

"Because the Preacher was wise, he still taught the people knowledge; yes, he gave good heed, and sought out, and set in order many proverbs. The Preacher sought to find out acceptable words; and that which was written was upright, even words of truth. The words of the wise are as goads, and as nails fastened by the masters of assemblies, which are given by one shepherd," Ecclesiastes 12:9-11.

Edinburgh,
Printed by *Thomas Turnbull*
Old Assembly Close, 1882

CAMBRIDGE
Printed by *John Field*, printer to the University,
and are to be sold at the sign of the *Seven Stars* in Fleet-street
near S. Dunstans Church, London.
1659.

CHARACTER OF THE WORK

TO THE PRINTER,
December, 1822.

Sir,

At your request we readily express our opinion, of Arrowsmith's *Armilla Catechetica*, or *A Chain of Principles*, a handsome New Edition of which you are about to publish. That opinion is in a high degree favorable. In an age when learned judicious Theologians were perhaps in an unparalleled degree numerous, Dr. Arrowsmith held a distinguished place. None of his writings are more worthy of his high character, than that you are about to republish, with the exception of the Assembly's *Shorter Catechism*, in the compilation of which he had a principal hand. His *Armilla Catechetica* exhibits the first Principles of the Christian Faith with remarkable accuracy, and supports them by the most satisfactory arguments. In reprinting this work, we consider you as having done an important service to the Christian world, and hope your success will be such as to encourage you to give a modern form to some more of the little known, but highly valuable, *Treatises* of the Nonconformist Divines.

John Brown, *Whitburn.*
James Simpson, *Edinburgh.*
William Goold, *Edinburgh.*
John Colquhoun, D. D. *Leith.*
Robert Culbertson, *Leith.*

PREFACE

It is the profession of the Apostle Paul to the Corinthians in regard of himself, that "as a wise master-builder he had laid the foundation," (1 Corinthians 3:10) by which he would signify and declare this much to them; that the laying of the foundation is the work of a master-builder, as also that some skill and wisdom is both required and shown in the right laying of it.

This has been eminently the care of the Reverend, and learned Author of these ensuing *Discourses*, who being sufficiently sensible of the defect, as well as necessity of a settled and well-grounded knowledge in the fundamentals of the doctrine of Christ (Hebrews 6:1) has therefore with all diligence applied himself here in this treatise, which he has left to the world.

Neither was this more seasonable for the time than it was proper and fitting for the place, in which at first it received its beginning, being in one of the schools of the prophets, and a principal seminary of divines, St. John's College in Cambridge. Where being at that time *master* (and having as yet no other public employment, which might take him up) he was willing, rather, to lay himself forth so much in this way of his ministry, by *Catechetical Lectures* in that Chapel on the evenings of the Lord's Day. As Elisha when he came to Jericho,[1] casting salt into those springs of water, for preserving of all savouriness and fruitfulness in them.

Now these sermons of his he had drawn up (so far as to the preaching of them) into a complete *body of divinity* in thirty distinct Aphorisms, with their respective *Exercitations*; being also the sum, and extract of most of his former labors in the whole course of his ministry; which he had intended (if God had permitted) to have fitted, and prepared for the press. But being prevented of this his purpose by a long and tedious

[1] 2 Kings 2:21.

sickness, and much weakness growing on him, and at last by death itself, he finished only these six, which are now presented to view; and authorized under his own hand, for those which he allowed of as his, exclusively to any other besides. And he committed them to our care alone for the management of publishing of them; which accordingly we have endeavored to do with all fidelity.

The book is not unfitly described (and that by the author himself) *A Chain of Theological Principles*. For such is the nature of the truths propounded in it; as in order to other points of divinity, which are founded on them, so likewise to the life of a Christian, which is regulated greatly by them in their right improvement. Every article of Christian Religion has somewhat in it of principle to a gracious and holy conversation to which it is carried and directed. Here 1 Tim. 3:16, it is said, "Great is the mystery of godliness, God manifested in the flesh," *etc.* The incarnation, passion, resurrection, ascension of Christ and the like, are all matters of godliness; because they tend to godliness in their nature and discovery, as also promote godliness in the true compliance and closing with them.

It is called *A Chain of Theological Principles* for various reasons.

First, from the connection, which they have one with another. For like as in a chain there are diverse links joined together, and these in a mutual dependence, concomitance and subordination, even so is it likewise with the doctrines and principles of Christian Religion. They are connected and so knit together, as that there cannot be a denial of one, but more will consequently fall with it. Look as in things necessary to be done, there is a dependence and connection of commands, so that he, who breaks one law is interpreted to break *all the rest*, and to be guilty of a universal transgression; because he sins against that general authority, by which all the rest were given, so also in things necessary to be believed; he that denies one article of faith which is offered to him by

God to be received, denies the faith itself in its latitude,[2] as sinning against the general veracity of him that propounds it, and weakening all other truths, which are dependent on it. Though perhaps in so doing, he may not always actually intend it.

Secondly, it is a chain also for that special concord and agreement which it breeds (and ought to breed) in those that profess it, notwithstanding all collateral and circumstantial differences whatever. The principles of Christianity as they are united within themselves, so they do marvelously unite those who do really and cordially embrace them, and make them to speak the same thing that there are no divisions among them.[3] But they are to be perfectly joined together in the same mind, and in the same judgment, as the apostle expresses it. There it comes to pass, that there is so much distraction in opinion.[4] The primitive believers, while they were all of one faith, they were answerably all of one heart and of one soul; and so preserving the unity of the spirit in the bond of peace.[5]

Thirdly, A chain also for the worth and dignity of it, Proverbs 1:9, "They shall be an ornament of grace to thine head, and chains about thy neck." Persons of quality and authority are accustomed to wear their golden chains by which they are set out and adorned. It is the expression of Christ to his church, Song of Songs 1:10. "Thy cheeks are comely with rows of jewels: Thy neck with chains of gold." And again, Song of Songs 4:9. "Thou hast ravished my heart, my sister, my spouse, thou hast ravished my heart with one of thine eyes, with one chain of thy neck." This system and body of truth which is here in part commended to us, is the precious and glorious chain on the neck of the true spouse of Christ, which makes her look pleasingly, and amiably in the eyes of her beloved, and distinguishes her from all false and

---

[2] 1 Timothy 5:8.

[3] 1 Cor. 1:10.

[4] Acts 4:32.

[5] Eph. 4:3.

counterfeit lovers.

To all this we may finally add, what it is in the very work itself, and the contrivances of it: in which (not to anticipate the thoughts of others that shall peruse it) soundness of judgment with elegance of expression, sublimity of sentiment with sobriety of spirit, variety of reading with accuracy of composure; sweetness of wit with savouriness of heart, do seem to be linked together in so rare, and happy a conjunction, as makes this *Chain of Theological Principles* to be a chain of *pearls*.

The Lord by his Holy Spirit set home the truths in it on the hearts of all those who shall be made partakers of it. "To him be glory in the church by Christ Jesus throughout all ages world without end." Amen.

THOMAS HORTON.
WILLIAM DILLINGHAM.
Cambridge, November 2, 1659.

MEET JOHN ARROWSMITH

A Short Account of the Life and Character of John Arrowsmith, D.D. (1603-1659)

John Arrowsmith was born at Gateshead, near Newcastle on Tyne, in the county of Northumberland, in England, on the 29th day of March, in the year 1603, educated in St. John's College, Cambridge, and afterwards chosen fellow of Katherine Hall in the same University. It is remarkable, that this eminent divine was born in the same year, on the same day, and almost even at the same hour, with that much celebrated English divine, Dr. John Lightfoot.[6] Divine providence raised up most seasonably many very eminent men, about this time, who were great ornaments to the Reformed Church; and who have acquired immortal fame by their valuable writings, and have carefully transmitted their great usefulness to succeeding generations, in their learned and pious productions.

Respecting the early life and education of the illustrious subject of this Memoir, it is difficult to procure any particular account: but it is evident by his writings and employments, that he had been highly favored with a well-directed and liberal education. He was elected one of the University preachers, was sometime preacher of the gospel at Lynn or King's-Lynn, an ancient sea-port town, in the county of Norfolk, afterwards preacher at St. Martin's, Iron-monger Lane, London, and was called to sit in the Assembly of Divines at Westminster.[7] Here he was eminently distinguished by his abilities, learning and piety. Mr. Robert Baillie, one of the Commissioners from the Church of Scotland to the Assembly of Divines at Westminster, says when writing for Scotland

---

[6] *Lightfoot's Life*, prefixed to the folio edition of his *Works* 1684, and 1686.

[7] See Neal's list of the Assembly of Divines at Westminster. *Hist. Purit.* vol. iii. chapter ii. Bakers *MS. Collec.* vol. i. page 265.

respecting the business of the Assembly, "Our letter to foreign churches, formed by Mr. Marshall, except some clauses belonging to us put in by Mr. Henderson, is now turned into Latin by Mr. Arrowsmith a man with a glass eye, in place of that which was put out by an arrow, a learned divine, on whom the Assembly put the writing against the Antinomians."[8] He constantly attended during the Session and united with several of his brethren, was principally engaged in drawing up the Assembly's *Catechism* as he was one of the divines approved by the parliament to be consulted in ecclesiastical matters.

While the Reformation was advancing, several improvements were requisite, highly deserving the attention of our reformers, to render the English Universities more capable of answering the noble ends of their institution. Disgraceful charges were brought against these useful seminaries of learning: and our zealous ancestors consulted both the honor and interest of these venerable foundations, by endeavoring to amend in them what was amiss. Laudable attempts were made to restore the credit of their *Alma Mater*. Learning and piety were now the chief recommendations for offices. Accordingly, the utmost exertions were made, that all departments might be supplied with learned and pious men. The famous Earl of Manchester was appointed to visit the University of Cambridge, in order that he might correct what was wrong in it. Among other things, he ejected some heads of Colleges, and made choice of some divines, who were then sitting in the Assembly at Westminster, to be masters in their places: among whom was the illustrious subject of this memoir. Mr. Baillie, above-mentioned, who was then at Westminster, says, "When we were going to the rest of the propositions concerning the Presbytery, my Lord Manchester wrote to us from Cambridge, what he had done in the University, how he had ejected, for gross scandals, the heads of five Colleges: and that he had made choice of five of our

---

[8] Baillie's *Letters*, vol. i. page 414.

number, to be Masters in their places, Mr. Palmer, Vines, Seaman, Arrowsmith, and our countryman, Young, requiring the Assembly's approbation of his choice; which was unanimously given; for they are all very good and able divines."[9] Agreeably to this account, Mr. Arrowsmith having been first examined, and approved by the Assembly of Divines at Westminster, was constituted master of St. John's College, in the University of Cambridge, April 11, 1644, when Dr. Beale was ejected, in the following manner, "The Right Honorable Edward Earl of Manchester, in pursuance of an ordinance of Parliament, for regulating and reforming the University of Cambridge, came in person into the chapel of St. John's college, and, by the authority to him committed, did, in the presence of all the fellows then resident, declare and publish Mr. John Arrowsmith, to be constituted master of said college, in room of Dr. Beale late master there, but now justly and lawfully ejected; requiring him the said John Arrowsmith, then present, to take on him the said place, and did put him into the said master's seat or stall, within the said chapel; and did likewise straightly charge all and every of the fellows, etc. to acknowledge him to be actually master of the college, and sufficiently authorized to execute the said office."[10]

On his admission, he was required to make and subscribe a solemn declaration, of which the following is a copy;[11] "I, John Arrowsmith, being called and constituted by the right honorable Edward Earl of Manchester (who is authorized thereto by an ordinance of parliament) to be Master of St. John's College, in the University of Cambridge, with the approbation of the assembly of divines now sitting at Westminster, do solemnly and seriously promise, in the presence of Almighty God, the searcher of all hearts, that, during the time of my continuance in that charge, I shall faithfully labor to promote piety and learning in myself, my

---

[9] Baillie's *Letters*, vol. i. page 489.

[10] Neal's *Hist Purit.* vol. iii. chapter iii.

[11] Baker's *MS. Collec.* vol. xii. page 169, 170.

fellows, scholars and students, that do, or shall belong to the said college, agreeably to the late solemn league and covenant, by one sworn and subscribed, with respect to all the good and wholesome statues of the said college, and of the university, correspondent to the said covenant; and by all means to procure the welfare and perfect reformation both of that college and university, so far as to me appertains. JOHN ARROWSMITH."

During the above year he was one of the committee of learned divines which united with a committee of the lords and commons, to treat with the commissioners of the Church of Scotland, concerning an agreement in matters of Religion.[12]

By what our reformers did in this affair, they certainly made berth the public in general, and the University in particular, their debtors; however little they might both be disposed to acknowledge the obligation. This reformation attracted much notice; and was warmly praised by some persons, and as violently censured by others.[13] Mr. Neal says, "The Lord's Day was observed with uncommon rigor; there were sermons and prayers in all the churches and chapels both morning and afternoon. Vice and profaneness were banished, insomuch, that an oath was not to be heard within the walls of the University; and if it may be said without offence, the Colleges never appeared more like nurseries of religion and virtue than at this time." The same author adds, "I have before me the names of fifty-five persons, who, after they had been examined by the Assembly were put into vacant fellowships in the compass of the year 1644, and within six months more, all the vacancies were in a manner supplied, with men of approved learning and piety. From this time, the University of Cambridge enjoyed a happy tranquility, learning revived, religion land good manners were improved, at a time when the rest of the nation was in blood and confusion. And

---

[12] *Papers of Accem.* page 13.

[13] See Walker's *Attempt*, Part 1. respecting the Regulation of the University of Cambridge.

though this alteration was effected by a mixture of the civil and military power, yet in a little time things reverted to their former channel, and the statutes of the University were as regularly observed as ever." When our author was promoted to be Master of St. John's College, one of the schools of the prophets, and a principal seminary of divines, he conscientiously discharged the duties of his office, and pursued his studies and researches, with the most unceasing assiduity. While he had no other public employment, he delivered catechetical lectures in that chapel on the evenings of the Lord's Day, laying a good foundation of the doctrine of Christ, like a wise master-builder. As Elisha, when he came to Jericho, casting salt into the springs of water, for the preservation and health of all those persons who were in the place, he used his best endeavors to supply what was lacking, and to correct what was amiss. He explained the genuine sources of religious knowledge, in a most judicious and prudent manner, in order to promote a spirit of practical piety, and vital religion, in the hearts of his hearers, and especially of the candidates for the holy ministry. He was peculiarly attentive to the advancement of solid and useful learning in his College. Solid learning and true piety were most intimately connected in himself, and they were so connected in all his instructions to others. They ought always to go hand in hand, in the public teachers of Christianity. When he was master of this College, he began to apply himself, with eminent success, to that most elaborate and truly excellent work, *A Chain of Theological Principles*. This most beautiful and very important *Chain* was designed to form a complete Body of Divinity in thirty distinct *Aphorisms*, with their respective *Exercitations*. And the laborious author intended to have prepared these learned and pious productions for the press, if the Lord had spared and afforded him health: but sickness and death put an end to his labors, when he had finished only these six *Aphorisms*, with their respective *Exercitations*, which have been published to the world, and are entitled, *A Chain of Theological Principles.*[14]

He took his doctor's degree in the year 1647, and was chosen vice-chancellor of the University of Cambridge the same year. In the year 1651, he was presented to the rectory of Somersham, and was also constituted Professor of divinity, in this famous University, which office he resigned in 1665, and was succeeded by Dr. Tuckney.[15] In the year 1655, on the death of Dr. Hill, our illustrious author was removed to be Master of Trinity-College, in said University, which Wood says is the best preferment in it. In a situation so peculiarly agreeable to the views and habits of a scholar and of a divine, he eminently displayed his ardent zeal and great fidelity in the honorable service of his great Master. And the infinitely wise and sovereign Disposer of all things certainly regarded the University of Cambridge with peculiar favor, when he placed this learned and pious divine in such eminent stations there, where he was made the instrument of great usefulness. It was an observation of Tacitus, that advancement rarely mended the disposition of the human mind; only Vespasian was changed to the better. And Evagrius gives it as the high praise of the Emperor Mauritius, that in the height of all his majesty, he retained his ancient piety. It may be considered, by good information, as the high praise of the subject of this Memoir, as he was seemingly the subject of the unsearchable riches of divine grace, that in the height of all his preferments, he retained his former piety; and even improved greatly in literature, and in the disposition of his mind. There is growth both in knowledge and in grace.[16]

He was a very eminent and useful preacher of the glorious gospel of the grace of God. There is one remarkable instance of this transmitted to posterity, respecting Mr. John Machin, of Jesus' College, Cambridge. Mr. Machin was born

---

[14] Preface to the *Chain*, by Messrs Horton and Dillingham.

[15] Kennet's *Chronicle*, page 601, 935.

[16] Wood's *Athenae Oxon.* vol. ii. Col. 505. Calamy's *Account*, vol. ii. page 78. 294. Baker's *MS. Col.* vol. i. page 265.

at Seabridge in Staffordshire, Oct. 2, 1624. He spent his youth in vanity and sin. When about twenty-one years of age, he went to the University, without any view to the holy ministry, or to a continuance there. But God was pleased, on his first going thither, to effect a gracious change in him, chiefly by the preaching of Dr. Hill; and that of Dr. Arrowsmith was much to his comfort and edification. No sooner did he find this blessed change in his heart, than his friends found it by his letters; by which, together with his exemplary conversation afterward, he is said to have been the instrument of converting his three sisters, and there was room to hope, both his parents.[17]

Dr. Arrowsmith was also reckoned an eminently learned and highly useful professor of divinity. He was truly a turning and shining light, able to distinguish truth from error, and pure worship from superstitious devices. He was an enlightened leader, and careful instructor of others. He was well qualified to write and discourse on theological subjects with precision, elegance, ease, and perspicuity. By his great ingenuity and erudition, he was enabled to throw light on many difficult passages of the sacred writings that had been ill understood, and not well applied. Great dexterity, good judgment, profound and admirable learning, with true piety, were very conspicuous, both in his ministry, and in the divinity chair. He acquired a distinguished reputation in the University, by his excellent wit, amiable manners, singular prudence and plainness. His wit and erudition, being sanctified by the grace of God, were successfully employed by him, as weapons against the adversaries of truth and of religion.

He continued to labor with indefatigable zeal in his Master's service, until he was seized with a lingering sickness, terminating in death, which prevented the completion of his noble designs.[18] Information respecting the manner of the death of this eminent divine is not attainable. He died in

---

[17] Palmer's *Nonconformist's Memorial*, under Whitley, in Cheshire.

[18] See Prefaces to his *Chain*, and *God-man*.

February, 1659, aged 57 years, and his remains were interred in Trinity college chapel, the 24th of the same month.[19]

Four lines of a little poem Mr. Smart's, on the death of a Mr. Newbury, after a lingering illness, which are appropriate, may be here introduced.

> Hereforth be every tender tear suppressed.
> Or let us weep for joy that he is blest!
> From grief to bliss, from earth to heav'n remov'd,
> His memory honored, as his life beloved.[20]

Mr. Neal says, "Dr John Arrowsmith was of an unexceptionable character of learning and piety. He was an acute disputant, and a judicious divine, as appears by his *Tactica Sacra*, a book of great reputation in those times."[21] He was undoubtedly a real friend to true-religion, and has transmitted to posterity a shining example of piety and diligence in his Master's service. His name ought to be in the list of the eminent divines and, men of learning, who were real ornaments to the Reformed Church in the seventeenth century.

Dr. Arrowsmith is a writer of distinguished excellence. He may be justly numbered among the benefactors of English literature. By one who appears to have been well acquainted with him, he is characterized "as a burning and a shining light who, by his indefatigable study of the sublime mysteries of the gospel, spent himself to the utmost, to explicate the darkest places of scripture. This he did with a view to enlighten others in the knowledge of Jesus Christ. He was a holy and learned divine: firm and zealous in his attachment to the cause of Christ, from which no worldly allurement would shake his

---

[19] Wood's *Athenae Oxon.* vol. ii. Col. 505. page 371. and title-page of Arrowsmith's *Chain*. Calamy's *Account*, vol. ii. page 78, 294. Baker's *MS. Col.* vol. i. page 265.
[20] Monthly Review Enlarged, Jan. 1792. vol. vii.
[21] Hist. Purit. vol. iii. 1644.

faith, or move his confidence. He was a man of a thousand. Those who knew him could give testimony of his diligence, his zeal, his integrity. His public ministry discovered his great dexterity, sound judgment, admirable learning, and indefatigable labors. His soul aspired after more than his weak and sickly body was able to perform. He put forth his energy beyond his strength to do good."[22]

In his writings, we clearly see the beautiful image of a mind which was judicious and serious, richly furnished and adorned with the comely ornaments both of learning and of piety. His writings *are:*

1. *The Covenant-Avenging Sword Brandished.* A sermon preached from Lev. 26:25 before the House of Commons, at their solemn fast, Jan. 25th, 1642. 4to. pp. 28. London, 1643. This sermon was also printed at Dumfries, 1797. Subsequently printed by *Puritan Publications* in 2011.
2. *England's Ebenezer*: or, *Stone of Help.* A sermon preached from 1 Sam. 7:12 to both Houses of Parliament in Christ's church, the Lord Mayor and Aldermen of the city of London being present, on a day of solemn thanksgiving, March 12th, 1644. 4to. pp. 34. London, 1645.
3. *A Great Wonder in Heaven*: or, *A Lively Picture of the Militant Church, drawn by a divine Pencil.* A sermon preached from Rev. 12:1, 2. before the Commons, at Westminster, Jan. 27th, 1647. 4to. London, 1647.
4. *Tactica Sacra*, sive de milite Spirituals Pugnante, Vincente, & Triumphante, Dissertatio, Tribus Libris comprehensa, 4to. pp. 363. Cantabrigiae, 1657. This learned dissertation, which is divided into three books, respecting the spiritual soldier fighting, conquering, and triumphing, well deserves the perusal of the scholar, who can read Latin.
5. *A Chain of Principles:* or, *An orderly Concatenation of Theological Aphorisms and Exercitations; in which the Chief Heads of Christian*

[22] Arrowsmith's *God Man*, Preface, edition 1660.

Religion are asserted and improved. 4to. pp. 490. Cambridge, 1659. This is a book of real worth; and it is strange that it has not been oftener printed. It will amply repay the trouble of a perusal. It occurs still in the catalogues of books, especially in London. It was formerly cheap, 6*s.* or 7*s.* but now 15*s.* It appears in several parts of Scotland, where it is an ornament to many good libraries.

6. *God-Man.* An Exposition of the first eighteen verses of the first chapter of the gospel according to John. 4to. pp. 311. London, 1660. Sells now in London at 7*s.* 6*d.* Dr. Cotton Mather, in his *Student and Preacher*, says, "Everything of Arrowsmith is admirable." "The names of Lightfoot, Selden, Gataker, Greenhill, Arrowsmith, Twisse, Bishop Reynolds, Wallis, *etc.* will always be famous in the learned world."[23]

[23] Neal's *Hist. Purit.* vol. iii. chapter x.

OUTLINE OF THE WORK

APHORISM[24] I

Man's blessedness does not consist in a confluence of worldly accommodations, which are all vanity of vanities, but in the fruition of God in Christ who only is the strength of our hearts, and our portion forever.

EXERCITATION[25] I.
Psalm 144. End opened. Blessedness, what Solomon's scope in Ecclesiastes. Why he describes himself *Qoheleth*. His testimony concerning the creatures. Their threefold transcendent vanity. Intellectual accomplishments brought under the same censure, by reason of the folly, enmity, anxiety, and insufficiency that attend them. An apostrophe to the world.

EXERCITATION II.
A gloss on Psalm 36:8. God in Christ: a soul-satisfying object. The circular motion of human souls, and their only rest. A threefold fullness of God and Christ opposite to the threefold vanity of the creatures.

EXERCITATION III.
Two conclusions from Psalm 73:26-26. The Psalmist's case stated. The frequent complication of corporal and spiritual troubles. How God strengtheneth his people's hearts against their bodily distempers; how under discouragements of spirit. The secret supports of saving grace. What kind of portion

[24] An *Aphorism* is a pithy observation that contains a general truth. A concise statement of a scientific principle, typically by an ancient classical author.

[25] An *Exercitation* is an act of the mind in the practice or training for logical thinking. It can also be the performance of a religious observance; an act of worship. In this work it is the performance of worship in logical thinking and *exegesis* pertaining to the fundamental truths of the Scriptures outlining the beliefs of the Christian Religion.

God is to the Saints. A congratulation of their happiness in this.

EXERCITATION IV.
The first inference grounded on Isaiah 55:1, 2. by way of invitation, backed with three encouragements to accept it, *viz.* The fullness of that soul-satisfaction which God gives, the universality of its tender, and the freeness of its communication. The second by way of expostulation, and that both with worldlings and saints. A conclusion by way of soliloquy.

APHORISM II.

We are conducted, to the fruition of God in Christ by Christian religion, contained in the divine oracles of Holy Scripture.

EXERCITATION I.
The safe conduct of saints, signified by the pillar in Exodus, performed by the counsel of God himself, the abridgement in which we have in the doctrine of Christian religion. How that tends to blessedness.

EXERCITATION II.
The insufficiency of other religions for bringing men to the enjoyment of God inferred from their inability to discover his true worship. John 4:24 opened. God to be worshipped in and through Christ a lesson not taught in nature's school. Faults in Aristotle's *Ethics.*

EXERCITATION III.
Oracles of God vocal, or written. Books of scripture so called in five respects, *viz.* In regard of their declaring and foretelling, their being consulted, prized and preserved.

EXERCITATION IV.

How Scripture-oracles far excel those of the heathen in point of perspicuity, of piety, of veracity, of duration and of authority. The divine authority of Scripture asserted by arguments. An inference from the whole Aphorism.

APHORISM III.

Scripture oracles, supposing it sufficiently clear by the light of nature, that there is a God, make a further discovery of what he is in his essence, subsistence and attributes.

EXERCITATION I.
1 Cor. 15:34 expounded. Opinionists compared to sleepers and drunkards. Three observations from the end of the verse. What knowledge of God is unattainable in this life. What may be had. The knowledge we have concerning God distinguished into Natural, Literal, and Spiritual.

EXERCITATION II.
That there is a God, the prime dictate of natural light; deducible from man's looking backward to the creation, forward to the rewards and punishments dispensed after death, upward to the angels above us, downward to inferior beings, within ourselves to the composition of our bodies, and dictates of our consciences, about us to the various occurrences in the world.

EXERCITATION III.
Reason's three ways of discovering God fall short of manifesting what he is. The expression in Exodus 3:14 most comprehensive. A brief exposition of it. Satan's impudence. Nature and art are both unable to discover the Trinity. What Scripture reveals about it, Basil's *memento.* Julian's *impiety.* Socinians branded. The three persons compared to those three wells in Genesis 26.

EXERCITATION IV.
Divine Attributes calling for transcendent respect. They are

set down in the Scripture so as to curb our curiosity, to help our infirmity, to prevent our misapprehensions, and to raise our esteem of God. Spiritual knowledge super-adding to literal clearness of light, sweetness of taste, sense of interest, and sincerity of obedience.

APHORISM IV.

Goodness and Greatness are attributes so comprehensive, as to include a multitude of divine perfections.

EXERCITATION I.
God described from goodness and greatness both without and within the Church. A lively portraiture of his goodness in the several branches of it. Exodus 34:6-7. Bowels of mercy implying inwardness and tenderness. Our bowels of love to God, of compassion to brethren. Mercy not to be refused by unbelief, nor abused by presumption.

EXERCITATION II.
Grace what? From it spring Election, Redemption, Vocation, Sanctification, and Salvation. A *caveat* not to receive it in vain. It purges and cheers. Glosses on Titus 2:11-12 and 2 Thess. 2:26-27. The exaltation of free grace exhorted to. Longsuffering not exercised towards evil angels, but towards men of all sorts. It leads to repentance, is valued by God, and must not be slighted by us. A dreadful example of goodness despised.

EXERCITATION III.
The bounty of God declared by his benefits, *viz.* giving his Son to free us from hell, his Spirit to fit us for heaven, his angels to guard us on earth, large provisions in the way, and full satisfaction at our journey's end. John 3:16, James 1:5 and Psalm 24:1 glossed. Isaiah 25:6 alluded to. Inferences from Divine Bounty, beneficence to Saints; not dealing niggardly with God, exemplified in David, Paul, and Luther. Truth in God is without all mixture of the contrary. It appears in his

making good of promises, and threatenings, teaching us what to perform and what to expect.

EXERCITATION IV.
Keeping mercy for thousands explained. Men exhorted to trust God with their posterity. Luther's last *Will and Testament*. Iniquity, transgression and sin, what they are. Six scripture expressions setting out the pardon of it. God's goodness in it. Faith and repentance the way to it. Pardon in the court of heaven, and of conscience. The equity and necessity of forgiving one another. We are to forgive as God for Christ's sake forgives us, *viz.*, heartily, speedily, frequently, and thoroughly. A twofold remembrance of injuries, in *cautelam, et in vindictam.*

EXERCITATION V.
The latter clauses of Exod. 24:7 so translated and expounded as to contain an eighth branch of goodness, *viz.* clemency in correcting. Equity in visiting iniquities of the fathers on the children. Clemency in stopping at the third and fourth generation. A lesson for magistrates. A speech of our queen Elizabeth. God's proclamation in Exodus 34. Improved by Moses in Numbers 14.

EXERCITATION VI.
Job 11:7-9 expounded of Divine Greatness. Three reasons of that exposition, with the resolution of a question about it. The height of God's universal, unaccountable, omnipotent sovereignty proved and improved.

EXERCITATION VII.
The depth of divine omniscience seen in discerning the deep things of man, yes of Satan, yes of God. Our ignorance discovered and acknowledged. The longitude of God's perfection stated. Eternity proper to him. Not assumed by, or ascribed to men without blasphemy.

EXERCITATION VIII.
Divine immensity shadowed out by the breadth of the sea Divine omnipresence cleared and vindicated. The proposal of it as an antidote against sinning in secret. Five practical Corollaries from the greatness of God in general.

APHORISM V.

The goodness and greatness of God are both abundantly manifold by his decrees of election and preterition, together with his works of creation and providence.

EXERCITATION I.
How predestination comes to be treated of here. Election described from the nature, antiquity, objects, products and cause of it. Rom. 11:33, 2 Tim. 1:9, with Titus 1:2. Ephesians 1:4, with Matthew 25:34 opened. Of acts supposing their objects. Of acceptance of persons, what it is; and that predestination does not import it. Acts 13:48 expounded and vindicated. Whether one elect may become a reprobate? The negative maintained, and 1 Cor. 9:24-26 cleared. Eph. 5:11 enlightened. Concerning the good pleasure of God's will, and the counsel of it.

EXERCITATION II.
Preterition described. The term defended. Eph. 1:4 compared with Rev. 17:8. Eph. 1:9 and Rom. 11:13 expounded. God not bound to any creature, except by promise. The parable in Matt. 20 urged. The three consequents of negative reprobation. Dr. Davenant's *animadversions* against Mr. Hoard's book recommended. The goodness of God manifested in election, as in a most free, peculiar, ancient, leading and standing favor.

EXERCITATION III.
An Introduction to Romans 9. Most part of that chapter expounded, together with various passages in chapter 10 and

11 for proof of these two conclusions. 1. That Paul in Rom 9. doth on occasion propound and prosecute the doctrine of predestination. 2. That he derives the decree of preterition from the sovereign greatness of God. A confectary showing how useful the said doctrine is to sober minds.

EXERCITATION IV.
Creation what. Pythagoras and Trismegistus. Hebrews 6:3 opened. Scripture philosophy. *Ex nihilo nihil fit*, how true. Creature what. God's goodness in the works of creation, particularly in the framing of Adam. The consultation on which, pattern after which, parts of which he framed. Two histories, one of a priest, the other of a monk. The original body and soul improved.

EXERCITATION V.
The same, and other attributes of God declared from his providential dispensations, the interchangeableness in which largely discoursed of and applied from Ecclesiastes 7:14. A gloss on Isaiah 10:11. Cheerfullness a duty in six respects; crosses how to be considered.

APHORISM VI.

Providence extends itself not only to all created beings and to all human affairs, especially those that concern the church; but even to the sins of angels and men.

EXERCITATION I.
Introduction concerning the contents of this Aphorism. Providence over all created beings. Preservation of men to be ascribed to God himself, not to good men, yes, not to good angels, in whom heart-searching and patience are wanting. Providence reaching to human affairs; economical, civil, military, moral and ecclesiastical. Anastasius' design frustrated. Rome and our nation instanced in. J.G. castigated.

EXERCITATION II.

Deuteronomy 11:12 opened. God's care proved from the provision he makes for inferior creatures. From Israel's conduct. From the experiments and acknowledgements of saints in all ages. Experiments of the Virgin Mary, Hechelters, Musculus, acknowledgements of Jacob, David, Psalmist, Augustine and Urain. From God's causing things and acts of all sorts to cooperate to the good of the Saints, Isaiah 27:2-3 explained. The Church preserved from, in, and by danger.

EXERCITATION III.
Hard-heartedness made up of unteachableness in the understanding, untractableness in the will, unfaithfulness in the memory, insensibleness in the conscience, and unmoveableness in their affections. Metaphors to express it from the parts of man's body, stones and metals, a soft heart. Mischief, searedness and virulency attendants of hardness. God's concurring to it by way of privation, negation, permission, presentation. Tradition to Satan. Delivering up to lusts and infliction.

EXERCITATION IV.
Objections against, and corollaries from the foregoing propositions. The least things provided for. Luther's admonition to Melancthon. Maximilian's address. Pliny's unbelief. The Psalmist stumbles at the prosperity of the wicked. His recovery by considering it was not full, was not to be final. The superintendency of providence over military and civil affairs in particular. The church's afflictions. Promises cautioned. Duty of casting care on God. He no author of sin. The attestation of this state, and of this writer.

APHORISM I

Man's blessedness does not consist in a confluence of worldly accommodations, which are all vanity of vanities; but in the fruition of God in Christ who only is the strength of our hearts, and our portion forever.

EXERCITATION I.

Psalm 144. End opened. Blessedness what. Solomon's scope in Ecclesiastes. Why he describes himself Qoheleth. His testimony concerning the creatures. Their threefold transcendent vanity. Intellectual accomplishments brought under the same censure, by reason of the folly, enmity, anxiety, and insufficiency that attend them. An apostrophe to the world.

This is a case which has long since been determined by the Prophet David, who in Psalm 144th, after he had twice charged those whom he calls *strange children*, with a *mouth speaking vanity*, once in the 8th and again in the 11th verse, goes on to record (as good interpreters,[26] ancient and modern do conceive) the substance of their vain talk in a way of boasting about their flourishing condition in reference to the thriving of children, *Our sons*, say they, *are as plants grown up in their youth*, (not wishing they might, as we read it, but boasting they *were*) *our daughters as corner-stones, polished after the similitude of a palace*; to plenty of provision, *Our garners are full, affording all manner of store*; to increase and usefulness of cattle. *Our sheep bring forth thousands and ten thousands in our streets; our oxen are strong to labor*; to peace and tranquility of estate, *There is no breaking in, nor going out, no complaining in our streets.* On this they applaud themselves, and as placing their happiness in such outward accommodations, say, (as it is in the former part of verse 15.)

[26] Augustan. Genebrard. Ainsworth. John Baptist. Folengius in Psalm 144.

Happy are the people that are in such a case.[27] (Which sense is extremely favored, not only by the vulgar Latin, inserting *Dixerunt*, but also by the Septuagint, who render it by ἐμακάρισαν, both concurring to have it read, They pronounced the people blessed that were in such a case.) Then comes in the last words according to this interpretation, as the Psalmist's resolution in the point, by way of *epanorthosis*, or in express contradiction rather to so gross a mistake, *yea blessed are the people who have the Lord for their God.*

§2. There is one *center* in which the desires of all men meet, however distanced in the *circumference*; one port, for which, they are all *bound*, although embarked in several vessels, and affecting different winds to sail by. That center and port is *blessedness*, which may admit of this description. It is the acquiescence of rational appetites in an object so full of real and durable goodness, as to be able fully to satisfy all their longings. The question debated in *Ecclesiastes* is whether anything under the sun is such an object. The Preacher resolves it in the *negative*, by reason of that universal vanity which overspreads the whole creation. Therefore it is, that the eye (as he tells us) is not satisfied with seeing, nor the ear with hearing, (Eccl. 1:8) because these two senses of discipline, when they have given their utmost intelligence, cannot present, the soul of man with any created accommodations perfectly good without deject, and *perpetually* good without *decay*. Solomon was one that had both *men* and *money* at command, to assist him in making difficult and costly, experiments; a *wise* heart able to dive into nature's secrets; a peaceable reign, in which he met with nothing to take him off from the work, or disturb him in it; *strong inclinations* and constant *endeavors* to find out the utmost of what could possibly be discovered in any creature; yet he it is that concludes, on trial, not on hear-say, or conjecture, "*Vanity*

[27] *Beatum dixerunt populum cui haec sunt.*

of vanities," *Qoheleth* says, "*vanity of vanities, all is vanity*," (Eccl. 1:1).

§3. Qoheleth, which is the style he gives himself in that book, comes from a root, that signifies to *collect* and *gather*, and, though it is of a feminine termination, is, for lack of a common, gender, in the Hebrew tongue, (as other words of the like form) capable enough of a masculine construction. To him it may be thought agreeable on four different notions, each in which contributes much validity to what he testifies. First, as a *Preacher*, who having gathered various arguments to convince the sons of men of the insufficiency of all things below God himself to render them happy, in that discourse speaks as to a Congregation; where in the Proverbs he had spoken as to one man, frequently using this compellation, *My son*. So Jerome, and Cajetan. Secondly, as a writer, who had collected into a Synopsis all the opinions of those who had been taken for wise men by their several followers concerning happiness, confuting such as were erroneous. So Grotius. Thirdly, as a student, who had gathered much wisdom by observation and experience, of which he there gives demonstration. So Broughton. Lastly, as a penitent, who having by his gross idolatry and other sins fallen from communion with the people of God, and being desirous to have his return stand on record, and to testify his repentance in that book, for the church's satisfaction gathers together many experiments of his own personal folly, and makes an humble confession of them: whereon he was restored, and again *gathered* into the bosom of the Church. So Cartwright and Junius. The witness we see is beyond exception.

§4. In his testimony, "*vanity of vanities, vanity of vanities, all is vanity*," the assertion is repeated as in Pharaoh's dream, to show its certainty; and the term of vanity doubled, partly to manifest the transcendence of it, as the most holy place was described *The Holy of Holies*, and the most eminent canticle *The Song of Songs*: and partly to note the *multiplicity*, as Scripture calls that the *Heaven of Heavens*, which, being highest, contains many heavens within its circumference. For there is in the creatures a threefold transcendent vanity as may appear in that *they are:*

First, so unprofitable, as to be hurtful with. On this the Preacher seems to have had a special eye, because after all is *vanity*, he subjoins immediately, "What profit has a man of all his labor, which he has taken under, the sun?" (Eccl. 1:3). He has done nothing but filled his hands as it were with air, who has been toiling all his days to replenish his chests with wealth, "*And what profit has he that has labored for the wind?*" (Eccles. 5:16). Just so much, and no more, than that Emperor got,[28] who having run through various and great employments, made this open acknowledgement, *Qmnia fui, sed nihil profuit*, I have been all things, but it has advantaged me nothing at all. Neither are they simply unprofitable, but this sore evil did Solomon see under the sun, namely, "*Riches kept for the owners of it to their hurt*," (Eccl. 5:13). They often prove prejudicial to the outward man, exposing it to danger. Whoever robbed a poor beggar, or begged a poor fool? more often to the inward, where that of Agur, *Give me not riches, but feed me with food convenient for me; lest I be full, and deny thee, and say who is the Lord?*"[29] As if abundance made way for Atheism in those that know not how to manage it. Plenty betrays many souls to slavery. Which made the good Emperor Maximilian second of that name, when a mass of treasure was brought in, refuse to have it hoarded up, professing himself *a keeper of men, and not of money*,[30] and fearing lest by falling into love therewith he should cease to be a Sovereign Lord, and become a servant to the mammon of unrighteousness.

§5. Secondly, so deceitful as to frustrate expectation when men's hopes of advantage by them are at the highest, Let

---

[28] Septimius Severus.

[29] Proverbs 30:8-9.

[30] *Hominum non opum mihi demandata est custodia; quibus si semel capiar illico e Rege servus futurus sum.* Beyerlinck. *Apophtheg. Christian*, page 210.

him that would rightly conceive of vanity (a late Casuist says)[31] imagine the idea of a thing made up of nothing as the matter, and a lie as the form of it. Scripture speaks of *lying vanities*, and useth the terms deceitful and vain as equipollent. "Favor (Bathsheba says) is deceitful, (Proverbs 31:30) and beauty is vain." The Poet interprets Vanus by *mendax*;[32] and in old Latin *vanare* was the same with *fallere*. The creatures are accustomed shamefully to frustrate men's hopes, and seldom to make good to the *enjoyer* what they promised to the expectant. Yes as Jonah's gourd (having done him no service in the night, when he did not need it) withered in the *morning*, when he hoped for most benefit by it against the ensuing heat of the day: so the blessings of this World frequently wither at such times as we looked to find the most freshness in, and refreshments from them. None but Haman was invited with the King to Queen Esther's banquet; this filled his mind with windy hopes, which ended soon after in his ruin.

§6. Thirdly, so inconstant and mutable as to be gone all on the sudden without giving their owners warning. That is said to be vain which vanishes. "Man is like to vanity, his days are a shadow that passeth away," (Psalm 144:4). Accordingly the two sons of the first man carried in their names a memorandum of what they and their posterity were to expect. *Cain* signifies possession, *Abel* vanity. All the possessions of this world are of a vanishing nature, and liable to a speedy decay; or rather, they are not possessions but pageants, which while they please us, pass away from us in a moment.[33] Those we have here are running banquets, delicate, and served in with state, but soon over. How many does swift destruction snatch every day out of the arms of worldly felicity, and stab to the heart at one blow! Behold Belshazzar in the midst of his cups and concubines struck into a deadly trembling. Herod,

---

[31] D. Sanders, *praelect de Jurament*. page 40. Jonah 2:8.

[32] Virg. *Aeneid*. 2. carm. 80.

[33] *Quod miraris pompa est. Ostenduntur istae res, non possidentnr, & dum placent traseunt*. Senec. *epist*. 110.

when the people had newly invested him with a *godhead*, presently, after it was well on, had it pulled over his ears, and became a prey to worms. The rich man in our Savior's parable invited himself to a feast of delicacy, and talked of prosperity laid up for many years; but that very night was his soul required of him to pay the reckoning.

§7. These things duly weighed, I could not but be affected with that gallant speech of a Christian writer, "If the fruition of all the World were to be sold, it would not be so much worth as; the labor of one's opening his mouth only to say, I will not buy it," yet wondered less at it, when I remembered how much some even heathen philosophers[34] have disdained to think of scraping to themselves a happiness out of the world's dunghill, how generously they have professed their living above such accommodations as it affords. I am really greater (could Seneca say) and born to far greater things then that I should become a slave to my outward man.[35] For there are some higher acquits gloried in by more sublimed flesh and blood, as much more conducing to blessedness, I mean intellectual accomplishments of wisdom and learning. Yet, as when the enquiry was, "Where shall wisdom be found, and where is the place of understanding? The depth said it is not in me, and the sea said it is not with me," (Job 28:13-14). So, if the same question is put concerning *happiness*, worldly wisdom itself must return the same answer, and say *It is not in me*, by reason of the folly, enmity, anxiety and insufficiency that attend it, so that the preacher might well determine even of it, "This is also vanity," (Eccl. 2:15).

§8. I. Folly. "The wisdom of this world is, foolishness with God," (1 Cor. 3:19). So the Apostle, who speaking elsewhere of those who bore the name of most knowing men, saith, "they became vain in their imaginations and their foolish heart was darkened, professing themselves wise, they became

---

[34] P. De la serv's *myrrhour*, page 85.

[35] *Major sum, el ad majora genitus, quam ut mancipium sim mei corporis*, Senec. *epist.* 65.

fools," (Rom. 1:21-22). With men indeed a little science may make a great show; but he only is wise in God's esteem who is wise to Salvation. Give me a man as full of policy as was Achitophel, of eloquence as Tertullus, of learning as the Athenians, were in Paul's time. If with Achitophel he plot against the people of God, with Tertullus have the poison of asps under his lips, with those Athenians be wholly given to superstition; for all his policy, eloquence, and learning often may be bold to call him *fool* in Scripture's language. The learned *Logician*, whom Satan daily deceives by his sophistry, and keeps from offering up to God reasonable service, is no better than a fool for all his skill. Nor the subtle Arithmetician who has not learned to number his days that he might apply his heart to sifting wisdom. Nor the cunning Orator, who although he is of singular abilities in the art of persuading men, is of Agrippa's temper himself but *almost persuaded to be a Christian*.

§9. II. Enmity. "The wisdom of the flesh is enmity against God," (Rom. 8:7). He that calls it so, found it to be so indeed in his own experience. For Paul, was nowhere more opposed than in Greece (Acts 17:16, 18, 32) the eye of the world, more derided than at Athens the eye of Greece. Where it is that St. James, not contenting himself with the epithets of earthly and sensual[36] brands it also with the name of *Devilish* wisdom. What else was Matchievel but the devil's professor in politics, as Arius, Socinus, (and such like masters of error) have been in Divinity! And of such *Devilish* wisdom what other issue can be expected but that it should lead men to the devil from whom it came? Where Bernard leaves them saying, "Suffer the wise men of this world to go wisely down to hell."[37]

§10. III. Anxiety. Wisdom is neither attained with ease, as requiring much study which is a weariness to the *flesh*;

[36] James 3:15.

[37] *Sinete sapientes hujus seculi alta sapientes, & terram liquentes sapienter descender in infernum.* De vita solitar.

neither does it, when attained, administer ease, but the contrary rather; for when study has been midwife to knowledge, knowledge becomes nurse to grief. Let Solomon speak, "I gave my heart to know wisdom, I perceived that this also is vexation of spirit. For in much wisdom is much grief and he that increaseth knowledge increaseth sorrow," (Eccl. 1:17-18). Many and dreadful are the damps that seize on such as dig deep in the mines of learning. Sharp minds like sharp knives often cut their owner's fingers. The deep reach of a prudent man makes him aggravate such evils as are already come on him, by considering every circumstance so as to accent every sad consideration, and anticipate such as are yet to come, by galloping in his thoughts to meet them. Had not Achitophel been so wise, as to foresee his inevitable ruin in the remote causes of it, when Hushai's counsel was embraced, he would never have made so much haste, as he did, to hang himself.

§11. IV. Lastly, insufficiency to render men either *holy* or *happy*. For when the worldly-wise have dived into the bottom of nature's sea, they are able to bring up from there instead of these pearls of price, nothing but hands full of shells and gravel. Knowledge indeed and good party managed by grace are like the rod in Moses' hand, wonder-workers; but turn to serpents when they are cast on the ground, and employed in promoting earthly designs. Learning in religious hearts, like that gold in the Israelites earrings is a most precious ornament. But if men pervert it to base wicked ends, or begin to make an idol of it, as they did a golden calf of their ear-rings, it then becomes an abomination. Doubtless these later times, in which so many knowing men are of a filthy conversation, and have joined feet of clay to their heads of gold, would have afforded good store of additional observations to him that wrote the famous book concerning the vanity of sciences,[38] which appears in nothing more than their inability to produce suitable deportment in such as enjoy

[38] *Corn. Agrippa.*

them; without which there can be no solid foundation laid for true happiness.

§12. Wherefore think to yourself at length, O deluded world, and write over all your school-doors, "Let not the wise man glory in his wisdom," (Jer. 9:23), over all your court gates, "Let not the mighty man glory in his might," over all your exchanges and banks, "Let not the rich man glory in his riches." Write on your looking-glasses that of Bathsheba, "favor is deceitful and beauty is vain;" (Prov. 31:30), on your mews and aruntilery-yards that of the Psalmist, "God delighteth not in the strength of a horse, he taketh not pleasure in the legs of a man;" (Psa. 147:10), on your taverns, inns, and ale-houses, that of Solomon, "wine is a mocker, strong drink is ringing, and whosoever is deceived thereby is not wise," (Prov. 20:1), on your magazines and wardrobes, that of our Savior, "lay not up for yourselves treasures on earth, where moth and rust doth corrupt, and in here thieves break through and steal, (Matthew 6:19). Write on your counting houses that of Habakkuk, "woe to him that increaseth that which is not his, how long? and to him that ladeth himself with thick clay," (Hab. 2:6). Write on your play-houses that of Paul, "lovers of pleasure more than lovers of God," (2 Tim. 3:4). Write on your banqueting houses, that of the same holy apostle, "meats for the belly and the belly for meats, but God shall destroy both them and it;" (1 Cor. 6:13). Yes on all your accommodations that of the preacher, "all is vanity and vexation of spirit," (Eccl. 1:14).

EXERCITATION II.

A gloss on Psalm 36:8. God in Christ: a soul-satisfying object. The circular motion of human souls, and their only rest. A threefold fullness of God and Christ opposite to the threefold vanity of the creatures.

§1. What shall we then say? Are the sons of men, in whom such strong desires and longings after blessedness are implanted, left without all possible means of attaining that in which rational appetites may acquiesce? God forbid. "They shall be abundantly satisfied with the fatness of thy house, and thou shalt make them drink of the river of thy pleasures," (Psa. 36:7-8). So David to God concerning such as put their trust under the shadow of his wings. Creature comforts are but lean blessings in comparison, there is a fatness in God's house, such as satisfies, and that abundantly. They afford but drops, where Christ is a river of pleasures. Look as when an army of men comes to drink at a mighty river, a Jordan, a Thames, they all go satisfied away, none complaining of a lack, none envying another, because there was water enough for them all. Where if they all had come to a little brook there would not is has been found enough to quench the thirst of every one. So here note it. The creatures are small brooks that have but a little water in them, "yea broken cisterns that hold no water," (Jer. 2:13). No wonder if souls return empty from them. But Christ has a river for his followers, able to give them all satisfaction. We must not expect more from a thing then the Creator has put into it. He never intended to put the virtue of soul-satisfying into any mere creature, but has reserved to himself, Son and Spirit the contenting of spirits as a principal part of divine prerogative. To such as expect it elsewhere, that person or thing they rely on may say as Jacob did to Rachel, "*Am I in God's stead?*" (Gen. 30:2).

§2. It is certain that none can make our souls happy but *God* who made them, nor any give satisfaction to them but *Christ* who gave satisfaction for them.[39] They were fashioned at first according to the image of God, and nothing short of him who is described "the brightness of his Father's glory, and the express image of his person, can replenish them."[40] As when there is a curious impression left on wax, nothing can adequately fill the dimensions and lineaments of it but the seal that stamped it. Other things may cumber the mind, but not

---

[39] *Neque enim facit beatum hominem nisi qui fecit hominem Deus.* Aug. epist 52.

[40] Heb. 1:3, *Ad imaginem Dei facta anima rationalist caeteris omnibus occitparis potest, repleri non potest.* Bernard. *Serm. de bonis deserend.*

content it. As soon may a trunk be filled with wisdom as a soul with wealth; and bodily substances nourished with shadows, as rational spirits fed with bodies.

Whatever goodness creatures have is derivative, whatever happiness they enjoy stands in reduction to the origin of their being. The motion of immortal souls is like that of celestial bodies purely circular. They do not test without returning back to the same point where they issued, which is the bosom of God himself. Fishes are said to visit the place of their spawning yearly, as finding it most commodious for them; and sick patients are usually sent by physicians to their native soil, for the sucking in of that air from which their first breath was received. Heaven is the place where souls were produced; the spirit of man was at first breathed in by the Father of spirits, and cannot acquiesce until he is enjoyed, and heaven in him.

§3. Witness was born to this truth by the *Amen*, the faithful and true witness, when speaking of those whom the Father had given him, he uttered that remarkable assertion, "This life eternal that they may know thee, and Jesus Christ whom thou hast sent," (John 17:3). Also, when he made his followers that promise of rest, "Come to me all ye that labor, and are heavy laden, and I will give you rest. Take my yoke on you, *etc.* and ye shall find rest to your souls," (Matthew 11:28-29). God would not rest from his works of creation until man was framed; man cannot rest from his longing desires of indigence until God is enjoyed. Now since the fall God is not to be enjoyed but in and through a Mediator; therefore when any man closes with Christ, and not until then, he may say with the Psalmist, "Return to thy rest, O my soul, for the Lord has dealt bountifully with thee." That which the King of Saints testified will be most readily attested by all his loyal subjects. Enquire of such as are yet militant on earth, in which their happiness consists, the answer will be in their having "fellowship with the Father, and with his Son Jesus Christ," (1 John 1:3). Let those who are triumphant is asked what it is that renders their heaven so glorious, their glory so incomprehensible, you shall have no other account but this, it is because they have now attained a complete fruition of that all-sufficient, all-satisfying, ever-blessed and ever-blessing object *God* in *Christ*.

§4. Nor can it easily be denied by such as consider that in this object there is found a threefold fullness, opposite to the threefold vanity in the creatures, which I spoke about before. First a fullness of utility opposite to their unprofitableness. Infinite goodness extends itself to all cases and exigents without being limited to particulars, as created goodness is. Here in the scripture God and Christ are compared to things most extensive in their use, and of most universal concernment. Philosophers look at the Sun as a universal cause. Christ is called the "Sun of Righteousness" (Mal. 4:2) by the Prophet, and "The Lord God," (Psalm 84:11) the Psalmist says, is a Sun and Shield. In a tree the root bears the branches, and the branches fruit. Christ is *both* root and branch. A root, in Isaiah, "In that day shall there be a root of Jesse, which shall stand for an ensign of the people; to it shall the Gentiles seek, and his rest shall be glorious," (Isa. 11:10). A branch, in Zechariah, "Behold I will bring forth my servant the branch," (Zech 3:8). In a building the foundation and cornerstone are most considerable in point of use. Christ is both. "Thus saith the Lord God, behold I lay in Sion for a foundation a stone; a tried stone, a precious cornerstone, a sure foundation," (Isa. 28:16). In military affairs what more useful for offence than the sword, for defense than the shield? The Lord is both. "Happy art thou O Israel; who is like to thee, O people, saved by the Lord, the shield of thy help, and who is the sword of thine excellency!" (Deut. 23:29). In civil commerce money is of most general use for the acquiring of what men need, of which Solomon therefore says, "It answereth all things," (Eccl. 10:19). (Where it is that worldlings look at a full chest as having a kind of Deity in it, able to grant them whatever their hearts desire.) *All things* of God in Christ, it is most true. He only can answer all the desires, all the necessities of his people; and is accordingly said to be their silver and gold, as Junius renders the place in Job.[41] To him a soul may not only say as Thomas did, "My Lord and my God," but as another, "*Deus meus & omnia*, My God and my all."[42]

§5. Secondly, a fullness of truth and faithfulness opposite to their deceit. The creatures do not, cannot perform whatever they promise, but are like deceitful brooks, frustrating the thirsty traveller's expectation. We read of Semiramis that she caused this motto to be engraven on her tomb, "If any King stand in need of money, let him break open this monument." Darius, having perused the inscription, ransacks the sepulcher, finds nothing within, but another writing to this effect, "Hadst thou not been unsatiably covetous, thou wouldst never have invaded a monument of the dead." Such are all the things of this world. They delude us with many a promising motto, as if they would give us hearts ease; but when we come to look within, instead of contentment, afford us nothing but conviction of our folly in expecting satisfaction from them. With God it is otherwise. He is faithful that promised, (Hebrews 10:25) says the apostle; and again, "Faithful is be that calls you, who also will do it," (1 Thess. 5:24). "I am the way," says Christ of himself, "the truth and the life," (John 14:6). In him believers find not less, but more than ever they looked for; and when they come to enjoy him completely are enforced to cry out, as the Queen of Sheba did, "The half was not told me," (1 Kings 10:7).

§6. Thirdly, a fullness of unchangeableness opposite to their inconstancy. This God challenges to himself, "I am the Lord, I change not," (Mal. 3:6). And Jesus Christ is said to be "the same yesterday, and today, and forever," (Heb. 13:8). Another apostle, speaking of the Father of lights, "from whom descends every good and perfect gift," (James 1:17), (in this

---

[41] *Quicquid nummis praesentibus opis, et veniet; clausum possidet arca Jovem.* Petron. Arbit.

[42] Erit Omnipotens lectissimum aurum suum, et argeatum, viresque tibi.

alluding, as Heinsius[43] conceives, to the High Priest's Urim and Thummim, that is lights and perfections; to Urim in these words *Father of lights*, to Thummim in these *perfect gifts*) tells us that with him is "no variableness neither shadow of turning."[44] The metaphor is thought by some to be borrowed from the art of painting, in which pictures ane first rudely shadowed, then drawn to the life. In the creatures we find a full draught and lively portraiture of mutability; but not so much as the rudiments of a draught, as the least line or shadow of it in God and Christ.

EXERCITATION III.

Two conclusions from Psalm 73:26-26. The Psalmist's case stated. The frequent complication of corporal and spiritual troubles. How God strengthens his people's hearts against their bodily distempers; how under discouragements of spirit. The secret supports of saving grace. What kind of portion God is to the Saints. A congratulation of their happiness in it.

§1. From that pathetical passage in one of the Psalms, "Whom have I in heaven but thee? And there is none on earth that I desire besides thee. My flesh and my heart fails; but God is the strength of my heart, and my portion for ever," (Psa. 73:25-26); these two conclusions may be raised; 1. There is no person or thing in heaven or earth short of God in Christ to be looked on and desired as our utmost good. 2. The fruition of God in Christ is able to make and to continue a man happy even in the midst of utmost extremity.

The former I have treated of in the foregoing exercitations, intending to handle the latter in this. That I account an utmost extremity as to kind, (though as to degrees it may be either more intense or more remiss) when there is a complication of sufferings both in body and mind at once. Such was the Psalmist's case here. It is not flesh alone, or heart

[43] Heinsius *in locum*.

[44] Τροπῆςἀποσκίασμα. Pareus *in loc*.

alone, but "my flesh and my heart" in conjunction, both failed him at one and the same time. Such is the sympathy of soul and body, that when it fares ill with one, the other commonly is disturbed. If the soul is in an agony, the body languishes. Satan's buffeting Paul with blasphemous thoughts, as some conceive, proved a thorn to his flesh.[45] On the other side, if the outward man is tormented, the inward is accustomed to be dismayed, even to failing of heart. The Stoics indeed, those magnificent boasters, talk of an apathy, and Plutarch tells us that Agesilaus, when he lay, sick of the gout, and Carneades, who came to visit him, observing what pains he conflicted with, was about to leave him as one not in case to be spoken to, bade him stay, and pointing at once to his own feet and to his heart, said, "Nothing comes from there hither,"[46] as if his mind were in no way disquieted for all the sufferings of his flesh. But far better men than any of them have born witness to the contrary. "Our flesh had no rest, but we were troubled on every side; without were fightings, within were fears," (2 Cor. 7:5). So says Paul. David in one of his Psalms in this way, "O Lord heal me, for my bones are vexed; my soul also is sore vexed," (Psalm 6:2-3). In another this way, "There is no-soundness in my flesh; I am feeble and sore broken, I have roared by reason of the disquietness of my heart," (Psalm 38:7-8).

§2. But as when Peter walking on the waves, and perceiving how boisterous the winds were, began to sink, Jesus immediately stretched forth his hand and caught him; so when the Psalmist's flesh and heart failed, God even then was the strength of his heart; according to the original, the rock of it. Rocks are not more fortifying to cities and castles built on them, than God is to his people's hearts. A sincere believer's soul is therefore assimilated by our Savior to a house founded on a rock, (Matt. 7:25), which was every way assaulted; in the roof by rain descending on that, in the foundation by floods

---

[45] 2 Cor. 12:7. Σκόλοψ τῄ σαρκι.

[46] *Mane Carneades, nihil enim illinc huc pervenit.*

washing on it, in the walls by winds blustering against them; and yet stood because it *was strong*, was strong because founded on a rock. Suck a *rock* is our God, and that even in such a case as has been described.

§3. Hezekiah whom God had chosen to life, (Isa. 38:1) was sick to death. Lazarus whom Jesus loved, became sick and died (John 9:3). Timothy had his often infirmities (1 Tim. 5:23). The Psalmist's flesh failed him, or to speak in Paul's phrase, his outward man perished (2 Cor. 4:16); yet God meanwhile was the rock and strength of his sick servant's heart. First, by preserving in it an expectation of such fruit as saints use to reap from those trials; fruit which relates partly to sin, and partly to grace. To sin by way of cure. Diseases when sanctified drain the inward as well as the outward man, and help to spend out the bad sicknesses of both. Sickness (Isidore says) woundeth the flesh, but healeth the mind; is the body's malady, but the soul's medicine.[47] For instance, weakness kills the itch of worldliness. Let pleasure open all her shops, and present a sick man with her choisest parties: let Mammon bring forth all his bags and jingle them in his ears; produce all his crowns, sceptres, mitres, and lay them at his feet, how ready will he be to cry out, "Away with them." Behold I am at the point to die (as Esau once reasoned) and what can these vanities profit me? The same may be said of self-confidence and pride which are also frequently antidoted by diseases. A special end (as Elihu tells Job (Job 33:17)) which God aims at in his chastening with pain is to hide pride from man, that is, to *remove* it, as what we hide is removed out of sight. A Christian Emperor, one of the Ferdinands, when his chaplain Matthias Cittardus came visit him as he lay on his death-bed, and according to the mode of the court described him most Invincible Emperor,[48] finding himself

---

[47] *Adversa corporis remedia sunt animae. Aegritudo carnem vulnerat mortem curat*. Isidor. Lib. 3. *De sum*. Bono.

[48] *Ab. Scultetus Idea Concion*. In *Isaiae* c. page 9. page 147. *In agone invictissimi titulum agnoscere nolebat, etc*.

overcome with sickness, would not admit of that compellation, but charged him not to use it more; on which the chaplain made his next address on this wise, "Go to dear brother Ferdinand, ending hardship as a good soldier of Jesus Christ."

§4. Next to grace, in point of growth. The rise of grace is sometimes occasioned by a sore disease. Beza[49] tells us of himself, that God was pleased to lay the foundation of his spiritual health in a violent sickness which befell him at Paris. The growth of grace is always promoted when God makes use of this means. It is not more usual with children to shoot up in length, than with Christians to become greater in grace in or after a sickness. See it exemplified in the famous protestant divines. Olevian said on his death-bad, "In this disease I have learned to know aright what sin, and what the majesty of God is."[50] Rollock on his, "I am not ashamed to profess that I never reached to so high a pitch in the knowledge of God, as I have attained in this sickness."[51] Rivet on his, "In the space of ten days since I kept my bed, I have learned more, and made greater progress in divinity, than in the whole course of my life before."[52]

§5. Secondly, by infusing and exciting a principle of Christian patience, which is therefore able to support and strengthen the heart when philosophical, stoical patience cannot do it; because itself is strengthened from such divine topics, as philosophy knows but little, if anything of. I shall instance in two, the pains of hell deserved *by* us, and the pains of Christ endured *for* us. Well may the consideration of hell torments due to us all, as being by nature children of wrath, conduce to the working of patience in us under these petty sufferings in comparison. For what are these rods to those scorpions? A fever to those everlasting burnings? The stone or

---

[49] *Morbus iste verae sanitutis principium*, &c. Epist. *paefix Confessioni*.

[50] Mel. Adam. *In vitis Germ. Theol*. page 601.

[51] Idem in *vitis Exterorum*. page 189.

[52] Dauberu Ora. Funeb. in *excessum Andrae Riveti*, page 90.

gout to that fire and brimstone? A sick bed to hell, where the sickness never goes off, "the fire never goeth out, the worm never *dieth*?" (Mark 9:44). So also when on our beds of sickness we think of that garden in which Christ lay prostrate on the ground, in our fits of his agony, and our sweats of his water and blood, the consideration of his torments, and of our interest in them, may well mitigate the sense of our present sufferings, if not wholly swallow them up, as Aaron's rod devoured those of the magicians. Are you afflicted with sore pain in this or that part? He had hardly any member free. Are your spirits feeble and faint? "His very soul was exceedingly sorrowful even to death," (Mark 26:38). Do you cry, *My God, my God, why hast thou afflicted me?* Jesus cried with a loud voice, "My God, my God, why hast thou *forsaken* me?" (Matt. 27:46).

§6. Yes, but however manifest it is that when the flesh fails, the heart may be strengthened, how the heart itself should fail and yet be strengthened, is not so evident. I am therefore to make it appear in the next place, that these two clauses, "My heart faileth," and God is the "strength of my heart," may both be verified at once without a paradox in different respects. By reason of remainders of unbelief in the most regenerate on this side heaven, when Satan's temptations shall strike in with their corruptions, holy men may be induced in a fit of dejection, because the Lord has cast them down, to conceive and say he has cast them *off*. David once said, "I had fainted, unless I had believed to see the goodness of the Lord in the land of the living," (Psalm 27:13). Such fainting show from not believing; such unbelief is much fermented by not considering that (as no outward blessing is good enough to be a sign of eternal election, seeing God often fills their bellies with hidden treasure, who treasure up to themselves wrath against the day of wrath,) so no temporal affliction is bad enough to be an evidence of reprobation, seeing the dearest Son of God's love was "a man of sorrows and acquainted with grief," (Isa. 53:3). Yet may the same heart at the same time be strengths and from another cause, namely,

God, who easily can, and usually does supply such effectual grade as is able to keep the head above water when the rest of the body is under it, able to preserve the Spouse in a posture of "leaning on her beloved in a wilderness," (Song of Songs 8:5); to make one with Abraham believe in hope against hope (Rom. 4:18), and say with Job, "Though he kill me, yet will I trust in him," (Job 13:15). Faith can support when nature shrinks; call God Father when he frowns, and make some discovery of a sin through the darkest cloud. When it sees no light it may feel some influence, when it cannot close with a promise, it may lay hold on an attribute, and be ready to make this profession, "Though both my flesh and my heart fail, yet divine compassions fail not. Though I can hardly discern at present either sun, or moon, or stars, yet will I cast anchor in the dark, and ride it out until the day break." There was a time when Jonah said, "I am cast out of thy sight," (Jonah 2:4, 7) but added with the same breath, "yet will I look again toward thy holy temple;" and presently after, "when my soul fainted within me, I remembered the Lord," *etc.*

§7. The connection of these words in the psalm, "My heart faileth, but God is the strength of my heart and my portion for ever,"[53] may seem to imply some such thing; in other words, that in times of languishing, God affords a strengthening support in secret by encouraging a believer to wait on himself as his portion forever, notwithstanding all his sufferings for the present. There can be no better, or more sovereign cordial than this, if we consider the suitableness, and sufficiency of God to this purpose. In the choice of a portion as of a wife, fitness is chiefly to be regarded; she is a wife indeed, who is a meet help, that a portion indeed which is suitable to the soul of man. God only is so. For the soul is a spiritual and immortal substance, therefore to her, worldly accommodations are unsuitable, because they are, most of them corporal, all of them temporal. But God who is a *spirit*

[53] *Quaecunque me angustiae corpis aut animae urunt, Tu meo animo es robur, dum te aeternam mihi haereditatem fore spere.* Simmius in *Psalm* 73.

(John 4:24) and who only has immortality, fits her exactly in both respects. The uncreated Spirit becomes a portion forever to this his everlasting creature (1 Tim. 6:16). As for sufficiency, the soul's appetite is too vast for any creatures to fill up the measure of her capacity: but when she has once pitched on God self-sufficient in his being, all-sufficient in his communications, she then has enough, and is ready to profess With David, "The Lord is the portion of mine inheritance and of my cup: the lines are fallen to me in pleasant places, yea I have a goodly heritage," (Psalm 16:56). Indeed what can one wish in a heritage that is not to be found in God? Would we have large possessions? He is immensity. A sure estate? He is immutability. A long term of continuance? He is eternity itself. I shall therefore finish this with a serious congratulation to the saints, and a high applause of their blessedness. Happy, three times happy are you, dearly beloved in the Lord,[54] because when those men of the world which have their portion in this life, as David speaks, part with theirs (as they must all do at death, if not before) you are led to a fuller fruition of your portion. Theirs at the best is but some good blessing of God, that will in time be taken from them; yours is the good God himself, blessed and blessing you forever. He is so at present, and he will be so to all eternity; a portion of which you can never be plundered. Impoverished you may be, but not undone; discouraged, but not disinherited. Your flesh perhaps, yes, and your hearts too may fail, but "God will be the strength of your hearts, and your portion for ever." I shall add no more, but only remind you of what is written in the hundred forty and sixth psalm, "Happy is he that has the God of Jacob for his help, whose hope is in the Lord his God," (Psalm 146:5).

EXERCITATION IV.

[54] *Quid potest eo esse felicius cijus efficitur suus conditor census; & hereditas ejus dignatur esse ipsa Divinitas?* Prosper *de vit. Contemplate*. Lib. 2 c. page 16.

The first inference grounded on Isaiah 55:1, 2. by way of invitation, backed with three encouragements to accept it, viz. The fullness of that soul-satisfaction which God gives, the universality of its tender, and the freeness of its communication. The second by way of expostulation, and that both with worldlings and saints. A conclusion by way of soliloquy.

§1. In the synagogues of old on the eighth day of the feast of tabernacles, called by the Jews *Hosanna Rabbah*, the great *Hosanna*, and by the evangelist, "The last day, the great day of the feast,"[55] four portions of scripture were accustomed to be read, *viz.* those of the fifth book of Moses, called Deuteronomy, the last words of the prophet Malachi, the beginning of Joshua, and that passage concerning Solomon's rising up from his knees after his prayer, and blessing the people with a loud voice in the eighth chapter of the first book of Kings. Then Jesus, who was the end of the law and the prophets, the true Joshua and Solomon, stood up, saying, "If any man thirst, let him come to me and drink. He that believeth on me, as the scripture has said, out of his belly shall flow rivers of living water," (John 7:38). But why did he then speak of waters? Tremellius gives this account of that out of the Talmud.[56] The Jews, he says, on that day used with much solemnity and joy to fetch water from the river Siloah to the temple where, being delivered to the priests, it was by them poured on the altar, the people in the meantime singing out of Isaiah, "with joy shall it draw water out of the wells of salvation," (Isa. 12:3). Our Savior therefore to take them off from this needless, if not superstitious practice, tells them of other and better waters, which they were to have of him, according to what he had elsewhere said by the ministry of the same prophet in these most emphatical words, "Ho, every one that thirsteth, come ye to the waters; and he that has no money, come ye, buy and eat, yea come; buy wine and milk without money and without price. Wherefore do ye spend

[55] John 7:37. Vid. Ludov de Dieu in loc.
[56] Annot. in loc.

money for that which is not bread, and your labor for that which satisfieth not?" (Isa. 55:1-2). Words that, besides an intimation of the aforementioned truths concerning the creature's inability, and the sufficiency of God in Christ, to satisfy souls, clearly hold forth a double improvement; one by way of invitation, the other by way of expostulation.

§2. The invitation is set on with vehemence and importunity, *Ho come*, but as not content with that, he doubles it, *yea come ye*, and triples it, *yea come*. Not come and look on, or come and cheapen, but come and buy, buy and eat. They may be rationally said to come who frequent the ordinances, in which Christ is usually to be found; they to buy, who part with something, are at some cost and pains in pursuit of him; they to eat, who feed on him by a lively faith. Careless wretches will not so much as vouchsafe to come, by reason of their oxen, or farms, or some other impediment, the Lord must have them excused. Formal professors come indeed, but refuse to buy, will lay out no serious endeavors in searching the scriptures and their own deceitful hearts, but are merely superficial in such undertakings. Temporary believers (whose hearts are really, though not savingly worked on) seem to have bought, yet did not eat, for lack of that spirit of faith, which engrafts men into Christ, and makes them as truly one with him as the body is with the meat it feeds on. Do we lack encouragements to receive this invitation? The place itself presents us with three.

§3. One from the fullness of that satisfaction which is here tendered under the metaphors of water, wine, milk, and bread: the last in which is implied partly in those terms of opposition, for that which is not bread, (as if he had said, *you might have had that of me which is bread indeed*,) partly in the Word *eat*, which cannot so properly be applied to any commodity here mentioned, water, wine, and milk being liquids as to bread. Now there is somewhat in Christ to answer each of these. His flesh is bread, his blood is wine, his spirit is waters, (John 6:51; Matthew 26:28-29; John 7:38-39; 1 Peter 2:2) his doctrine is miLuke But because I conceive the Holy Spirit in this place does not so much intend a parallel of these, as a declaration of that sufficiency which is to be found in Christ and his benefits for saving to the utmost of all those that shall come to God by him; I shall only touch on that consideration, and by adding to this a same place in the revelation, briefly demonstrate from them both how all-sufficient a Savior he is. This in Isaiah holds forth somewhat proper to every sort of true believers. Milk for babes, water for such as are young and hot, wine for the aged,[57] bread for all. The other is that of Christ to the angel of the church of "Laodioea, I counsel thee to buy of me gold tried in the fire that thou mayest be rich, and white raiment that thou mayest be clothed and that the shame of they nakedness do not appear, and anoint thine eyes with eye-salve that thou mayest see," (Rev. 3:18), where he commends his gold for such as is tried in the fire, his raiment for such as will take away shame, and his eye-salve for a special virtue to make the blind see. Take them together, and there is in them enough to supply our principal defects, *viz.* unbelief the heart for which there is here gold tried in the fire, by which we may probably understand the grace of faith, concerning which we read in Peter, "that the trial of your faith, being much more precious than of gold that perisheth, though it is tried with fire, might be found to praise," (1 Peter 1:7). And unholiness in the life, for which there is the white raiment, if by it we understand inherent righteousness, according to that in the Revelation, "to her was granted that she should be arrayed in fine linen, clean and white, for the fine linen is the righteousness of the saints," (Rev. 19:8). Lastly, ignorance in the mind, for which there is his eye-salve to remove it, according to the apostle's prayer for his Ephesians, that God would give them "the spirit of wisdom and revelation, the eyes of their understanding being enlightened," (Eph. 1:17-18), *etc.*

§4. A second encouragement is from the universality of

---

[57] *Vinum Lac senum.*

this offer. "Ho. every one that thirsteth come;" so he do but thirst he shall be welcome, how unworthy whatsoever he may be in other respects. He will give grace to the thirsty *who enables them to thirst after grace.*[58] Christ is far from turning such persons away; yes but for such he would have no customers in the world; his commodities must lie by him dead for lack of sale; seeing others will not take them off, but leave them until on his hand, as things in which they see no need, have no esteem of. This let all men know for certain, that such as thirst so as to come, come so as to buy, buy so as to eat, will never have cause to repent of their bargain. I have somewhere read of a great commander, who being extremely tormented with thirst, sold himself and his army into enemies hands for a draught of cold water; which he had drunk he repented and said, "*O quantum ob quanuntilum!* How very little is that for which I have parted with so very much!" Believers may take up the like words, but in a far different sense: O how much grace, how much happiness have I got for a little thirsting, a little trusting in Jesus Christ!

§5. A third from the freeness of communication, amply declared in this clause, "Come buy vine and milk without money and without price." In the place hitherto insisted on, the word *money* occurs thrice, twice in the first verse and once in the second, but not in the same signification. In the first it is clearly interpreted by price, and signifies merit; they are said to have no money, who being conscious to themselves of their having nothing of their own to answer divine justice with, to fetch them in pardon, peace and righteousness, wholly disclaim all self-sufficiency, and come to Christ as to one that expects not to receive but to be received; looks for little or nothing from us but that we be nothing in ourselves, desirous to have all from him, and to partake of his fullness grace for grace. In the second it is expounded by labor, and denotes industry. Men are said to spend money for that which they lay out their pains about. Money answers all, the

[58] *Dabit desideranti gratiam, qui dat gratiam desiderii.*

preacher says (Eccl. 10:19): the heathens have a proverb which ascribes as much to labor.[59] We do not say with them, that God sells his benefits to us for our pains; but this we acknowledge, he gives them so as to require our industry about them. Yet is not this any prejudice to the freeness of his grace, or any contradiction to that clause, "Buy without money and without price," because our labor can in no way merit his blessings. As when a school-master teaches a boy *gratis*, the youth cannot possibly attain to learning unless he is industrious, and take pains at his book; but it does not therefore cease to be free on the teacher's part, because the learner's pains are required. So it is here.

Yet some in all ages have been so vain as to dream of bringing their money with them whenever they come; I mean that, which if not in itself, yet in their opinion seems to deserve what they come for. So it is with the Pharisees of old, and the papists of late. Insomuch as *Cornelius a lapide*, in his comment on this very place,[60] which makes altogether for the contrary doctrine, countenances the popish tenets of free-will and merit of congruity.[61] So elephants, they say, are accustomed before they drink to mud themselves in the water, which, if it were suffered to remain dear, would discover their deformity to them.

§6. I proceed to the expostulation contained in the next words, "Wherefore, do ye spend money for that which is not bread, and your labor for that which satisfieth not?" Words applicable both to worldlings, and to such believers as have not yet got clear of the world. First, to worldlings, who manifestly do not spend their money only, but their souls for that which is not bread. In the Lord's Prayer, *bread* is put for all necessaries, and used in the Lord's Supper, to signify the absolute necessity of receiving Christ, by whom spiritual life is supported, as the natural life is by bread. Now the

[59] *Dii laboribus omnia vendunt.*

[60] *Emptio est dispositio jjberi arbitrii.*

[61] *Emitur pretio non condigno, sed congruo.*

accommodations doted on by men of the world, and often purchased with the loss of salvation, are justly said not to be bread, because they are neither absolutely necessary to be had, nor able to support such as enjoy them. A man's life, our Savior Says, "consisteth not in the abundance of the things which he possesseth," (Luke 12:15). Wealth indeed is a necessary good, but no necessary blessing. None are made really happy by it, (though Latinists use the same word *Beatus*, to signify both rich and blessed.) A Christian may be happy without it; really happy, yes, and really wealthy too, for he is abundantly rich that possesses Christ in the midst of poverty;[62] and does not make treasure his God, as the servants of mammon do, but God his treasure.

§7. Furthermore, as the expression there is, "They spend their labor for that which satisfieth not."[63] A late Jesuit tells us a story of a feast made in Germany by a certain magician for noblemen, who while they sat at table with him, received good content, and fared to their thinking very deliciously, but when they departed, found themselves hungry, as if they had eaten nothing at all; which indeed was their case if the Jesuit's relation of the magician's art and fact may be credited. Such entertainment does this present world afford its principal guests. They are not fed with satisfying substances, but rather with deluding shadows. "Surely every man walketh in a vain show, surely they ate disquieted in vain," (Psalm 38:6). David speaks it of such as heap up riches, of whom also Solomon says, "The rich man's wealth is his strong city, and was a high wall in his own conceit," (Prov. 18:11). A strong city in his conceit, but indeed a castle in the air. One that applies the scaling ladders of Scripture and reason to such walls, may easily climb so high as to reach and pull down those ensigns of vanity, which makes such a flourish on the battlements of it. Sooner shall men gather grapes of thorns, and figs of thistles, than find that a fountain

---

[62] *Affatim dives est qui cum Christo pauper.*

[63] *Cornel. A lapide* comment. in Isa. 55:2.

of all good to any soul, the love in which Paul has branded "for the root of all evil," (1 Tim. 6:9-10). It drowns in perdition; how can it then crown with happiness? O that ever so rich an heir, as the soul of man, should run away with so servile a thing as money is, or give the least consent to a match so far below her birth and breeding.

§8. Let authority be added to wealth, and great honors to great revenues, yet will the product of both sums are not soul-satisfaction and blessedness, but vanity and vexation of spirit. How often is the sword put into mad men's hands, and bramble advanced to rule over better trees, and walls of mud shined on while marble pillars stand in shade? How often do goats clamber up the mountains of preferments, while the poor sheep of Christ feed below? Yes, how often is greatness acquired by base, and confounded by weak means? Flattery held Absalom's stirrup.[64] He that is every one's master now, was a while since, at every one's service. Well might Stella call ambition, charity's ape;[65] for it also believes all things, hopes all things, yes, and bears all things too until what it hoped for be attained, then grows intolerable itself. It may further be observed, that God usually takes a course to break the staff of such pride, by confounding the powers of worldly potentates, not with lions and tigers, but as Pharaohs of old, by frogs and lice. The apostle, I remember, says, "an idol is nothing," and yet the silversmiths cried out, "great is Diana of the Ephesians." Diana then was a great *nothing*. Such are those men of place idolized by common people, when the Lord begins to blow on them in his wrath, like those nobles of Idumea, concerning whom Isaiah said, "all her princes shall be nothing," (Isa. 34:12).

§9. Secondly, as for those saints whose wings are still somewhat clogged with the bird lime of this world, I humbly

---

[64] *Ambitio te ad dignitatem nisi per indigna non ducit. Senec. Natural, quaest.* in *Praefat.* lib. 1.

[65] *Ambitio charitatis simia, Charitas patiens est pro aeternis, arabitio pro terrenis.* Didac. *Stella de Contemptu mundi*, part 1. page 88.

desire them to consider, how ill it becomes the offspring of heaven to go licking up the dust of this earth, the woman's seed to content itself with the serpent's food; any one of the posterity of Japhet, after he has been persuaded into the tents of Shem, to bring on himself Canaan's curse, "a servant of servants shalt thou be," by subjecting his soul to that which God made to serve its servant, the body. Verily, if this present world, or anything in it is over precious in thy sight, O Christian, thou art become vile in the eyes of God, yes, in thine own: for none can set a high price on things without him until he have first undervalued his soul.[66] Time was when Satan showed our Savior all the kingdoms of this world, and the glory of them. If ever the world appears to you temptingly glorious, suspect it for one of Satan's discoveries. Sure I and the Scripture use diminishing terms, when it speaks of creature-comforts, as in styling the pomp of Agrippa (Acts 25:23) and Bernice much fancy, no reality; in calling men's temporal estates, this world's goods (1 John 3:17), not theirs but the world's, deceitful and uncertain richest (Matt. 13:22), thick clay (1 Tim. 6:17), and dust of the earth (Hab. 2:6), wind (Amos 2:7), grass (Eccl. 5:16), and the flower of grass, the least things (James 1:11), hardly things. Solomon brings them down to the lowest degree of entity, yes, to nullity, saying, "Labor not to be rich, wilt, thou set thine eyes on that which is not?" (Luke 16:10-15).

§10. Let Diotrephes then say, *It is good for me to have the preeminence*, Judas, *it is good for me to bear the bag*, Demas, *it is good for me to embrace this present world.* But do you, O my soul, conclude with David, "It is good for me to draw near to God," (Psalm 73:28). You are now as a bird in the shell, a shell of the flesh which will shortly break, and let out the bird: this crazy bark of my body after long will be certainly split on the fatal rock of death; then must thou its present pilot forsake it, and

---

[66] *Cujus anima in occulis ejus est pretiosa, in ejus oculis mundus est parvus. Dictum Hebraeorun apud Buxtorf. in florileg.* page 225. *Pecuniam habes? vel teipsum vel pecuniam vilem habeas necesse est.* Senec.

swim to the shore of eternity. Therefore, O everlasting creature, see and be sure you do not content yourself with a transitory portion. I do not, Lord, you know I do not. Of a small handful of outward things, I am ready to say, It is enough, but that which I long so passionately for, is a large heart full of God in Christ. You are my sun, the best of creatures are but stars, deriving the luster they have from thee: did not thy light make day in my heart, I should languish for all them in a perpetual night of dissatisfaction. There are within me two great gulfs, a mind desirous of more truth, and a will capable of more good then finite beings can afford; thou only canst fill them, who art the first truth, and the chief good. In thee alone shall "my soul be satisfied as with marrow and fatness, and my mouth shall praise thee with joyful lips," (Psalm 63:5).

APHORISM II.

We are conducted, to the fruition of God in Christ by Christian religion, contained in the divine oracles of holy scripture.

EXERCITATION I.

The safe conduct of saints, signified by the pillar in Exodus, performed by the counsel of God himself, the abridgement in which we have in the doctrine of Christian religion. How that tends to blessedness.

§1. There is no possibility of arriving at blessedness without a safe conduct, nor at glory without guidance; no infallible guidance but by the counsel of God himself. All which the Psalmist is like to have had in his eye, when in his humble address to God, he expresses himself in this manner, "Thou shalt guide me with thy counsel, and afterward receive me to glory," (Psalm 73:24). The husband's duty in relation to his wife is to be "the guide of her youth," (Prov. 2:17). Such has Christ (one of whose names is Counsellor (Isa. 9:6)) been to his church in former times, is at this day, and will continue to the end of the world. In Exodus we meet with the history of the Jewish Church, her youth, and her strange manner of guidance; which when the Levites, in Nehemiah came to commemorate they do it thus, "Thou in thy manifold mercies forsookest them not in the wilderness the pillar of the cloud departed not from them by day to lead them in the way, neither the pillar of fire by night to show them light, and the way in which they should go," (Neh. 9:19). It was not only a seasonable act of mercy to them in that age; but may be looked on as an emblem of that safe conduct, which the church in all ages may expect from Jesus Christ. For as in that cloudy fiery pillar there were two different substances, the fire and the cloud, yet but *one* pillar; so there are two different natures in Christ, his divinity shining as fire, his humanity darkening as a cloud, yet but one person. As that pillar departed not from them by day or by night, all the while they travelled in the wilderness so while the church's pilgrimage lasts in this world, the safe conduct of Christ by his spirit and ordinances shall be continued. But as at their entrance into Canaan, a type of heaven, the pillar is thought to have been removed, because not mentioned in the sequel of the story, and because the pillar but the ark going before them; so when the church shall arrive at heaven her resting place, the mediatory conduct of Christ is to cease, and the ordinances, which are here of use, to disappear.

§2. Meanwhile this infallible counsel of God has been most effectually administered by the prophets and apostles, especially by Christ himself, whose words were such as led directly to everlasting bliss. Insomuch as when Jesus said to the twelve, "will ye also go away? Peter answered him, *Lord, to whom shall we go? Thou hast the words of eternal life*," (John 6:67-68). As if he had said, *go whither we will to other teachers, we shall be sure not to meet with words of eternal life anywhere else*. Such are proper to Christ's school, taught only by himself, and his under officers: in which one has left this profession on record, "That which we have seen and heard declare we to you, that ye also may have fellowship with us: and truly our fellowship is with the Father, and with his Son, Jesus Christ," (1 John 1:3). So the disciple whom Jesus loved in his first epistle. Another this, "I take you to record this day, that I am pure from the blood of all men: for I have not shunned to declare to you all the counsel of God," (Acts 20:26-27). So Paul in his valedictory speech to the elders of Ephesus. Which he could not have said, had not the doctrine he preached among them been sufficient to have led all his hearers to the fruition of God in Christ, and therein to complete happiness. That by the counsel of God he intended to decipher Christian religion is manifest, because that was the sum of all his ministry, as we find him declaring elsewhere, "Having obtained help of God, I continue to this day witnessing both to small and great, saying none other things than those which the prophets and Moses did say should come: that Christ should suffer, and that he should be the first that should rise from the dead," (Acts 26:22, 27) *etc.*

§3. Counsel it is, and therefore described sometimes mystery, and that a great one, "Without controversy great is the mystery of godliness," (1 Tim. 3:16). Τής ευσεβείας, of religion, as others render it; meaning the Christian, an epitome in which follows, God manifest in the flesh, and sometimes wisdom, and that not among punies and novices, who do not see into the depth of things, but among them that are perfect. Sometimes, "the wisdom of God in a mystery, even the hidden wisdom, which God ordained before the world to our glory," (1 Cor. 2:7). Which made an ancient writer affirm, that "the mysteries of our religion art above the reach of our understanding, above the discourse of human reason, above all that any creature can comprehend."[67] Yes it will be found the counsel of God himself, and not of man, if we but consider a few of its materials; *viz.*, "principles above the reach of man's mind," a resurrection of the dead; a mystical union of all believers among themselves and to their head; a trinity of persons in one essence, two natures in one person; God reconciled to men by the blood, men to God by the spirit of Christ, with others of the like elevation. Doctrines contrary to the bent of man's will, as that of original sin, which represents him to himself as a child of wrath, worthy, before he see the light, of being cast into outer darkness. And that of self-denial, which takes him off from confidence in his own abilities; where proud nature challenges self-sufficiency, and will hardly be content with less. Lastly, promises and threatenings beyond the line of human motives and dissuasives, exhibiting to the sons of men, not temporal rewards but punishments only, but the gift of eternal life, and the vengeance of eternal fire: Things which not any of the most knowing law-givers and princes of this world did or could hold forth, until the only wise God was pleased to reveal and urge them in the

[67] Υπέρ τϖν, ύπίρ λόγος κατάληψις κλιςης φυσεας τά ήέτερα. Just. Mart. *Expos. Fidei.*

sacred authentic records of Christianity.

§4. Now Christian religion promotes our guidance to the fruition we treat of, these two ways, *viz.* by discovering God in Christ, and by uniting to him; the former it performs as Christian, the latter as religion.

First, As Christian it discovers God in Christ, which other religions do not. "No man has seen God at any time, the only begotten Son, which is in the bosom of the Father, he has declared him," (John 1:18). So the Evangelist, or as others think, the Baptist. "All things are of God, who has reconciled us to himself by Jesus Christ, and has given to us the ministry of reconciliation, *in other words*, that God was in Christ, *etc.*," (2 Cor. 5:18-19). So the apostle says. The poor pagan knows neither God nor Christ, but ignorantly turns the truth of God into a lie, worshipping creatures, and instead of Christ is directed by his *theology* to the service of a middle sort-of divine powers called daemons;[68] and looked at as mediators between the celestial sovereign gods, whom the Gentiles worship, and mortal men. The modern Jew acknowledged the true God of his fathers, Abraham, Isaac, and Jacob, but does not own Jesus the son of Mary for the true Christ; yes disowns him so far, as not only to expect another Messiah, but (if writers do not deceive us) to blaspheme and curse him and his followers. The deluded Islamic confesses one God, the creator of heaven and earth; yes conceives so well of the Lord Jesus, as not to suffer any Jew to take up the profession of a Muslim, until he has first renounced his enmity against Christ, yet he will neither acknowledge his satisfaction, on which our salvation is founded, nor his divinity by virtue in which that satisfaction is meritorious. Where the true and pious Christian is by his religion taught to say with Paul, in direct opposition to all the three aforementioned sects, "We know that an idol is nothing in the world; and that there is none other God but one. For though there be that are called gods, whether in heaven or to earth (as there be gods many and Lords many) yet to us there

[68] See M. Mede's *Apostasy of the latter times*, pages 9-10, and subsequent.

is but one God the Father, of whom are all things, and we in him; and one Lord Jesus Christ, by whom are all things, and we by him," (1 Cor. 8:4-6).

§5. Secondly, as religion, (a term which both Augustine and Lactantius derive *a religando* because by the true religion improved men's souls are tied and fastened to the Supreme Being) it unites us to God and to Christ. The graces of union are especially faith and love. Christian Religion is made up of these two, "Kiss the Son," (Psalm 2:12), David says, which implies the affection of love, "Blessed are all they that put their trust in him," which holds forth an expression of faith. "Hold fast the form of sound words," Paul says, "which thou hast heard of me, in faith and love, which is in Christ Jesus," (2 Tim. 1:13). Love is the fulfilling of the law, faith the fulfilling of the gospel, both the fulfilling of Christian Religion. These two pipes being rightly laid from a Christian's soul to the fountain of living waters fetch in there a daily supply of such grace as will certainly end in a fullness of glory: where worldlings (all the pipes of whose spirits are laid to cisterns, broken cisterns that can hold no water,) must needs continue empty still; and for lack of Christ (who is not seen but by those two eyes, nor embraced but by those two arms) fall short of happiness, how eminent whatsoever they may be in the pursuit of by-ways. So to discover and to unite are acts of prerogative not communicable to other professions. For to maintain (as some do) that a man may be saved in an ordinary course (I do not meddle with extraordinary dispensations, but leave the secrets of God to himself) by any religion whatever, provided he live according to the principles of it, is to turn the whole world into an Eden; and to find a tree of life in every garden, as well as in the paradise of God.

EXERCITATION II.

The insufficiency of other religions for bringing men to the enjoyment of God inferred from their inability to discover his true worship. John 4:24 opened. God to be worshipped in and through Christ a lesson not taught in nature's school. Faults in Aristotle's Ethics.

§1. It has appeared already in part by what has been before discoursed, that as the other patriarch's sheaves made obeisance to Joseph's, so other religions must bow down to Christianity, by name those three grand competitors, Paganism, Judaism, and Mahometism: as also those other leading books, by name the Talmud, the Koran, and the much applauded writings of heathen philosophers, must all do homage to the Bible. Yet it will not, I suppose, be unworthy of my pains and the reader's patience further to clear the insufficiency of all exotic doctrines by an argument taken from divine worship, to which I proceed by certain steps.

I. Religion is a thing which distinguishes men from beasts more than reason itself does. For some brute beasts have appearances of reason, none of religion. Man is a creature addicted to religion may perhaps, be found as true a definition, as that which is commonly received (man is a living creature endued with reason).

II. Some kind of deity is acknowledged everywhere throughout the world, and wherever a deity is acknowledged, some kind of worship is observed. Should a synod of mere philosophers be convened to consult about the matters of God, I make no question but in the issue of their debates they would pronounce an *Anathema* against Atheism, and another against irreligion. Among the Romans to worship sparingly was accounted the next door to being an Atheist.[69]

III. None but the true God can discover what the true worship of God is. As that glorious eye heaven is not to be seen but by its own proper light: a million of torches cannot show us the sun.[70] So it is not all the natural reason in the world that can either discover what God is, or what worship he expects, without divine and supernatural revelation from himself.

---

[69] *Parcus Deorum cultor et infrequens.* Horat. lib. 1. *Ode* 34.

[70] *Desine cur nemo videat sine Numine Numen Mirari; Solem quis sine sole videt?*

§2. IV. Before the settling of Christianity and spreading of the gospel throughout the world, many everywhere were unsatisfied concerning the worship they performed, and inquisitive after some teacher who might help them in this by his advice. This may be gathered not only from that which was said by the woman of Samaria in that dispute of hers with our Savior about worship, "I know that Messiah comes, which is called Christ: when he is come, he will tell us all things,"[71] but also by what Ficinus reports concerning Plato, in other words, that being asked by one of his scholars, how far forth, and how long his precepts were to be obeyed, he returned this answer, "Until there come a more holy one, by whom the fountain of truth shall be opened, and whom all may safely follow."

V. The precepts and practice of such as teach and profess other religions, are inconsistent with those gospel rules which Christ and his apostles have given for the regulating of divine worship. Two in which I shall instance in. The first is that which fell from our Savior's own mouth, "God is a Spirit, and they that worship him must worship him in spirit and in truth." [72] Where *Spirit* in the latter clause seems to stand in opposition partly to the formality of the Jews, who did so wholly addict themselves to outward observances in a spiritless way, as to give our Savior occasion of saying, "Well has Isaiah prophesied of you hypocrites, as it is written, This people honoreth me with their lips, but their heart is far from me. In vain do they worship me, teaching for doctrines the commandments of men," (Matthew 15:9). Partly to the idolatry of the Gentiles, who instead of tendering service suitable to a Spiritual Being, worshipped God in and by representations and images of this or that visible creature. The word *Truth* in the same manner may probably seem to be opposed partly to the typical worship of the Jews, in which

---

[71] John 4:25. *Donec in terries apparuerit sacratior aliquis qui fontem veritatis aperiat*, &c. Marsil. Ficinus in vita Platonis Vid. Livium Galan. *Praefat* page 8.

[72] John 4:24.

there were many resemblances and shadows of things to come, as sacrifices, incense, and other rites, the truth in which was exhibited in Christ and in gospel service; partly to the perfunctory worship of the Gentiles, who for want of scripture light, framed to themselves sorry forms of devotion, which the wisest among them were altogether unsatisfied with, yet as knowing no better, and being loath to give offence, observed them only for fashion's sake, so worshipping in show, rather than in truth.

§3. Doubtless what Seneca professed in his time, was a principle, which the most judicious heathen walked by, both in that and the ages foregoing. He, speaking of their religious observances, plainly said, "A wise man will keep them all as things commanded by our laws, not as things acceptable to the gods; for custom rather than conscience sake."[73] By this showing (as Augustine observes) that he himself misliked what he practiced, and did not approve his own adoration. What else was this but mock worship? And although it must be granted that some of them were more serious in that way of superstition which the Gentiles' theology prescribed, yet was not their worship in truth; for being destitute of Christ, who is "the way, the truth and the life," (John 14:6) they lacked that "truth in the inward parts," (Psalm 51:6) required by God in all holy services. The Pelagians indeed were of opinion that those virtues which appeared in heathen philosophers and others of eminent note for morality, though they had not received the knowledge of Christ, were true graces. But if Augustine[74] may be credited, this above all their corrupt tenets was that for which the Christian church did most abominate them and their doctrine. Yes, Paul, whom we are bound to believe, in the fourth chapter of his epistle to the

---

[73] *Qui omnia sapiens servabit taanquam legibus Justus son tanquam Diis grata. Sic adorabimus ut meminerimus cultum magis ad morem quam ad rem pertinere etc.* August. *De Civit Dei* lib. 6. c. page 10.

[74] *Hoc est unde vos maxime Christiana detestur Ecclesia Contr*. Julian. *Pelag*. Lib. iv. c. page 3.

Ephesians, is thought to have concluded the contrary. We find there "the life of the Gentiles clearly opposed to the life of God, which they, *he says*, were alienated from; as also to the truth as it in Jesus, and to that true holiness, or holiness of truth, by which every spiritual worshipper is endued."[75] And so far is the apostle in that place from excepting their philosophers, that as Grotius thinks, he aims especially at them; because his phrase in the seventeenth verse, "That ye walk not as other Gentiles walk, in the vanity of their mind,"[76] is fully parallel with that in. his epistle to the Romans, "They became vain in their imaginations," which is certainly meant of their philosophers, for it follows (professing themselves to be wise) σοφοί (the name by which that sort of men were commonly known, witness the seven wise men of Greece) before Pythagoras invented that other of φιλοσοφοί lovers of wisdom, as more modest.

§4. The second grand direction about the manner of worship is, that it is performed in the name, and through the mediation of Jesus Christ, who saith of himself, "I am the way, no man comes to the Father but by me," (John 14:6). And of whom Paul says, "Whatever ye do in word or deed, do all in the name of the Lord Jesus," (Col. 3:17); also here Luther was bold to assert, "That all the preachings, teachings, and actings of men out of Christ are idolatry and sin in the sight of God."[77] Now although the first direction was not altogether unknown to some of the Gentiles, as may be gathered from various passages in their writings, cited by Grotius in his notes on John the fourth at the twentieth verse, and by doctor Meric Casaubon in his second book *De cultu* the third chapter. Yet of this second they had no knowledge at all; for it is not a lesson to be learned in nature's school. The heavens indeed, and so the earth, with all the creatures in them both, "declare the

---

[75] Ephesians 4:17-18, 21, 24.

[76] *Vide* Grotium in Ephes. 4:17, and in Rom. 1:21-22.

[77] *Quicquid oratur, docetur et vivitur extra Christum est idololatria coram Deo et peccatum*. Luther, *tom*. 3. edit. Jenens. page 300.

glory of God" in himself; but the glory of God in the face of Christ as mediator is not declared by any of them. Insomuch as Paul tells the Ephesians, that while they were Gentiles, "they were at that time without Christ," (Eph. 2:11-12); although Ephesus then was full of philosophers and eminent scholars, witness the proverb of Ephesian letters, and that story in the Acts, which mentions the burning of boots there to the value of fifty thousand pieces of silver, by such as were taken off from the study of curious arts on their conversion to the faith.[78] As for Jews and Mahometans, the former we know have espoused long since another Messiah, and the latter set up impostor Mahomet for their mediator.

§5. Now this argument built on the foundation of these premised considerations stands in this way, no religion or doctrine can bring us to the fruition of God but such as instructs us how to worship him aright; no religion or doctrine but Christianity teaches the right worship of God; therefore, none but it can bring us to enjoy him. The proposition is bottomed on that necessary connection which is between the fruition of God and his adoration; he being accustomed to communicate himself in or after acts of worship, according to these and the like places. "He that has my commandments and keepeth them, he it is that loveth me: and he that loveth me shall be loved off my Father, and I will love him, and will manifest myself to him," (John 14:21). "Behold I stand at the door, and knock: if any man hear my voice and open the door, I will come in to him, and will sup with him, and he with me," (Rev. 3:20). The assumption has been already cleared. But if further proof is needful, I shall add one more argument. So far is the light of nature from making a full discovery of what belongs to divine worship, that the wisest philosophers in their moral tractates have not only been silent as to faith in Christ, and repentance from dead works and such other eminent duties of religion, but commended to their readers, some habits and actions, some

[78] Εφίσια γραμματτα Acts 19:19.

virtues and duties, which in Scripture are represented as vices and sins. For example, Aristotle, one of nature's high priests, in his ethics, one of the choicest pieces of morality extant, makes a virtue of *eutrapelia*, which Paul under that very term prohibits as a thing inconvenient for Christians, "neither filthiness, nor foolish talking, nor *eutrapelia* jesting, which are not convenient," (Eph. 5:4). So also *nemesis*, that is, grief and indignation at the prosperity of unworthy men, is by him reckoned among such affections as are near of kin to virtues, but condemned at large by David in the 37th Psalm, and by Solomon in the Proverbs, saying, "Fret not thyself because of evil men, neither be thou envious at the wicked," (Prov. 24:19). Another of his virtues is μεγαλοψυχια, magnanimity, which he describes to be the judging of a man's self-worthy of great things when he is so. Where our Savior directs us even "when we have done all things that are commanded us," (Luke 17:10) yet to say we are unprofitable servants. He would have such a person a despiser and contemner of others, which is plainly pharisaical;[79] thinks all that favors of humility unworthy of his magnanimous man, where Solomon tells us, "It is better to be of an humble spirit with the lowly, than to divide the spoil with the proud," (Prov. 16:19). Yes, he allows him in case of contumely to speak evil of his adversaries, where our Savior's rule is, "Bless them that curse you, pray for them that despitefully use you," (Matthew 5:44).

EXERCITATION III.

Oracles of God vocal, or written. Books of scripture so called in five respects, viz. in regard of their declaring and foretelling, their being consulted, prized and preserved.

§1. In the epistle to the Hebrews, these two phrases, "The first principles of the oracles of God," and "the principles

[79] Ὑπερέπληι κί καταφροιηπκόν.

of the doctrine of Christ,"[80] import one and the same thing, implying also that Scripture records are the *only* store house and conservatory of Christian Religion. I shall therefore from here take occasion to show, that books of Scripture are oracles of God, why they are so called, and in which they excel other oracles. For the first, there were two sorts of oracles belonging to God, *vocal* and *written*. The vocal were those answers he gave from between the cherubim on the top of the Mercy-seat which covered the Ark,[81] by reason in which, the Holy of Holies, where that Ark stood, was described the Oracle.[82] The written are the two tables of the law, called by Stephen the lively oracles, and the canonical books of Scripture, as well those of the Old Testament, of which Paul speaks, when he declares it as the great privilege of the Jews, that "to them were committed the oracles of God," (Rom. 3:2) as those of the New, to which Peter is like to have had a peculiar respect in. that saying of his, "If any man speak, let him speak as the oracles of God," (1 Peter 4:11), ώς λὸγια Θεοῦ. Especially if his meaning be to admonish such as speak in congregations, public teachers, or as another apostle describes them "ministers of the New Testament," (2 Cor. 3:6) that they are careful to deliver Scripture truths in Scripture words, New Testament matter in New Testament language, taking the particle ός in that text for a note, not of similitude, but of identity; as when it is said, "We beheld his glory, the glory as of the only begotten of the Father," (John 1:14), it is not meant of a glory like his, but the very same; so let him speak as the oracles of God, that is, the self-same things which-God has spoken in his word.[83]

§2. The word λωγια, by which heathen writers had been accustomed to express their oracles, (chiefly such as were uttered in prose, went under the same of χρησμοί) was

[80] Hebrews 5:12 and 6:1.

[81] 1 Kings 6 often and chapter 8:6.

[82] Acts 7:38.

[83] Vide Gerhard *Comment*, in 1 Pet. 4. pages 631 and 634.

enfranchised by the Holy Spirit, and applied to the books of Scripture, to intimate (as I conceive,) that these books were to be of like use to Christians, as those oracles had been to infidels; in which take a five-fold account.

I. Those declared to heathen men the will of their idols, where also they had their names of λὸγια from λέγειν and "oracula from orare, quod inerat illis Deorum oratio," as Tully gives the etymology, because they contained what the gods spoke, and delivered to be their mind. The scriptures in like manner contain the mind of Jehovah. Somewhat of his nature we may learn from the creatures, but should have known little or nothing of his will, had no canonical scripture revealed it. We use to call a man's testament his last will, because in it he makes a final declaration of what he would have his executors do. He that would exactly know the will of God, must look into his two testaments: there he shall find it fully expressed, and nowhere else.

§3. II. Those foretold future events, which made them he so much frequented by such as thirsted after knowledge of things to come. These read every one's destiny, and acquaint him afore-hand with what he may or may not infallibly expect, according to his present and future qualifications. Not to mention prophesies in the New Testament, in which the principal magazine is the apocalypse, the old contains very many predictions beyond the activity of human foresight. For although such effects as depend on natural causes (which are uniform in their workings) may be foretold by a skillful naturalist and a wise statesman, observing the present constitution of a government, may prognosticate what events are like to ensue on those counsels and curses which he sees taken. Yet the quickest eye on earth cannot foresee such future contingents as have their dependence on the mere free will of persons yet unborn; and where or when they are born, not common principles, but heroic impulses must incline them. Where in the scriptures we meet with the name of Josiah and Cyrus, and with their performances long before they had a being. We find old Jacob foretelling the respective fates of all his children, and of their posterity; Isaiah speaking of Jesus Christ, as if he had written a history rather than a prophecy; and Daniel, who lived under the first monarchy, describing the several revolutions under all the others, as if he had seen them with his eyes.

§4. III. Those gave advice in doubtful cases, and were in all undertakings of moment consulted with by devout heathens, who, as Strabo[84] testifies, in their chief affairs of state relied more on the answers of their oracles than on human policies. These were Dave's delight and his counsellors,[85] as we use to advise with those friends, in whom we take most pleasure. He had many wise men about him, but in all their meetings for advice the word of God was still of the *quorum*, and nothing to be concluded of in the result without its consent. Scripture must not only be heard in all our debates, but when any thing comes to be voted, always have a negative voice. Concerning Ahitophel's advice it was said, "what he counselled in those days was as if a man had enquired at the oracle of God," (2 Sam. 16, to the last); which words (being, as it is well said by Peter Martyr, *comparatio non aequiparatio*, a comparison only, not a parallel) sufficiently intimate that all the oracles of God are to be consulted, and also that their counsel is to be rested in. I shall therefore be bold to say to him that reads, whoever he is, as Jehoshaphat once did to Ahab, "Enquire I pray thee of the word of the Lord today," (2 Chron. 18:4); as Paul to his Colossians, "Let the word of Christ dwell in you richly in all wisdom," (Col. 3:16) yes as Christ to his hearers, "Search the scriptures," (John 5:39). Other books may render men learned to ostentation, none but these can make them really wise to salvation. Philosophical speculations, quaint notions and strains of wit, if compared with these oracles, are but as so many spider's webs to catch flies, more fit for the taking of fancies than the saving of souls.

---

[84] Lib. 16 *descript*. Judaeae.
[85] Psalm 119:24.

§5. IV. Those were exceedingly prized by such as enjoyed them, as the great advantage of their states, and the great donative of their gods, who were thought to gratify their worshippers by nothing more than by oracular discoveries. These are certainly the highest privileges by which a people can be gratified; witness that discourse of Paul in the beginning of his third chapter to the Romans, where he handles and decides the controversy between Jew and Gentile about precedency. Consent in religion is accustomed to tie the fastest knots of mutual accord; but there are no greater animosities than those that arise from diversity of professions. The Jews of old abhorred the Gentiles as uncircumcised, ignorant idolaters; the Gentiles on the other side derided the Jews for their circumcision, as favoring of obscenity, and for their sabbaths, as savoring idleness.[86] Paul who was by birth a Jew, by office a teacher of the Gentiles, well knew what feuds, and also what odds there were between them; yet equally involves them in the guilt of original sin throughout the whole second chapter. And because the Jew, who stood on his points, esteeming himself every way the better man, would be ready to take offence at this, and to say, as it is in the first verse of the third chapter, "What advantage then has the Jews, or what profit is there of circumcision?" The Apostle answers by way of concession. And though he holds his conclusion firm (which is that both Jews and Gentiles, considered in their naturals, are all under sin, (Rom 3:9-22) and that in this respect there is no difference) yet he readily grants that in some regards the Jews far excelled the rest of the world. Diverse of their privileges are insinuated in the former part of the second verse, "Much every way;" in the latter, one instanced in, as most considerable, "Chiefly because to them were committed the oracles of God."

---

[86] *Religionum vincula sunt arctissima. Religionum odia sunt acerbissima.—Reddimus obscaenae convitia debita genti.—Quae genitale caput propudiosa metit—Septima quaeq; dies turpi damnata veterno.—Tanquam lassati mollis imago Dei.* Rutil, *Itiner.* lib. 1.

§6. V. Those were preserved with much solicitude. History tells us how great care the Romans took for the safe custody of the Sibylline oracles in their capitol after Tarquin had bought them:[87] when the capital was burnt and those books in it, what means were used to get other copies out of Greece; and how a College of priests was appointed to keep them safe. These surely deserve as much and more care in every suitable possible way. The ancient Jews preserved the letter of Scripture entirely, but lost the sense; as the papists now keep the text, but let go the *truth*. A good Christian will not be backward in giving all diligence to hold fast both, by laying the scripture up in his judgment, conscience and memory. We are all desirous to have fair and well printed Bibles. Believe it, the fairest impression of the Bible is to have it well printed on the reader's heart. Mr. Fox tells us of one Mr. Crow a sea-man, who being shipwrecked lost all his wares, and also cast five pounds in money into the sea, but kept his New Testament hanging still about his neck, so swimming on a broken mast, until after four days (all the rest of his company being drowned) he was discovered and taken up in that posture alive.[88] The only way of preserving souls from being drowned in eternal perdition, is having the grace and truth of Scripture so bound on the heart as to be willing to part with money or anything else, for the safety of them. It is well worthy of our best consideration how much and how often Solomon in the Proverbs presses this. It is known how careful the most are to get and keep silver and gold, but "Receive my instruction (wisdom says there) and not silver; my knowledge rather than choice gold," (Prov. 8:10). Yet as well as men love money, they will rather let go that than lose their members, in which none are more dear than the apple of the eye. "My son (He says) keep my words, and lay up my commandments with thee: keep my commandments and live, and my law as the apple of thine eye," (Prov. 8:1-2). Yet skin

[87] Vid. *Molinaei Vates*, lib. iii. c. page 12.

[88] *Acts & Monum.* vol. 3. last edition, page 705.

for skin and all a man has will he give for his life: if the loss of a member or two will save that, they shall go. His advice to his son is, "Take fast hold of instruction, let her not go; keep her, far she is thy life," (Prov. 4:13). Yet the martyrs parted even with their lives to save their souls; our keeping of these is really of as great concernment as the keeping of our very souls, for so saith Solomon, "He that keepeth the commandment, keepeth his own soul," (Prov. 19:16).

EXERCITATION IV.

How Scripture-oracles far excel those of the heathen in point of perspicuity, of piety, of veracity, of duration and of authority. The divine authority of Scripture asserted by arguments. An inference from the whole Aphorism.

§1. Having showed in which they agree, I am bow to make known in which these Scripture-oracles differ from and excel those other, *viz.*

1. In point of perspicuity. Apollo's oracles were delivered in so dark and ambiguous terms, as gave the Grecians, though they were his chief worshippers, occasion to style him by the name of λοξιας,[89] because he seldom answered directly in doubtful cases, but used such a form of words as might be diversely interpreted, to the end his credit might be saved, whatever event the business had about which he was consulted, where Scripture is so framed, as to deliver all things necessary to salvation in a clear and perspicuous way. There are indeed some obscure passages in it to exercise our understandings,[90] and prevent our loathing of overmuch plainness and simplicity: yet whatever is needful for us to satisfy hunger, and nourish our souls to life eternal, is so expressed (I do not say that it may be understood, but so) as men that do not wilfully shut their eyes against the light,

---

[89] Euseb. *praeparat. Evangelic.* lib. 4.

[90] *Pascimur apertis, exercemur obscuris, illic fames pellitur, hic fastidium.* Augustine.

cannot possibly but understand it.

§2. II. In point of piety. The heathen were put on many ungodly practices by their oracles, if good historians may be credited,[91] even by those of the Sibyls,[92] which were of greatest esteem for sanctity. But the frame of Scripture is according to godliness. Piety sparkles in every leaf, and throughout the whole there runs a constant exaltation of God in Christ. There are near all sorts of poems (to instance in them) with which we meet in human writings have their parallels in the Canonical books; but they are such as carry in them a genius and strain of godliness far beyond anything that occurs in the poems of men. There are Επινίκια, Songs of victory; but such as exalt, not the prowess of man, but the glory of God. So Exodus the fifteenth: Επινίηδια, funeral songs, but such as celebrate Christ's death and the good will of God in it; so Psalm the twenty second, and Isaiah the fifty third. Επωτικά songs of love, but such as set forth the love of Christ to his Spouse the church, and her mutual affection to him. So Psalm the forty fifth, and the Canticles. There are also βακολινοί, sacred pastorals, but such as magnify no other Shepherd but God atone, so Psalm twenty third. Yes γεωρεκά too, but such as ascribe all to him. So Psalm sixty fifth. Let Virgil is asked *Quid faciat laetas segetes*, he will wholly insist on this or that secondary cause of fertility. Ask David, he presently falls in his Georgics on praising God as the author of all fruitfulness. "Thou visitest the earth and waterest it; Thou makest it soft with showers; Thou blessest the springing of it; Thou crownest the year with thy goodness; Thy paths drop fatness, *etc.*" in the end of that forecited Psalm.

§3. III. In point of veracity. Many falsehoods were littered, much flattery practiced by their oracles. As when Socrates was declared by the father of lies to be the wisest man on earth,[93] notwithstanding the two great prophets

[91] Plutarch, in *Publicola*. Livius lib. 21-22.
[92] Sir Walt. Raleigh, lib. 5. pages, 374, and 393.
[93] Helvicus, page 18.

Haggai and Zechariah were his contemporaries. And when Apollo was said φιλιππίζεμ by reason of his so palpably favoring of King Philip in his responses.[94] Where Scripture is free, not only from all degrees of falsehood (for of it we may say, *verity of verities, all is verity*) but of flattery too. Insomuch as it may be observed concerning the pen-men of holy scripture, that, contrary to the custom and guise of human writers, they are not more free, full and impartial in any relations, than in those which concern their own failings, and theirs who were nearest and dearest to them. Moses' unbelief, David's blood guiltiness, Jonah's pettishness, Jeremiah's impatience, Paul's persecution, are recorded by their own pens. And where the other evangelists in the enumeration of Christ's apostles barely name Matthew for one, without setting any brand on him, he himself tells us what he had been before Christ called him, Matthew the publican (Matthew 10:3). Yes where Paul in his epistle to the Galatians had brought in a charge against Peter for Judaizing, and spoken of his own "resisting him openly, because he was indeed to be blamed," (Gal. 2:11); yet Peter for all this, in his second epistle (which was written a good while after) describes him his "beloved brother Paul," (2 peter 3:15-16) and does not commends his wisdom only, but all his epistles, even that in which he himself was reproved. As for their carriage toward others, Moses who loved the Hebrews so well as to wish himself blotted out of God's book, rather than they should perish, yet does not spare to relate their many rebellions, with the aggravations of it to the full. The idolatry of his brother Aaron, the murmuring of his sister Miriam, the frowardness of his wife Zipporah, are as freely recorded by him as any other historical passages whatever. Luke, who was Paul's companion and scholar, tells us in the Acts what havoc he had made, and how sore an enemy he had been to the church of Christ. Mark, whom Peter describes his son, aggravates the story of his dear father's sin against Christ,

---

[94] Vide Sirenium *de fato* l. 9. c. 12 and 13.

more than some of the other evangelists.[95] Luke and John tell us barely of his denying; but Mark adds further, that "he began to swear and curse, saying, I know not the man."[96]

§4. IV. In point of duration. Satan, who is God's ape in very many things, had his oracles also of both sorts, vocal; as at Delphi and Dodona, which Ovid in that respect joins together in one verse, *Non mihi si Delphi, Dodonaque diceret ipsa*; written, as in the Sibyl's books contained at first in three volumes, two in which, as it is said, were purposely cast into the fire by her that presented them, because Tarquin would not meet their price; the third sold for as much as was demanded in the beginning of the treaty for all three.[97] Now providence so ordered things, that there was a remarkable failing of the former sort on the coming of Christ in the flesh, and a total cessation of them not long after his death, insomuch as Plutarch wrote a book of their defect; and a destruction of the latter after Christianity had taken root in the Roman empire, when Stilico burnt the Sibyl's books as fermenters of paganism and profaneness.[98] He that was manifested to destroy the works of the devil stopped the mouths of those evil angels that gave answers by oracles. The *Sun of Righteousness* arose, and those wild beasts were forced to betake themselves to their dens, Then was the prince of this world judged and his angels dislodged, for the Lord Christ had ejected them. But the Old Testament scriptures received a strong affirmation from Christ by his appealing to them, arguing from them, and expounding of them. Yes, so far were the oracles of God from any diminution by his coming, preaching and dying, that they did not receive a confirmation only, but a glorious augmentation, in that within a while after there was added to them by his secretaries, the evangelists

---

[95] 1 Pet. last. 13.

[96] Mark 14:68, 70-71.

[97] Plin. *natur. hist*. lib. 13. c. page 13.

[98] *Sibylina fata cremavit opis*. Vide Baron, *tom*. 4. ad annum Christi 389. n. 56. et *Molin. Vates*, page 182.

and apostles, another volume, I mean the books of the New Testament, on the publishing in which there came out from God as it were a second edition of his oracles much enlarged.

§5. Fifthly and lastly, in point of authority. Those were from the father of lies, as has been said; but these from the Father of lights. Scripture is of divine authority, "Holy men of God (Peter says) spake as they were moved by the Holy Spirit," (2 Peter 2:1). They wrote accordingly, "All scripture, *Paul says*, was given by inspiration of God," (2 Tim. 3:16). It is not more true that they are oracles for their use, than that they have God for their author. Many large volumes have been written to make good this assertion. It is a thing in which the Spirit of God, who indited the scripture, gives such abundant satisfaction to the spirits of godly men, as to make other arguments, though not useless, yet to them of less necessity: he alone bearing witness to the divinity of holy writ, and to the truth of his own testimony, so putting a final issue to that controversy. But because there is need of other reasons for the conviction of other men, I have produced certain arguments elsewhere, and shall here make an addition of two more, which are not mentioned in that discourse, one from consent, another from continuance.[99]

§6. From consent so, writings of men differ exceedingly one from another, which made Seneca say, "Philosophers would then be all of one mind, when all clocks were brought to strike at one, and the same time."[100] Yes, it is hard finding an author that does not differ from himself more or less, if he write much, and at various seasons. But here is a most harmonious consent. The word, since written fully agrees with that which in former times was delivered to the Patriarchs, and transmitted by word of mouth. As the word God is the same today, yesterday and forever, although not incarnate until the fullness of time came, and then made flesh. So the word of God was for substance the same before and

---

[99] *Tactica Sacra*. lib. 2. c. page ult.

[100] *Tunc inter Philosophos conveniet quando inter Horologia*.

after, although until Moses received a command to put it in writing, there wanted that kind of incarnation. And as the written word agreed with the unwritten, so one part of that which is written harmonizes with another. The two Testaments, Old and New, like the two breasts of the same person give the same miLuke As if one draw water out of a deep well with vessels of different metal, one of brass, another of tin, a third of earth, the water may seem at first to be of a different color, but when the vessels are brought near to the eye, this diversity of colors vanishes, and the waters tasted have the same relish: so here, the different style of the historiographers from prophets, of the prophets from evangelists, of the evangelists from apostles, may make the truths of Scripture seem of different complexions until one look narrowly into them, and taste them advisedly, then will the identity both of color and relish manifest itself.

§7. From continuance in this way. Notwithstanding all the confusions that have happened in the world, all the fires that have been kindled, the massacres that have been executed, and the battles that have been fought against the true Christian Religion, the store house of it has continued to this day, and these oracles of God been preserved in spite of hell. Solomon's philosophical treatises, against which the world had no spleen but a liking of, are long since lost; where his canonical writings are extant still. When the earth opened up to swallow up Korah and his company, there are some who think some of his children were taken up by the hand of God into the air until the earth closed again, then set down without having received any harm, because in the titles of various Psalms, mention is made of the sons of Korah,[101] whom they suppose then preserved to propagate these whose service the Lord had a purpose to use so long after. How often has persecution opened her mouth from age to age, and swallowed up millions both of men and books! Yet the Bible has been continued still by the over-ruling hand of heaven,

[101] Tirinus in *Numer.* 16. *nota ultima.*

yes, which makes it more remarkable, God has so befooled the devil in this, as to preserve his own book many times by the hands of his and its enemies. It is too well known how small friends the Jews are and have here before been to the truth contained in the Old Testament, yet of them did the Lord make use to keep it, and they proved to be careful in trust for making over the assurances of life to us Gentiles. Concerning one book of the New Testament, *viz.* the Apocalypse, it is very observable that when its authority was questioned of old, the Church of Rome struck in with her testimony, and was a special means to have it kept in the number of canonical books; not without a special providence. God, who made Pharaoh's daughter a second mother to Moses, whom he had appointed to bring destruction afterwards on her father's house and kingdom, made the Romish Church a dry nurse to preserve this Book (whose meaning she did not know,) that it might bring desolation on herself and her children afterwards. Well may we therefore conclude, and say of the Holy Bible, as Gamaliel once did of the apostle's preaching (Acts 5:38-39), "Had this work been of men it would have come to nought long ere this," but being of God, the devil and his accomplices have not been able to overthrow it.

§8. We learn also from what has been said, to magnify the grace of God who in order to the promoting of our blessedness, has brought us of this nation to the knowledge, of Christian Religion, for a lack in which many millions in other parts still sit in darkness and the shadow of death. It was a memorable act of Witekindus, one of the Dukes of Saxony, who flourished about the nine hundredth year of Christ[102] after his renouncing paganism, and receiving the faith of the gospel, he caused the black horse, which he had formerly born in his military colors, to be laid aside, and instead of it, a white horse to be born, in testimony of his triumphant joy for that great change; perhaps because among the Romans, the manlier was to make use of such colored

[102] Sir H. Spelman in *Aspilogia*, page 71.

steeds in their triumphs.[103] It put me in mind of what we read in Revelation 6 and in the 2nd where Christ is described as going out in the ministry of the gospel, which was then newly embraced by that Prince, "Behold a white horse, and he that sat on him had a bow, and a crown was given to him, and he went forth conquering and to conquer." Yes, where there are various modes of the Christian Religion, we are therefore to have our hearts and mouths filled with the highest praises of God, because we have it in the purest, that is, the Protestant way, which allows the people in general a free use of bibles in their native language. In various parts even of Europe it is far otherwise, particularly in Spain, where the bible in their vulgar tongue is reckoned among prohibited books,[104] and suffices to bring him that reads it into danger of the *Inquisition*. Therefore let such as list make their boast of other things which England is said to be famous for, as beautiful churches, bridges, women, *etc*.[105] If I were asked what advantage have Englishmen, and what profit is there of living in that Island, my answer should be, much every way; but chiefly, because to them are committed the oracles of God, and liberty to read their father's mind in their mother tongue.

---

[103] *Qui candore cum nive certabant*. Pompon. *Laetus*.

[104] *In Hispania in indice librorum prohibitorum regula sexta sic habet. Prohibentur Biblia in vulgari lingua cum omnibus suis partibus*. Azor. *Instit. moral*. Tom, 1. lib. 8. c. page 26, page 714.

[105] *Anglia, mons, pons, sons, ecclesia, faemina, lana*.

APHORISM III.

Scripture-oracles, supposing it sufficiently clear by the light of nature, that there is a God, make a further discovery of what he is in his essence, subsistence and attributes.

EXERCITATION 1.

1 Cor. 15:34 expounded. Opinionists compared to sleepers and drunkards. Three observations from the end of the verse. What knowledge of God is unattainable in this life. What may be had. The knowledge we have concerning God distinguished into Natural, Literal, and Spiritual.

§1. "Awake to righteousness and sin not: for some have not the knowledge of God; I speak this to your shame," (1 Cor. 15:34). These are the apostles express words to his Corinthians. Which will be better understood, if we *consider*,

I. That there was a time, when of all the nations in the world Greece was held the most licentious, and Corinth of all the cities in Greece; insomuch as in common speech revelers were said to play the Grecians, and fornicators to play the Corinthians.[106] Also that after, the grace of Christ (who came to call sinners to repentance) had appeared there in planting Christianity, this riotous humour was notably fed in false brethren by the false teachers, who opened a gate to all profaneness by denying the resurrection.

II. That of such teachers and professors Paul speaks in this chapter, "How say some among you that there is no resurrection?"[107] and calls on them in the beginning of this verse to awaken to righteousness, because the many and gross vapors that ascended from this heresy had cast them into a deep sleep, in which all their spiritual senses were bound. Heretics may perhaps pretend to the highest strains of

---

[106] Pregraecari. Κορινθιαζεσθαι.
[107] Verse 12.

devotion, and make their boast of strongest assurances. Yet all this is but like the talking or walking of men in their sleep, or like the quick and nimble phantasms of dreaming students. Their devotion is but a dream of piety, their assurance will prove but a dream of happiness.

§2. III. That the word Εκνήψατε there used by the apostle is very emphatic, and properly signifies an awaking out of such a sleep as has been occasioned by too much drink. So Noah awoke from his wine, and "awake ye drunkards saith Joel."[108] Neither will it be difficult to discern in as sensual opinionist the symptoms of a drunken man. You may see him reeling to and fro, now entertaining this odd conceit, tomorrow that, and the next day a third, unstable in all. Well if not vomiting too and casting out scornful reproaches on all that are of a contrary judgment, as on dark and low-spirited men. You may perceive him full of tongue, as drunkards commonly used to be, prating, and venting his own apprehensions everywhere; yes perhaps pasting of himself and his party as too many, too hard for all their opposites. So one drunkard, our proverb says, is forty men strong. Who so attempts to reason with him will easily find him as incapable of conviction, as Nabal was of Abigail's narration until his wine is gone out of him (1 Sam. 15:37).

IV. That the cause was manifest why such men had a charge given them not to sin, awake to righteousness, the apostle says, and sin not. For that the desperate opinion they had embraced was a high-way to abominable courses. The denial of a resurrection has a natural tendency to looseness of life, inclining men to say, as they did, "Let us eat and drink, for tomorrow we shall die," (1 Cor. 15:32). And the more licentious any man is, the more willing to close with such an opinion. Accordingly among the Jews, where most of the common people adhered to the Pharisees, who professed strictness, and amused them with outward forms of godliness, the gentry and such as gave themselves most to

---

[108] ἐξενηψε Gen. 9:24. Εκνήψατι, Joel 1:5.

voluptuousness became followers of the Sadducees, who denied the resurrection. Such men (Theophylact says)[109] are not so easily persuaded of a resurrection, because they are afraid of punishments in another life, if any be.

§3. V. That these especially were the *persona* whom Paul there censures for gross ignorance, such as they had just cause to be ashamed of. He had said before in the twelfth verse, "Some among you say there is no resurrect ion," in the thirty-fourth verse speaking still of the same men, "Some have not the knowledge of God," (1 Cor. 15:12). Only where in case of personal affiants to himself and his fellow preachers he had appeared touch more mild in the fourth chapter, "I write not these things (he says there) to shame you, but as my beloved sons I warn you." Here he sets an edge on his rebuke, and tells them he spoke it to their shame; because the heresy he strikes at, struck at the root of all religion, and became an inlet to epicurism, yes to atheism.

VI. That from the latter part alone, "Some have not the knowledge of God, I speak this to your shame," three observations may be raised without offering violence to the words, one as implied, the rest as expressed, in other words,

1. There is a knowledge of God to be had.
2. Some do not have it.
3. The lack of it is a matter of shame.

All which I intend to insist on in this and the following exercitations.

§4. Concerning the first. There is a knowledge of God to perfection, which is always saving; and another to salvation indeed, but as yet imperfect. The former had been proudly challenged by some sons of delusion, and accounted attainable in this life by the sole improvement of reason. For we read of Aetius that be dared to say, "I so know God, as I do myself; yea I do not know myself so well as I do God."[110] A certain

---

109 Οι γάρ έαυτοῖς ουτεῖδοτες καπά είπίθονται εἶται ανάςασιν διὰ τῶν [βαλαζοειαν]. Theolphyl. in 1 Cor. 15.

110 Ουτως όιδ ατόν Θεόν ώς παρ έμαυτόν κί α τοσᾶτόν όιδα έμαυτόν ώς τόν

evidence to make it appear that the wretch neither knew himself nor God. And Peter Abelard is said to have maintained this assertion, "that the whole of God's essence may be comprehended by human reason."[111] But the truth is, it is neither attainable in this life, as being reserved for another world (according to the apostle's doctrine, (1 Cor. 13:9-10) "We know but in part. When that which is perfect is come, then that which is in part shall be done away,") nor at all by the sole improvement of reason. The less cannot comprehend the greater, "God is greater than our heart," (1 John 3:2) St. John says, therefore in-comprehensible by the shallow reason of shipwrecked nature. He and the Sun are alike in this, both refresh wary beholders, but put out the eyes of curious pryers. However faith may look on God with much comfort, for reason to stare too much on him is the way to lose her sight. When she has tired and wildered herself in searching after the true God her return must be *non est inventus*, he is not to be found, at least not by me. Faith only can find him out, yet not to perfection either, although to salvation it may and does.

§5. Which is the latter kind of knowledge above mentioned, and that I am now speaking to, as attainable here. Even the lowest rank of Christians, whom John describes his little children, are described by their having known the Father (1 John 2:13). And because the new covenant runs this way, "They shall all know me from the least of them to the greatest of them, saith the Lord," (Jer. 31:33); But although it is most true, that there is a saving knowledge of God attainable here, yet for any man to presume, that whatever knowledge of God he attains, it will certainly save him is a most strong delusion. For where there is a natural and a literal as well as a spiritual knowledge, it will be manifest by the sequel of this discourse, that none is saving but the third. The first is that which may be fetched out of the book of nature without any further

---

Θεόν. Epiph. *haeres.*

[111] *Totum quod Deus est humana ratione comprehendi posse*. Osiand. *Hist. Eccles. centur*. 12. page 265.

induction of higher principles. Antony, the religious monk, when a certain philosopher asked him how he did to live without books, answered he had the voluminous book of all the creatures to study on, and to contemplate God in.[112] "Believe me," said Bernard[113] to his friend, as one that speaks out of experience, "there is sometimes more to be found in woods, then there is in books. Trees and stones will teach thee that, which is not to be learned from other masters." The book of Scripture without doubt has the preeminence in worth by many degrees; but that of the creatures had the precedency in time, and was extant long before the written word. We may therefore well begin with it.

EXERCITATION II.

That there is a God, the prime dictate of natural light; deducible from man's looking backward to the creation, forward to the rewards and punishments dispensed after death, upward to the angels above us, downwards to inferior beings, within ourselves to the composition of our bodies and dictates of our consciences, about us to the various occurrences in the world.

§1 There are six several acts which every man of understanding is able to exert in a way of contemplation. He may *respicere, prospicere, suspicere, despicere, inspicere, and circumspicere.* Whosoever shall advisedly exercise any of these will undoubtedly meet, with some demonstrations of a deity; much more if he be industriously conversant in them all.

I. If he *respicere*, looks backward to the creation of the world (which the light of nature will tell him had a beginning) he will see and understand the invisible things of God by the things that are made, even his eternal power and

[112] Socrat. *Eccles. history*. Lib. 4. C. page 23.

[113] Bern. *Epist.* 107. *Aquid amplius invenies in sylvis quam in libris.*

God-head, as Paul speaks.[114] Basil therefore called the World a school in which reasonable souls are taught the knowledge of God.[115] In a musical instrument when we observe diverse strings meet in a harmony, we conclude that some skillful musician tuned them; when we see thousands of men in a field, marshaled under several colors, all yielding exact obedience, we infer that there is a General, to whose commands they are all subject. In a watch, we take notice of great and small wheels all so fitted as to concur to an orderly motion, we acknowledge the skill of an artificer. When we come into a printing-house and see a great number of different letters so ordered as to make a book, the consideration of this makes it evident that there is a composer, by whose art they were brought into such a frame. When we behold a fair building, we conclude it had an architect, a stately ship well rigged and safely conducted to the port, that it has a Pilot. So the same is said here. The visible world is such an instrument, army, watch, book, building, and ship, as undeniably argues a God, who was and is the Tuner, General, and Artificer, the Composer, Architect and Pilot of it.

§2. II. If he *prospicere*, looks forwards to the rewards and punishments, to be dispensed in another world, (which the heathen's Elysium and Tartarus show them to have had a slight knowledge of by the light of nature[116]) he cannot but acknowledge some supreme Judge, by whom they are dispensed; and that he is a searcher of hearts, in which piety and sin chiefly reside; seeing it is impossible for him otherwise to pass righteous judgment without mistaking good for evil, and evil for good. Some discourses of Plato, and some verses of Menander, besides many other testimonies, make it appear that the notion of these things was entertained by the wiser

---

[114] Rom. 1:20.

[115] Ψυχώς λογικαν διδατκαλοίον, κί της θεογνωσιας παιδεντηριον. Basil. *Hex.*

[116] Vid. Livium Galant. *Christian. Theolog. Cum Platonica comparat.* Lib. xii. Page 341 & subsequent.

sort both of philosophers and poets,[117] and that which they held of a world to come is a topic sufficient to argue from, for the being of a God in the world that is.

III. If he *suspicere*, looks upwards to a rank of creatures above himself, I mean good and evil spirits, of which the heathens were not ignorant; witness their large discourses of daemons, of intelligences, and of a *bonus et malus genius*. For if such creatures as angels be acknowledged, so good, holy, wise and powerful as they are said to be by all that take notice of them, they must have a maker, better, holier, wiser and more powerful than themselves; seeing the cause is always more noble than the effect, and has that perfection which it communicates much more eminent in itself. If there are devils, whose mischief and might are both of them so confessedly great, there must needs be a God to restrain and countermand them; else the world would soon be turned into a mere hell, full of nothing but abominations and confusion.

§3. IV. If he *despicere*, looks downward to things below himself, whose nature is inferior to that of man; the contemplation of elements, plants and brute beasts, will extort the confession of a deity. "The heavens declare the glory of God, and the firmament showeth his handy-work," (Psalm 19:1). Nor these alone, which have so much of magnificence in them: but the least fly, if it could be anatomized, would be found to have in it more miracles than parts; such proportion of members, distinction of offices, correspondence of instruments, as speaks the infinite power and wisdom of the Maker. Well might Job say, as he did, "Ask now the beasts and they shall teach thee, and the fowls of the air, and they shall tell thee: or speak to the earth, and it shall teach thee, and the fishes of the sea shall declare to thee. Who knoweth not in all these that the hand of the Lord has worked this?" (Job 12:7-9).

V. If he *inspicere*, looks within himself, and that either

---

[117] Μηδέν πλανήθης ές ν Άδαικρισις, ής περ ποίήσει Θεός ό πάντων δεσποτης. Menand.

to the composition of his body, or to the dictates of his conscience. We are so fearfully and wonderfully made (Psalm 139:14), that the great physician Galen, though a heathen, being amazed at the wisdom which he discovered in the frame of every member in man's body, could no longer contain himself, but fell to praising the Creator in a hymn.[118] As for conscience there is nothing more common than for wicked men after the commission of gross sins to be inwardly tormented and affrighted reason of something it suggests, the substance in which is, that there is a God, and that he will judge them for what they have done. Calvin tells us of a certain profane fellow who was ranting at his inn, and blasphemously wresting that of the Psalmist, "the heaven of heavens is the Lord's, and the earth has he given to the children of men," as if God left us to do what we wish on earth, confining himself and his providence to the heavens; by this as far as he openly dares disavowing a deity. On which he was struck suddenly with extreme torments in his body, and began to cry out, *O God, O God.* So natural it is even for the worst of mankind to acknowledge a God in their extremities and for others more ingenuous, even among those that want Scripture-light (as Tertullian has observed) to be frequently saying, "God seeth. I commend it to God; God will recompense," which drew from him an exclamation that must be warily understood, "O the testimony of a soul naturally Christian!"[119]

§4. VI. If he *circumspicere*, looks round about him to the various occurrences in the world; the great deliverances vouchsafed to some, the great calamities brought on others, both beyond all expectation, "The Lord is, and cannot but be known by the judgments which he executeth," (Psalm 9:16); so by the; blessings which he bestows. Who can see a Daniel

---

[118] Galen, lib. 3. *de usu partium, compono hic canticum in Creatoris nostri laudem, etc. Multa miser timeo, quia feci multa proterve, exemplique metu terreor ipse mei*. Ovid. 1. 1. *Amor. Eleg.* 1.

[119] *O testimonium animae naturaliter Christianae!* Tertull. *Apolog.*

rescued from reasonable lions, unreasonable men, a Moses preserved in an ark of bulrushes, a Noah in a deluge of waters, others in a furnace of fire? Who can behold a Pharaoh plagued, a Herod eaten up with worms, an Achitophel making away with himself, a Judas bursting asunder in the midst, an Arius voiding of his bowels, and not cry out, as it is in the Psalm, "Verily there is a reward for the righteous; doubtless there is a God that judgeth in the earth?" (Psalm 58 to the last.) We meet with a passage in Atheneus not unworthy, as I conceive, to be taken notice of, and recorded here. When at a public meeting in some place of receipt, a beam of the house suddenly falling had dashed out the brains of a notoriously wicked man in the sight of many by-standers to whom he was known; one Stratonicus broke out into a speech so emphatic in the Greek, that it can hardly be translated without much loss, yet take it this way: *Sirs, he said, the beam of light which I have, convinces me that there is a God; if any of you are otherwise minded, this beam of wood may suffice to beget in him the same persuasion.*[120]

§5. But notwithstanding all this, as it fared with the wise men from the east, who, although they were assured by the appearancel of a star that a King of the Jews was born, yet needed the prophet's manuduction to give them notice who he was, and where they might find him. So though natural reason improved can make it appear that there is a God, yet there is a necessity of Scripture revelation to inform us who and what he is, in regard of his essence, subsistence, and attributes; in all these the written word goes far beyond whatever was or could be discerned in nature's school, and becomes the fountain of that literal knowledge of which we are now to treat.

EXERCITATION III.

Reason's three ways of discovering God, fall short of manifesting what he

[120] Ἄνδρος δοκῶ εἰ σι θεοί. Εἰ δὲ μή εἰ σι δοκῶ εἰ σι. Athen. *Deipnosophist*. l. 8.

is. The expression in Exod. 3:14 most comprehensive. A brief exposition of it. Satan's impudence. Nature and Art both unable to discover the Trinity. What scripture reveals about it. Basil's memento. Julian's impiety. Socinians branded. The three persons compared to those three wells in Genesis 26.

§1. Divines tell us of three ways by which reason goes to work in her enquiry after God; but none of them all is able to make a full discovery of his essence. The first is *via causalitatis*, when from the creatures, in which God is the supreme universal cause, reason begins to contemplate him as their efficient, because they could not make themselves. But here it only discovers *quod sit*, that there is a God, to whom all things owe their beings; not *quid sit*, what he is. The second is *via remotionis*, when it considers the several imperfections of creatures, and removes them all from God, as inconsistent with a deity. So it conceives him as immortal, impassible, impeccable, because to die, suffer, sin, are imperfections. But this only shows, *quid non sit*, what he is not; she is still to seek for what he is. The third is *via eminentiae*, when reason considers the various perfections which are scattered here and there, among created beings, and ascribes them all to God in an eminent and transcendent way. As when finding in angels and men wisdom, holiness and strength, it conceives God to be most wise, most holy, and most strong. Yet even, this doth but show, *qualis sit, non quis*, what kind of being God is, not who is he. Reason for that must be beheld to revelation. In which respects I cannot but applaud the wise, answer of that philosopher, (Epictetus, as some, report) who when his hearers said to him, Sir, you have uttered many excellent things concerning God, but we cannot as yet understand what he is, told them plainly, "Were I able fully to set forth God, I should either be God myself, or God himself cease to be what he is."[121] *Si omnino ego Deum declararem, vel ego Deus essem, vel*

[121] Joh. De Carthag. *Homil. Catholic*. Lib. 1 homil. 8. page 47.

ille Deus non foret.

§2. Were all such passages set aside as are not originally the heathens own, but borrowed from Jewish or Christian authors, I should not be afraid to affirm that there is one very short expression in scripture, in other words, "I am that I am," (Exod. 3:14), which reveals more of God, than all the large volumes of heathen writers. An expression so framed as to take in all differences of time, according to the idiom of the Hebrew tongue, in which a verb of the future tense, as Ehieh is, may signify time past and present, as well as that which is to come. Here arises a great latitude of interpretation; for according to different readings it implies different things. Reading it, as we do, "I am that I am," it imports the supremacy of God's being. The creatures have more of non-entity than of being in them: It is proper to him to say, *I am.* Ειμλ ό ών as in the Septuagint. Or the simplicity of it; where in creatures the thing and its being, *ens* and *essentia* are distinguishable, in him they are both one. Or the ineffability; as if the Lord had said to Moses, enquiring his name; I am myself, and there is nothing without myself that can fully express my being. Which put Scaliger on inventing that admirable epithet, 'Αυταυτός, that is, *ipsisimus ipse.*[122] Or lastly, the eternity of it; since there never was, never will be a time, in which God might not, or may not say of himself, I am. Where it is that when Christ would manifest his "goings out from everlasting," (Micah 5:2) as Micah phrases it, he makes use of this expression, "Before Abraham was, I am, *not* I was; (for that might have been said of Enoch, Noah and others who lived before Abraham's time, yet were not eternal,) but *I am.*[123] If it is rendered *I am* what *I was*, as Piscator would have it, then it speaks of his immutability. I am in executing what I was in promising, yesterday and today and the same forever. If, as others, *I will be what I will be*, then it denotes his independency.

---

[122] Scalig. de Subtilit. *Exercit*. 365. §2.

[123] Quae verbulo hoc continentur omnium hominum capacitatem transcendunt. Andr. Rivet. in Exod. 3:14.

That essence which the creatures have depends on the Creator's will; none of them can say I will be, not having of and in itself any power to make itself persevere in being, as God has. It may perhaps intimate all these, and much more than the tongues of angels can utter. Verily it is a speech containing more in it (as a learned writer acknowledged) than human capacities can attain.

§3. I shall therefore forbear to enlarge on it. Let me only observe before I leave it the notorious impudence of apostate spirits. Satan not contenting himself to have got the name of *Jove*, in imitation of *Jehovah*, the incommunicable name of God, prevailed with his deluded followers to ascribe to him that, which the Lord of heaven and earth assumes to himself in this mysterious place of Exodus, saying, "I am that I am." For over the gate of Apollo's temple in the city of Delphi, so famed for oracles, was engraved in capital letters this Greek word *EI*, which signifies *You are*, by which those that came there to worship, or to consult Satan's oracle, were instructed to acknowledge him the fountain of being, and the only true God; as one Ammonius is brought in discoursing at large of this very thing in the last treatise of Plutarch's morals, to which I refer the reader.

§4. As to the point of divine subsistence, *Jehovah Elohim*, Father, Son and Holy Spirit; three persons, but one God; or in Leo's expression, "One God without division in a trinity of persons, and three persons without confusion in a unity of essence,"[124] it is a discovery altogether supernatural. Yes, nature is so far from finding it out, that now when Scripture has revealed it, he cannot by all the help of art comprehend, or set it forth as she does other things; grammar itself lacking proper and full words by which to express, logic strong demonstrations by which to prove, and rhetoric apt similitudes by which to clear so mysterious a truth. The terms essence, persons, trinity, generation, procession and such like, which are commonly made use of for lack of better, have been,

---

[124] Deus indivise unus in trinitate, et inconfuse trinus in unitate.

and will be caviled at as short of fully reaching the mystery in all its dimension. Of the similitudes usually brought for its illustration, that which Hilary said is most true, "They may gratify the understanding of man, but none of them exactly suit with the nature of God."[125] For example, not that of a root, a trunk, and a branch; the trunk proceeding from the root, the branch from both, yet but one tree. Because a root may for some time be without a trunk, and a trunk without a branch, but God the Father, never was without his Son, nor the Father and Son without their co-eternal Spirit. Neither that of a crystal ball held in a river on a sunshine day, in which case there would be a sun in the firmament, begetting another sun on the crystal ball, and a third sun proceeding from both the former, appearing in the surface of the water; yet but one sun in all; for in this comparison, two of the suns are but imaginary, none real save that in heaven; where the Father, Word, and Spirit are distinct persons indeed, but each of them truly and really God.

§5. Well therefore may rhetoricians say, *It is not in us*, and in our similitudes fully to clear this high point; logicians also, *It is not in us*, and in our demonstrations fully to prove it. For however reason be able from the creatures to demonstrate a Godhead, as has been said, yet it cannot from there a Trinity; no more than he that looks a curious picture, can tell whether it was drawn by an Englishman or an Italian, only that the piece had a artificer, and such a one as was a prime master in that faculty; because the limner drew it as he was an artist, not as one of this or that nation. So the world is a production of that essence which is common to all three, not any personal emanation from this or that subsistent; which is the reason why a deity may be inferred from there, but not any distinction of persons, much less the determinate number of a Trinity. The doctrine in which is like a temple filled with smoke, such smoke as not only hinder the view of the quickest

[125] Omnis comparatio homini potius utilis habeatur quam Deo apta. Hilar, lib. 1. *de Trin.*

eye, but hurts the sight of such as dare with undue curiosity pry into it. A mystery which my faith embraces as revealed in the word, but my reason cannot fathom. While others run themselves on ground, and dispute it until their understandings be non-plussed; may I be enabled to believe what Scripture testifies concerning an unbegotten Father, an only begotten Son, and a Holy Spirit proceeding from both; Three, yet but One: and in this to acquiesce without enquiring as Mary did, when the angel foretold her miraculous conception, *How can this thing be?* To which question my return should be no other but that of Augustine, who notwithstanding his fifteen books concerning the Trinity, modestly said, "Askest thou me how there can be Three in One, and One inThree? I do not know, and am freely willing to profess my ignorance herein."[126] Verily this light is dazzling, and our eyes are weak. It is a case in which the wisest clerks are ignorant, and the ablest orators infants.

§6. Yet is the mystery itself written in Scripture as it were with the sun-beams, I do not reject as invalid, but only forbear as less evident the places commonly cited out of Moses and the, prophets; choosing rather to insist on New Testament discoveries, when the veil which formerly hid the Holy of Holies from men's sight, was rent in pieces, and the secrets of heaven exposed to more open view, than while the church was in her minority. At our Savior's baptism there was a clearer manifestation of the Trinity than ever before; as if God had reserved this discovery on purpose to add the greater honor to his only Son's solemn inauguration into the office of Mediatorship, which was then most visibly undertaken. He who casts his eye on, the third chapter of the gospel according to Luke, will quickly discern the Father in an audible voice, heard but not seen, "This is my beloved Son, in whom I am well pleased," (Luke 3:21, 22) The, word, made flesh now in the waters, receiving baptism, and after praying so, both heard and seen. The Spirit like a dove descending and resting on.

[126] Nescio, et libentur nescire profiteor. August, serm. de tempore 189.

Christ, seen but not heard. Insomuch as the Catholics were accustomed in the times of Athanasius to said the misbelieving Arians to Jordan, there to learn the knowledge of a Trinity.

§7. Behold after this a clear nomination, of the three co-essential persons in that commission which Christ our Lord sealed to the apostles before his ascension, in the end of the gospel according to Matthew, when he sent them out to "make disciples in all nations baptizing them in the name of the Father, and, of the Son, and of the Holy Spirit." Who can but see a trinity here? How can any who by virtue of this institution has been baptized, refuse to believe it? "It becomes us (Basil[127] says) to be baptized as we have been taught, to believe as we have been baptized, and to glorify as we have believed, the Father, the Son, and the Holy Spirit." Of this the great apostate Julian, was not a little sensible; considering that he could not fairly disclaim the trinity, until he had renounced his baptism, he took the blood of beasts offered in sacrifice to the heathen gods (as Nazianzen[128] tells us from the report of his own domestic servants) and bathed himself in it all over; so as much as in him lay, washing off the baptism he had formerly received. Add to this that impregnable place (which has here, and will forever hold out against all the mines and batteries of heretics) in the first epistle of John, "There are three that bear witness in heaven, the Father, the Word and the Holy Spirit; and these three are one," (1 John 5:7). Where a trinity is proclaimed both in *numero numerante*, there are three; and in *numero numerato*, telling us plainly who they are, Father, Word, and Holy Spirit: and that the same essence is common to them all. For these three are one.

§8. Yet is there a late generation of men commonly known by the name of Socinians, who although they maintain

---

[127] Δες ἡμας βαπτίζεσθας ως παρελάβαμεν πισευειν ὡς βαπτιζόμεθα, δοξάζειν δε ὡς πεπιςευκαμεν, Πατέρα και υιον, και ἁγιον Πνευμα. Basil epist. 78.

[128] Nazian. Orat. 1. *Advers. Julian* circa medium.

against Atheists the personality and eternity of God the Father, have confounded Christian Religion by denying the eternity of the Son, whose personality they acknowledge; and the personality of the Spirit, whose eternity they confess. I think it fares with these three blessed persons, as with those three noted wells of which we read in the twenty-sixth of Genesis. For two of these Isaac's servants were forced to strive with the herdsmen of Gerar, which made him call the one *Esek*, that is, contention, the other *Sitnah*, that is, hatred. Of a third they got quiet possession, and he called the name of it *Rehoboth*, saying, *Now the Lord has made room for us.* The Father's Godhead is like the well Rehoboth, about which there was no strife; for the Son's divinity, like the well Esek, we are forced to contend; as also for the Deity of the Spirit, which is as Sitnah to the Socinians; they hate the thoughts of it, much more the acknowledgement,

But can any man say by the Spirit of God, that the Spirit is not God? Is it not as clear by scripture-light that Christ is God, as by nature's light that God is? Are they Christians and spiritual who deny the divinity of Christ and the Spirit? Let the judgment of charity enjoy its due latitude: but for my part, I would not for a thousand worlds have a Socinian's account to give at the end of this.

EXERCITATION IV.

Divine Attributes calling for transcendent respect. They are set down in the Scripture so, as to curb our curiosity, to help our infirmity, to prevent our misapprehensions, and to raise our esteem of God. Spiritual knowledge super-adding to literal clearness of light, sweetness of taste, sense of interest, and sincerity of obedience.

Next to essence and subsistence of God, his attributes are to be considered; concerning which I premise this rule.

§1. The degrees of our respect are to keep proportion

with degrees of worth in persons and things; ordinary worth requiring esteem, eminent calling for reverence, supereminent for admiration, yes, and adoration too, if it is an uncreated object. Here the psalmist on contemplation of God cries out as in an ecstasy, "O Lord our Lord, how excellent is thy name in all the earth!" (Psalm 2:1, 9). His attributes are his name; their worth so superexcellent, as far to transcend the utmost pitch of that observance, which we, poor we, are able any way to render. Seeing as the stars of heaven disappear, and hide their head on the rising of the sun that outshines them so creatures seem not to be, excellent, yes, not to be, when the being and excellency of their Maker displays itself, according to that, "All nations before him are as nothing; and they are counted to him less than nothing and vanity," (Isa. 40:7). The best of them have but some perfections. God either has (as manna is supposed to have had the relish of all meats) or consumes all; sovereignty comprehends inferior honors. The best of their perfections are mixed with some defects: but "God is light, and in him is no darkness at all," (1 John 1:5). They may be perfect and good in their kind: he is perfection and goodness itself. In them we may find matter of wonder, but of astonishment in him, witness that eminent place, Neh. 9:5. "Blessed be thy glorious name, which is exalted above all blessing and praise." Nature, though not altogether silent on this argument, in other words, the divine attributes, yet enjoys but a dim light to discover them by, where the scripture represents them most magnificently in various respects.

§2. First, so as to curb our curiosity. For which end it expresses diverse of them negatively, as when God is said to be infinite, immortal, invisible, unsearchable: by which we are taught that it is easier for us to know what he is not, than what he is; which is known only to himself. The best terms (as Scaliger has it)[129] for men to manifest, their understanding of God by, are those which manifest that they understand him

---

[129] Scalig. de Subtilit. *Exercit.* 365. §7.

not.[130] "Thou, O Lord, *Nazianzen says*, hast produced all those things of which we speak; but art unspeakable thyself. All that can be known by us is from thee, but thou thyself cannot be known." Yes, Augustine was not afraid to affirm that Nescience is the better way of knowing God."[131]

Secondly, So as to help our infirmity. For where we are not able by any one act of our finite understandings to comprehend that infinite essence, which is itself one simple act, but comprehensive of all perfections; Holy Scripture, condescending to our weakness, allows us to take up as it were in several parcels, what we cannot compass at once; and in contemplating the attributes to conceive some under the notion of divine properties incommunicable to creatures; such as are immensity, independence, eternity, simplicity, self-sufficiency, all-sufficiency, omnipotence, omniscience, omnipresence. Others under that of divine faculties; such are understanding, will, and memory ascribed to God. It gives us leave to look at some as divine affections; such are his love, hatred, anger, grief and delight. At others as divine virtues; such are his mercy, justice, patience, faithfulness, holiness, wisdom, *etc.* and at other some as divine excellencies resulting out of all the former; such are Majesty, Blessedness and Glory.

§3. Thirdly, so as to prevent our misapprehensions. The attributes of God however diversified in our conceptions (as has been said) are identified with his essence, which is but one: though to us they appear to be different each from other, and all from it, as the vast ocean, though but one, receives diverse names from the several shores it washes on: so however justice, mercy, power and the rest be several names suited to different operations; yet God is but one simple act under those various denominations. Lest we should therefore apprehend them to be such qualities as our virtues are really distinguishable, yes and separable from our being (as

[130] Μυνθ έων ΰφρμτος έπεί οσσα λαλέιται. Μανος εων αγιωσος έπεί τέχες οσεα νοειται. Nazianz. hymn, ad Deum.
[131] Melius scitur nesciendo. Aug. lib. 2. *de ordine*.

appeared when the first man fell from his holiness, yet continued a man still) scripture sometimes predicates them of God in the abstract: as when Christ is described "wisdom" (Prov. 8) when it is said "God is love," (1 John 6:8) and "the Spirit is truth," (1 John 5:6). Men may be called loving, wise and true: God is love, wisdom, and truth itself. The apostle tells us that if God swear, he does it by himself and no other, (Hebrews 6:13); yet we find him in the Psalm 4 swearing by his holiness (Psalm 89:35): where it follows that his holiness is himself. Christ is usually said to sit at the right hand of God; but in one place it is expressed by sitting "on the right hand of power," (Mark 14:62). Therefore God is power, as well as love. There is the same reason of all his attributes.

§4. Fourthly, So as to raise our esteem of God. Some there be which ate frequently called Communicable Attributes, because in them the creatures share, as being, immortality, goodness, and wisdom. Unless we should in this respect have lower thoughts of God than become us, Scripture is accustomed to ascribe them to him in such a way of supereminence as, (however they are participated by angels and men, yet) he only is said to have them. Witness these texts, "there is none besides me. Who only has immortality. God only wise. And there is none good but God," (Isa. 59:6, 1 Tim. 6:16 and Chap. 1:17. Matthew 19:17). Because in him they are all infinite, all eternal, all unmixed, and without the least allay of imperfection. An apostrophe borrowed from a devout, though popish, writer, shall shut up this. "O abyss of divine perfection. How admirable art thou, O Lord, who possessest in one only perfection the excellency of all perfections, in such excellent sort, that none is able to comprehend it but thyself!"[132]

§. 5. There is yet behind, a third kind of knowledge far exceeding both the former. A knowledge of God not proceeding from the light of nature alone, as the first does; nor of Scripture alone, as the second; but from effectual

[132] Fr. Sales' *Love of God*, lib. 2. c. page 1. §3. page 74.

irradiations of the "Spirit of wisdom and revelation," (Eph. 1:17) accompanied with purging and cheering influences from the same spirit. Look as the literal makes an addition of further discoveries to the natural, (which has been sufficiently proved) so this spiritual knowledge of God superadds even to the literal various particulars, not unworthy of our serious consideration, *viz.*,

First, clearness of light. Since the canon of Scripture was perfected, the things which the Holy Spirit discovers are no other for substance, but those very things which are contained in the written word: only he affords regenerate persons clearer light to discern them by, than any they had before their conversion. Take a man that is now become a learned critic, turn him to the same Author which he perused when he was a young student; he will find the self-same matter, but see a great deal further into it, because he has now got further light. So is it here.

Secondly, Sweetness of taste, "I sat down under his shadow with great delight, and his fruit was sweet to my taste," (Song of Songs 2:3). So the Spouse. O taste and see that the Lord is good," (Psalm 34:8). So the Psalmist. On which place the School-men have founded their distinction of knowledge of sight and a knowledge of taste. Spiritual science is steeped in affection; taking delight in the things known, and not barely apprehending, but reliving and savouring what it apprehends with abundance of love and complacency.[133] Where those expressions in Solomon's song, "Because of the savour of thy good ointments, thy name is as an ointment poured forth, therefore do the Virgins love thee," (Song of Songs 1:3). He does not know the things of God (a late writer well says) who does not desire and love them.[134]

§6. Thirdly, sense of interest. Of the Zidonians God

[133] Scientia visus and gustus.

[134] Nescit divina, qui non optat, qui non amat. Jo. Euseb. *Nicomb. Theopolit.* page 91.

said, "They shall know that I am the Lord."[135] but of his own people Israel, "They shall know that I am the Lord their God." Paul of the believing Ephesians concerning Christ, "In whom ye trusted, after that ye had heard the word of truth, the gospel of your salvation," (Eph. 1:19). Others may consider the gospel as a word of truth, and a doctrine holding forth salvation; but such as are savingly enlightened and sanctified by the Spirit, view the salvation it holds forth as theirs, and are ready of every truth therein ordained; This is good, and good for me. Happy man, whosoever you are, that cannot look by an eye of faith at the gospel, as the charter of thy liberties, at condemning law, as cancelled by the surety, in the earth as the footstool of thy Father's throne at heaven as the portal of thy Father's house, at all the creatures in Heaven and earth' as an heir is accustomed to look at his father's servants, which are therefore his, so far as he shall have need of them, according to that, "All are yours, and ye are Christ's and Christ is God's," (1 Cor. 3:22-23).

Fourthly, Sincerity of obedience. No doubt but Eli's two sons, being priests, had a literal knowledge of God; yet being profane, they are said expressly not to have known him. "They were sons of Belial; they did not know the Lord," (1 Sam. 2:12). When Lucius a bloody persecutor offered to confess his faith, in hope thereby to beget in the auditors a good opinion of his orthodoxy, Moses the religious monk refused to hear him, saying, "The eye might sometimes judge of one's faith as well as the ear: and that whosoever lived as Lucius did, could not believe as a Christian ought."[136] Fully consonant to this is that of James, "I will show thee my faith by my works," (James 2:18). That of John, "He that saith, I know God, and keepeth not his commandments is a liar, and the truth is not in him," (1 John 2:4). And of Job, "Behold the fear of the Lord, that is wisdom, and to depart from evil is understanding," (Job 28 to the last).

---

[135] Ezek. 28:22, compared with verse 26.
[136] Ruffin. *histor. Eccles*. lib. 2 c. page 6.

APHORISM IV.

Goodness and greatness are attributes so comprehensive, as to include a multitude of divine perfections.

EXERCITATION I.

God described from goodness and greatness both without and within the church. A lively portraiture of his goodness in the several branches of it Exod. 34:6-7. Bowels of mercy implying inwardness and tenderness. Our bowels of love to God, of compassion to brethren. Mercy not to be refused by unbelief, nor abused by presumption.

§1. The most learned among the heathen made account that they had sufficiently characterized their Jupiter,[137] when they described him good and great, yes, the best and greatest of beings. Neither can it be denied that these two attributes, if we take them in their latitude, comprehend very many of those perfections, which commonly go under other names. And this perhaps may be the reason why David in psalm one hundred forty fifth, (which the rabbins are said to have esteemed so highly as to determine, but with more superstition than truth, that whosoever repeated it thrice every day, might be sure of eternal life)[138] having set himself to extol God, and to bless his name, as appears by the first and second verses, insists chiefly on these two. "Great is the Lord, and greatly to be praised, and his greatness is unsearchable," (Psa. 145:5-8). Shortly after, "They shall abundantly utter the memory of thy great goodness. The Lord is gracious and full of compassion, slow to anger, and of great mercy. The Lord is good to all; and his tender mercies are over all his works," (Psalm 145:7-9) I shall accordingly treat of both, and first of his goodness.

---

[137] Εΰς τε μεγας τι. Optimus Maximus.
[138] Coppen in argumento psal. 145.

§2. Moses was skilled in all the learning of the Egyptians; yet as not content herewith, he becomes a humble suiter to God for some further and better knowledge, I beseech thee (he says) show me thy glory," (Exod. 33:18). Other notions may fill the head of a moral man: nothing short of the knowledge of God can satisfy the heart of a saint. Wherefore in answer to this request, the Lord makes him a promise, saying, "I will make all my goodness pass before thee," (Exod. 33:19). The thing desired was a sight of his glory; the thing promised a view of his goodness. Which intimates that however in themselves all the attributes of God are glorious, yet he glories most in the manifestation of his goodness, neither any brings him in so much glory from the creatures who are accustomed to magnify this most. "I will mention the loving kindnesses of the Lord, and the praises of the Lord, according to all that the Lord has bestowed on us and the great goodness towards the house of Israel, which he has bestowed on them, according to his mercies, and according to the multitude of his loving kindnesses," (Isa. 58:7). So the Church in Isaiah.

Now the forementioned promise made to Moses in Exodus 33, was made good in the thirty-fourth chapter, where the Lord is said to have passed by him, and proclaimed, "The Lord, the Lord God merciful and gracious, long- suffering and abundant in bounty and truth, keeping mercy for thousands, forgiving iniquity and transgression and sin, and that will by no means clear the guilty, visiting the iniquity of the fathers on the children, and on the children's children to the third and to the fourth generation."[139] All which clauses, (even the latter expounded by most of God's justice) may be so interpreted as to relate to his goodness rather.

It is twofold, one essential, that by which God is good in himself, the other relative, that by which he does good to his creatures. The former is here set forth by the term Jehovah,

---

[139] Exod. 34:6-7. Totum hunc locum ad bonitatem Dei pertinere asserit Ludovic. de *Dieu Animadvers.* in loc.

which is doubled, and does most fully serve to express it, as coming from a root, that signifies being. For goodness and entity are convertible, and everything so far forth as it partakes of being, partakes also of goodness.[140] Therefore God in whom all degrees of entity meet is undoubtedly most good. The latter in the title *El*, which as a learned Jew affirms, does not less clearly express his influence, than Jehovah does his essence.[141] *El* and *Elohim* in their most proper notion (as he tells us) signifies the author and producer of things by an infinite power. Of this relative goodness there are various distinct branches mentioned in this superexcellent text, which are spoken to in their order.

§3. The first is mercy. The nature in which may receive much light from the Hebrew word which is here made use of.[142] It comes from a root that signifies shutting up in one's bowels, as child-bearing women retain and cherish their dearest offspring within their wombs. Accordingly we read in Luke of the bowels of God's mercy; a phrase which implies both inwardness and tenderness. First inwardness, our bowels are the most inner parts: The mercy of God springs from within, and has no original cause without himself. Human affection is commonly both begotten and fed by somewhat without, in the thing or person beloved; as culinary fire must be kindled and kept in by external materials: But "God loveth because he loveth, (Deut. 7:7-8) and showeth mercy on whom he will show mercy," (Exod. 33:19); as celestial fire is fuel to itself. He freely extends mercy to us in making us good, then does us good for being so; is not this a merciful God? Secondly, tenderness. The forecited passage in Luke runs in this way in our translation. *Through the tender mercies of our God.* Of all parts the bowels relent and earn most. In them we are accustomed to find a stirring, when strong

[140] Diabolus in quantum est, bonus est. August. pede Natur. Boni.c. 5.

[141] Abarbanel apud Joann. Buxtorf. fil. in *Dissertat.* de Nominibus Dei Hebraice thes. 39 and 41.

[142] רחום a רחם intra viscera recepit, πλαγχια ελεας Luc. 1:78.

affections of love or pity are excited, as Joseph did on sight of Benjamin (Gen. 43:30). God speaking after the manner of men uses this pathetic expression concerning his people, "How shall I give thee up Ephraim? how shall I deliver thee Israel? how shall I make thee as Admah? how shall I set thee as Zeboim? Mine heart is turned within me, my repentings are kindled together," (Hos. 9:8). His people accordingly cry to him, "Where is thy zeal and thy strength? the sounding of thy bowels, and of thy mercies, are they restrained?" (Isa. 58:15). Of all human bowels those of mothers are the tenderest. Can a woman (the Lord says) forget her sucking child that she should not have compassion on the son of her womb?" (Isa. 49:15). Yet sooner shall all the mothers in the world prove unnatural, than he unmerciful: for so it follows, yes, they may forget, yet will not I forget you.

§4. Well may this notion of mercy put us in mind of returning bowels of love to God, according to what David said in the beginning of Psalm 18, "I will love thee, O Lord my strength,"[143] where the word comes from the same forementioned root, and intimates exercising love out of his most inward bowels: as also of extending bowels of compassion to those especially that stand in nearest relation to him, according to that of John, "whoso has this world's goods, and seeth his brother has need, and shutteth up his bowels of compassion from him, how dwelleth the love of God in him?" (John 3:17). But that is not all the improvement we are to make of this attribute. As it is a most tender affection, so is it to be most tenderly used. We take therefore diligent heed, as of refusing it by unbelief so, of abusing it by presumption.

First, of refusing mercy by unbelief (Jonah 2:8). Many as the phrase is in Jonah, forsake their own mercy, by giving way to objections arising from the flesh, like smoke out of that bottomless pit in Revelation. Do not say therefore God is so angry with me, the arrows of the Almighty stick so fast, and

---

[143] Ex intimus visceribus diligam te Psa. 18:1.

the poison of it so drinks up my spirit, that I cannot expect any mercy from him. Know that the Lord is accustomed even "in wrath to remember mercy," (Hab. 2:3): and that the correction which you at present look at as an argument of wrath, may perhaps be an evidence of love, and an act of mercy. God is not about to hew you down, as your unbelieving heart imagines, but to prune you for prevention of luxuriancy. Be sure the right hand of his clemency knows whatever the left hand of his severity does. You had better be a chastened son, than an undisciplined bastard. There is no anger to that in Isaiah, "why should ye be stricken any more? ye will revolt more and more," (Isa. 1:5). That in Ezekiel 16:42, "I will make my fury, towards thee to rest and my jealousy shall depart from thee; and I will be quiet, and will be no more angry." That in Hosea 4:17, "he is joined to idols, let him alone."[144] Then is God most angry of all, when he refuses to be angry; yes, there is no anger of his to be compared to this kind of mercy. Men that are fatted to destruction often go prosperously in the world, have few afflictions in their life, no bands in their death. But as Erasmus once said, "From this prosperity good Lord deliver us."[145]

Do not say I am unworthy, and must therefore despair; for mercy is free, and if God should show mercy to none but such as are worthy of it, he should show mercy to none at all, seeing all have sinned and come short, as of the glory, so of the mercy of God. Say not my sins are many and great, too many and too great to be pardoned: but oppose to the multitude of thy transgressions that multitude of tender mercies mentioned by the psalmist; not forgetting the gracious invitation by another prophet, "let the wicked, forsake his way, and the unrighteous man his thoughts; and let him return to the Lord, and he will have mercy on him, and to our God, for he will abundantly pardon, or *multiply pardon*,"(Psalm

[144] *Tunc magis irascitur quando non irascuitur. Super omnem iram miseratio ista.* Bernard.

[145] Absit a nobis, charissimi, talis felicitas. Erasm. in *concione de misericordia.*

51:1) as the original phrase imports. To the greatness of your sins oppose the riches of God's mercy, and greatness of his love spoken of by the great apostle. God, he says, "who is rich in mercy, for his great love by which he loved us," (Eph. 1:4). Lo here a vast heap, to which men may come with confidence, be it ever so much they have need of, because these riches are not impaired by being imported. The mercies of an infinite God are infinite mercies, and so able to swallow up all the sins of finite creatures. What, though you have before delighted in sin? Do not despair, for he "delighteth in mercy," (Micah 7:18), mercy pleases him, as much as ever any sin you did. What though your rebellion has been long continued? "The mercy of the Lord is from everlasting to everlasting on them that fear him," (Psalm 103:107). Yes what though to former guilt you have added back-sliding, and relapses to rebellion? Yet remember that in Jeremiah, "Return ye back-sliding children, and I will heal your backslidings," (Jer. 3:22): together with that in the last of Hosea, where Israel had no sooner said, "in thee the fatherless findeth mercy," but it follows immediately, "I will heal their backslidings, I will love them freely," (Hosea 14:3-4). But lest any should surfeit on these sweet meats, we take heed.

§5. Secondly, of *abusing mercy by presumption.* Mercy improved opens to us the surest refuge. Mercy abused brings on us the sorest vengeance. It would be considered that there is one kind of presumers on whom mercy itself is resolved to have no mercy so long as they continue such: in other words, those that dare expect it, notwithstanding their resolution to go on in their impenitence, and ignorance of God. For so the God of heaven says concerning him, "Who blesseth himself in his heart, saying, I shall have peace, though I walk, in the imagination of my heart," (Deut. 29:19-21) to add drunkenness to thirst, "the Lord will not spare him, but the anger of the Lord and his jealousy shall smoke against that man; and the curses that are written in this book shall lie on him; and the Lord shall blot out his name from under heaven; and shall separate him to evil." And again, "it is a people of no understanding; therefore he that made them will not have mercy on them, and he that formed them will show them no favor," (Isa. 27:11). Such shall at length find to their cost that the justice of God, as well as his mercy, endures forever: and that as nothing is more calm than a smooth, more raging than a tempestuous sea; nothing more cold than lead when it is taken out of the mine, nor more scalding when it is heated; nothing blunter than iron, yet when it is whetted nothing more sharp: so none more merciful than God, but if his patience be turned, to fury by our provocations, none more terrible. "Because I have purged thee, saith the Lord, and thou wast not purged, thou shalt not be purged from thy filthiness any more, until I have caused my fury to rest on thee. I the Lord have spoken it, and I will do it, I will not go back, neither will I spare, neither will I repent, *etc.*," (Ezek. 24:13-14). Woe and again woe to them all, against whom mercy itself shall rise up in judgment. Look as the power of God, though infinite, receives limitations from his will; (he could have made millions of worlds, would make but one). In like manner his infinite mercy is also limited by his will; and his word the interpreter of his will plainly tells us that, as physicians begin with preparatives, so he begets fear in their hearts, to whom he intends mercy. "Look as a father pitieth his children, so the Lord pitieth them that fear him. The mercy of the Lord is from everlasting to everlasting on them that fear him, to such as keep his covenant, and to those that remember his commandments to do them," (Psalm 103:13, 17-18). Not they that presume, but that fear; not such as break, but as keep his covenant; not those that forget, but that remembers his commandments to do them; or at least those whose earnest desires and endeavors are that way bent, may expect and shall receive mercy from him. They shall find by sweet experience the infallible truth of what Mr. Percock once said on his recovery out of a deep and long desertion, *viz.*, "That the sea is not more full of water, not the sun of light, than the Lord of mercy."

EXERCITATION II.

Grace what? From it spring Election, Redemption, Vocation, Sanctification, and Salvation. A caveat not to receive it in vain. It purges and cheers. Glosses on Titus 2:11-12 and 2 Thess. 2:26-27. The exaltation of free grace exhorted to longsuffering not exercised towards evil angels, but towards men of all sorts. It leads to repentance, is valued by God, and must not be slighted by us. A dreadful example of goodness despised.

§1. A second branch of God's goodness is grace, which relates to unworthiness, as the former did to misery. God is merciful to the ill-deserving, gracious to the undeserving. So far are we from being able to merit so much as the crumbs which fall from his table, that even temporal favors are from grace. Noah was preserved in the deluge (Gen. 6:8). Why? because "he found grace in the eyes of the Lord." Jacob was enriched and had enough. How did it come to pass? "Because God, said he to Esau, has dealt graciously with me," (Gen. 23:11). But beside that common favor in which all share more or less, there is a more special grace, which the Psalmist prays for, "remember me, O Lord, with the favor that thou bearest to thy people: O visit me with thy salvation," (Psalm 104:5).

§2. This third is drawn throughout the whole web of salvation, and there is not a round in the ladder to heaven, which does not give every one that steps on it just occasion of crying, *grace, grace*. Did the Lord elect you to life and glory, when so many were passed by? What reason can be given of this but free grace? Paul describes it the election of grace in his epistle to the Romans (Rom. 11:5); and tells his Ephesians (Eph. 1:4-6) that God had chosen them in Christ before the foundation of the world, according to the good pleasure of his will, "to the praise of the glory of his grace," (Eph. 1:7). Have you obtained redemption through the blood of Jesus? That also, he says there, flows from the riches of his grace. Has the Lord effectually called you? Bow down your head and adore free grace, as the cause of it. For he saves and calls us, the same holy apostle says, "with a holy calling, not according to our works, but according to his own purpose and grace," (2 Tim. 1:19). So in the Acts, when a great number believed, and were turned to Christianity, Barnabas saw the grace of God, shining forth in their conversion. Have you received any abilities tending either to your own sanctification, or to the edification of others? Do the like on this occasion too, as Paul did, saying, "By the grace of God I am what I am; and his grace, which was bestowed on me was not in vain; but I labored more abundantly than they all; yet not I, but the grace of God which was with me," (1 Cor. 15:10). In a word, do you find in yourself any beginnings of salvation, any hopes that it shall be perfected? Remember what that great asserter of free grace has left on record to all posterity, "By grace ye are saved through faith, and that not of yourselves, it is the gift of God," (Eph. 2:8). Remember it *so*,

§3. First; to beware of receiving the grace of God in vain, it being ordained for better ends, in other words, purging and cheering of such as receive it. "The grace of God that bringeth salvation, has appeared to all men, teaching us that denying ungodliness and worldly lusts, we should live soberly, righteously and godly in this present world," (Titus 2:11-12). All partakers of grace should not only deny that gross ungodliness of conversation, which the very sons of morality decry and abhor; but also worldly lusts, to which others are secretly indulgent. Neither should they content themselves with a negative purity, such as that of the Pharisee was, "I am not as other men; not as this publican: not an extortioner, not an adulterer," (Luke 18:11), (Logicians say of this particle *not* that it is of a malignant nature; divines know that the malignant church is much built up by such negatives) but also practice positive holiness, by living soberly, righteously and godly, and that too in tins present world: not putting on a vizard, of these, as the manner of some is, on a sick-bed, or death-bed, when they can no longer look at themselves, as men of this world, but of another. As for cheering, remarkable is that prayer made in behalf of the Thessalonians, "Now our

Lord Jesus Christ himself, and God even our Father, which has loved us, and has given us everlasting consolation, and good hope through grace, comfort your hearts," (2 Thess. 2:16-17). It implies that where we cannot possibly raise from ourselves any ground of hope, or have any lasting, much less everlasting consolation from the creatures, grace is a firm foundation for both. And this is it, which has put the prince of darkness (whose desire it has always been to keep men in as hopeless and comfortless condition as he can) on using his utmost endeavors in all ages of the church, either to obstruct the doctrine of free grace, as by Pelagian and Arminian tenets, or to poison this fountain with corrupt deductions and inferences, as by Antinomians and Familists. Wherefore remember it so, *as*,

§4. Secondly, in all thy tenets and discourses to magnify and exalt that to which you owe so very much, indeed your all that good is. Do not think it enough, with some, of a thousand parts to ascribe nine hundred ninety and nine to free grace, reserving but one for free-will; for as Prosper resolves the case well, "It is not devotion to give almost the whole to God, but deceit to retain the least part."[146] And again, grace is wholly repelled, where it is not wholly entertained.[147] I do not wish now to dispute the point: only let me have leave to commend to your reading and observation a paper of verses, inserted by certain divines that were present at the Synod of Dort, into their suffrage, and comprehending a brief decision of the five articles there debated, with a pious inference from there; because with me they have ever been of great esteem since I first met with them in the Acts of that Synod.[148]

Gratia sola Dei certos elegit ab aevo;

---

[146] Non est devotionis dedisse prope totum, sed fraudis retinuisse vel minimum.

[147] Gratia Dei tota repellitur, nisi tota suscipiatur.

[148] *Acta Synod. Dordrect.* in quarto, page 293.

Dat Christum certis gratia sola Dei;
Gratia sola Dei fidei dat munera certis;
Stare facit certos gratia sola Dei.
Gratia sola Dei cum nobis omnia donet,

In English it is this way,

Free grace alone elected some to bliss;
Free grace alone gave Christ to death for some;
In some free grace works faith that saving is,
Some by free grace to perseverance come.
Since God's sole grace doth all our good provide.

§5. A third branch of divine goodness is long suffering; by which God has been pleased to put a notable difference between angels that fell, and the fallen sons of Adam. Of them Peter says, "God spared not the angels that sinned, but cast them down to hell, and delivered them into chains of darkness, to be reserved to judgment," (2 Peter 2:4). This was quick and speedy work. But the Lord (the same apostle says) "is long-suffering to usward," (2 Peter 3:9). He exercises much patience, very much, even towards all, though vessels, of wrath. For so Paul, "What if God willing to show his wrath and to make his power known, endured with much long-suffering, the vessels of wrath fitted to destruction?" (Rom. 9:22). How profane was the old world? How wicked a place was Jericho? Yet was he one hundred and twenty years in warning those of that age, before he brought the deluge on them: and be that made the world in six, was seven days in destroying that one city. The great doctor of the Gentiles was not much more than thirty years old when God converted him; yet we find him looking at this as infinite patience, as all long-suffering, that he was borne with so long. "I obtained mercy (he says) that in me first Jesus Christ might show forth all longsuffering," (1 Tim. 1:16). How sensible then ought they to be of this attribute, with whom God has born forty, fifty, sixty years, and still continues to cry to, as it is in Habakkuk, "Wo to him that increaseth that which is not his: How long?" (Hab. 2:6). As in Jeremiah, "O Jerusalem, wash thine heart from wickedness, that thou mayest be saved: How long shall thy vain thoughts lodge within thee?" (Jer. 4:14). And again, "Wo to thee, O Jerusalem, wilt thou not be made clean? When shall it once be," (Jer. 13:27). All which places declare sufficiently that the long-suffering God does in a manner long to see our conversion to him.

§6. And that indeed is the most proper use we can make of it according to Paul's expostulation, "Despisest thou the riches of his goodness and forbearance, and long-suffering; not knowing that the goodness of God leadeth thee to repentance," (Rom. 2:4). Verily, we cannot meet on this side hell, with a worse temper of spirit than that which inclines a sinner to despise the forbearance of God, and to kick against the bowels of his goodness: as that profane Arias did, who was executed at Norwich, concerning whom Mr. Greenham acquaints us with this strange and prodigious narration. "This hellish heretic, he says, (for so were the deniers of Christ's divinity accounted of in those days, whatever thoughts be had of them in these,) a little before he was to be executed, afforded a few whorish tears, asking, whether, he might be saved by Christ or not? When one told him that if he truly repented he should surely not perish, he broke out into this speech. "No, if your Christ be so easy to be intreated indeed, as you say, then I defy him, and care not for him."[149] Horrible blasphemy! desperate wickedness for a man to draw himself back from repentance by that very cord of love, by which he should have been drawn to it. The next degree of impiety is, when men are therefore bold to continue long in sinning, because he with whom they have to do is a long-suffering God. A vice of which the preacher of old took notice, "Because sentence against an evil work is not executed speedily,

[149] Mr. Greenham in his treatise entitled, *A Sweet Comfort for an Afflicted Conscience*, on Proverbs 18:14. circa medium.

therefore the heart of the sons of men is fully set in them to do evil." But let such fear and tremble at what follows, "Though a sinner doth evil an hundred times, and his day be prolonged; yet surely I know it shall not be well with the wicked," (Eccl. 8:11-13). The Lord values every moment of his forbearance, as in the parable, "Behold these three years I come seeking fruit on this fig-tree, and find none," (Luke 13:7). Christ sets a high price on every exercise of his patience, as in the Song of Songs, "Open to me, for my head is filled with dew, and my locks with the drops of the night," (Song of Songs 5:2). Take we heed of slighting that which God and Christ value. Know and consider that patience may be tired, that however the Lord may be long-suffering, yet he will not suffer forever, but be weary of repenting, in case men will not be weary of sinning. Hear what was once said by himself to Jerusalem, "Thou hast forsaken me, saith the Lord, you are gone backward; therefore will I stretch out my hand against thee, and destroy thee: I am weary with repenting," (Jer. 15:6).

EXERCITATION III.

The bounty of God declared by his benefits, viz. giving his Son to free us from hell, his Spirit to fit us for heaven, his angels to guard us on earth, large provisions in the way, and full satisfaction at our journey's end. John 3:16 and James 1:5, and Psalm 24:1 glossed. Isaiah 25:16 alluded to. Inferences from divine bounty, beneficence to saints, not dealing niggardly with God, exemplified in David, Paul and Luther. Truth in God is without all mixture of the contrary. It appears in his making good of promises, and threatenings, teaching us what to perform, and what to expect.

§1. Our Bibles in the next clause, making use of the generic term, have it, *abundant* in goodness. I will make bold to vary a little from the common translation, and to read it, abundant in bounty, because the word, as Zanchy and others have observed, most properly signifies that kind of goodness, which we call bounty or benignity,[150] and which makes a fourth branch. In this God is abundant. Witness the greatest of his gifts, by which we are accustomed to measure the bounty of benefactors. I shall instance in some of the chief. He bestows on *us*,

First, his Son to free us from hell. "God so loved the world that he gave his only begotten Son," (John 3:16). He did not grant him on the request and earnest suit of fallen creatures;[151] but freely gave him unasked; not a servant but a Son; not an adopted son, such as we are, but a begotten, begotten, not (as saints are,) of his will by the word of truth (James 1:18), but of his nature; he himself being the word and the truth; not one of many, but an only Son thus begotten; and this not for the procuring of some petty deliverance, but "that whosoever believeth in him should not perish, but have everlasting life." Well might this gift of royal bounty be ushered in with a "God so loved the world." Majesty and love have been thought hardly compatible.[152] Yet behold the majesty of God bearing love, and that to the world, the undeserving, yes ill-deserving world of mankind. "Herein is love, (St. John elsewhere says, let me say, in this is bounty) "not that we loved God, but that he loved us, and sent his Son to be the propitiation for our sins," (1 John 4:10). *Loved*, and *so loved*; that particle is most emphatical, and notes the transcendence of a thing, either good or evil. Paul speaking of the incestuous Corinthian, deciphers him this way, "Him that has so done this deed," (1 Cor. 5:3) so impudently, so abominably, so unchristianly. The officers being astonished at our Savior's doctrine, cried out, "Never man spake so as this man," (John 7:46) so excellently, so powerfully, so incomparably. Here, "God so loved the world," that is, so freely, so infinitely, so unspeakably. The apostle himself, who

[150] הסר proprie significat benignitatem, seu liberalem beneficentiam. Zanch. de Natur. Dei. l. i. c. 18. Vide Fulleri miscellan. lib. l. c. 8.
[151] Non concessit, sed purissime dedit. Stella.
[152] Non bene conveniunt, nec in una sede morantur, Majestas et amor.

had been wrapped up to the third heaven, and there heard things not to be uttered, lacks words when he comes to utter this; and uses an accumulation of many, because no one could serve his turn to express it sufficiently. Not content to have described it love, mercy, grace; as not having yet said enough, he calls it great love, glorious grace, rich mercy, yes, exceeding riches of his glorious and merciful grace, in his second chapter to the Ephesians (2:4, 5, 7).

§2. Secondly, His Spirit to fit us for heaven. Our heavenly Father is he that "gives the holy Spirit to them that ask him," (Luke 11:13). The Spirit in this way given works in us regeneration, (we are therefore said to be born of the Spirit (John 3:5-6)) and that real holiness, concerning which the apostle says, without it no man shall see the Lord (Heb. 12:14): so preparing us for that place, which our Lord Jesus is gone before to prepare for us (John 14:2-3). A daily conversation in heaven is the surest forerunner of a constant abode there. The Spirit, by enabling us to here, first brings heaven into the soul, then conducts the soul to it. Where it is that Nehemiah, recording the acts of God's bounty to Israel, reckons this as one of the principal, "Thou gavest also thy good Spirit to instruct them," (Neh. 9:20).

Thirdly, His angels to guard us on earth after David had said, "The angel of the Lord, encampeth round about them that fear him, and delivereth them," (Psa. 34:7-8). He adds immediately, "O taste and see that the Lord is good herein good, in bestowing such a guard on us." It was an act of royal benignity towards Mordecai in king Ahasuerus, to make Haman the favorite his attendant as he rode through the streets. Think about it, here a far greater, the holy angels, those favorites in the court of heaven, "are all ministering spirits, sent forth to minister for them who shall be heirs of salvation," (Heb. 1:14). A task which they perform without grudging, (although in themselves more noble creatures than we are) both out of love to their younger brethren, of whom they have a most tender care, and out of obedience to God, their Father and ours, who has given them charge so to do, as it is in the Psalm, "He shall give his angels charge over thee, to keep thee in all thy ways."[153] Lay this to the former (as Bernard did) and we shall see the whole heaven at work for our preservation, God the Father sending his Son to redeem us; the Father and Son sending their Spirit to guide us; the Father, Son, and Spirit sending their angels to minister for us. O taste and see that the Lord is good, bountifully good!

§3. *Fourthly*, Large provisions in the way. We consist of body and soul; he provides plentifully for both, "giving us richly all things to enjoy," (1 Tim. 6:17) as one apostle phrases it, yes as another, "giving to all men liberally and not upbraiding," (James 1:5). Where ordinary benefactors, by reason of their stinted abilities give either but a few things, or to a few persons only, or if to many, but sparingly; and are besides, apt to corrupt and blemish their good turns by casting them in the receiver's teeth, and making their boast continually of them:[154] all these are here removed from God, while he is said to give to all men, and that liberally, yes, and so as not to upbraid; although whatever men receive, yes, whatever they are, (sin excepted) are wholly his. That of the Psalmist is very emphatic, and well deserves our consideration. "The earth is the Lord's, and the fullness of it, the world, and they that dwell therein," (Psalm 26:1). The house in which a man dwells, may be his landlords; but the furniture his own. Here we are told that not the earth only, but the fullness of it is the Lord's. Both house and furniture may be another's; but he that inhabits it, his own man. Here they that dwell in it are the Lord's, the inhabitants themselves, as the room and the stuff. To which agrees that of St. Paul "ye are not your own," (1 Cor. 6:19). And that of an ancient writer cited by Heinsius, our very being is none of ours; much less the things we have in possession.[155] As for

[153] Psalm 91:11. Mittis unigenitum, immittis Spiritum, ne quid vacet in caelestibus ab opere solicitudinis, angelos mittis in ministerium.
[154] Authores pereunt garrulitate sui. Martial.
[155] Nostrum non est quod sumus, multo minus quod habemus.

spiritual provisions, his people use not to be scanted in them. Another particular reckoned up by Nehemiah, when he set himself to celebrate the acts of divine bounty towards Israel, was the institution of ordinances. "Thou camest down also (he says speaking to God) on mount Sinai, and spakest with them from heaven, and gavest them right judgments and true laws, good statutes and commandments; and madest known to them thy holy Sabbath," (Neh. 9:13-14). One way by which great princes are accustomed to manifest their royal bounty is the making of great feasts, as Ahasuerus and Solomon did; we may safely allude to the prophet's expression (though the place have another meaning) and say of the church in that respect, "In this mountain doth the Lord of hosts make not all people a feast of fat things, of wine on the lees well refined," (Isa. 25:6). Good sermons and prayers are like well refined wines: and as Christ himself is a Savior full of merits, so is his Gospel a doctrine full of promises; his supper a sacrament full of mysteries; his Sabbath a day full of opportunities; all his ordinances fat things full of marrow.

§4. Fifthly, full satisfaction at our journey's end. Now indeed, as the natural, so the spiritual eye is not satisfied with seeing, nor the spiritual ear with hearing because "we so but as through a glass darkly, not face to face, and know not in past that of which we hear," (1 Cor. 13:12). Then shall eye and ear have enough, when we shall see God as he is and hear Christ saying, "Come ye blessed of my Father; inherit the kingdom prepared for you from the foundation of the world," (1 John 3:2). Here, although believing souls have fellowship with God in Christ sufficient to satisfy them as at a breakfast;[156] yet that degree of fruition is lacking which should satiate them fully, as at a feast, beyond that of ordinances. What shall there be enjoyed will satisfy every claim of rational appetites; the first truth, filling up our understandings, and the chief good our wills to the very brim. Then shall that be to the utmost verified, which David once said of regenerate

[156] Sistitur appetitus in via, satiatur in patria.

persons, "They shall be abundantly satisfied with the fatness of thy house; and thou shalt make them drink of the river of thy pleasures: for with thee is the fountain of life, in thy light shall we see light," (Psa. 36:8-9).

§5. For improvement of it. As our Savior once said, *Be ye merciful*, so be bountiful, let me say, as your Father is bountiful. St. Paul having praised the Macedonians for their deep poverty abounding to the riches of their liberality, urges the grace and benignity of Christ as a principal motive to excite his Corinthians to a like exercise of bounty towards the poor saints at Jerusalem. "For ye know," he says, "the grace of our Lord Jesus Christ, that though he was rich, yet for your sakes he became poor, that ye through his poverty might be rich," (2 Cor. 8:2, 9). More especially let us all learn from here not to deal niggardly with God himself; but to think no pains too great, no expense too much, no time too long that is spent in his service; not, as the manner of some is, who so manage the profession of religion, as if their main care and study were how to serve him with most ease, and to come off with the cheapest performances. David, Paul, and Luther, were men of another spirit. The first, as he delighted in the commemoration of divine bounty to him, saying, "I will sing to the Lord, because he has dealt bountifully with me," (Psa. 43:6): And again, "Return to thy rest, O my soul, for the Lord has dealt bountifully with thee," (Psa. 116:7); so he was no niggard in his returns, but ever and later enquiring what he should do to testify his thankfulness. "What shall I render to the Lord for all his benefits towards me?" (Psa. 116:12). And as providence offered occasion laying himself out for God; witness that his resolution testified to Araunah the Jebusite, not to offer to the Lord of "that which cost him nothing," (2 Sam. 24:24). The second was willing "to spend and to be spent," (2 Cor. 12:15) in the work of his ministry; and "not to, be bound only, but to die at Jerusalem, for the name of the Lord Jesus," who had there suffered not bonds only, but death for him (Acts 21:13). "The third, during his retirement in the castle Coburga for the safety of his person, having then more time to spare for devotion than his many public employments had been accustomed to afford him, was no niggard of it: but (as one Vitus Theodorus, who then lived with him informed Melancthon,) spent no less in prayer to God, than at least three hours every day, and those such hours as were fittest for study."[157] And yet, O the business of some men's spirits! whose services cost them very little or no intention, while instead of using the world, as if they used it not, they use good duties as if they did not use them; pray, as if they prayed not, hear as if they heard not, keep the Sabbath as if they kept it not, and repent as if they did no such thing: who although they profess believing in Christ, and know that "God spared not his own Son, but delivered him up for us all," (Rom. 8:32) yet deal so sparingly with the Lord, as to grudge him I say not every drop of blood but of sweat, yes, almost every minute of time that they spend in his immediate service. Let such men know, that to be over thrifty in our expenses on God, is the worst piece of husbandry in the world. I shall dismiss them with that of Moses to those unthankful men of Israel, "Do ye thus requite the Lord, O foolish people and unwise!" (Deut. 32:6).

§6. A fifth branch is faithfulness. One letter of this glorious name is abundant in truth, that is, in faithfulness. *Multus fide*, so Junius renders it. These two are frequently joined in scripture, as exegetical of each other. So when Christ is described "the Amen, the faithful and true witness," (Rev. 3:14) and the counsels of God said to be "faithfulness and truth," (Isa. 25:1). God abounds in it so as to have no mixture of the contrary, although the best of men have some. Where that of Paul, "Let God be true," (Rom. 3:4) that is, owned and acknowledged for such, but every man a liar. A lightsome body may have somewhat of darkness in it; for example, a precious stone some speck or cloud, but light itself admits of none. "God is light, and in him there is no darkness at all," (John 1:5): so God is truth, and in him there is no falsehood at

---

[157] Nullus abit dies quin ad minimum tres horas, easque studiis aptissmas in orationem parat. Melch. Adam, in vita Lutheris. page 138; page 142.

all. God that cannot lie," (Titus 1:2) the apostle says. Satan is the "father of lies," as that he does notwithstanding at times speak some truth, to the end he may deceive the better. God is "the Father of truth,"[158] as that he can never lie, no more than he can deny himself; which is utterly impossible! "If we believe not, yet he abideth faithful, he cannot deny himself."[159] Now his truth appears especially in two things.

First, the fulfilling of all his promises; which shall as surely receive their accomplishment in due season, as that of Christ's incarnation did, "when the fullness of time was come," (Gal. 4:4) and that of bringing the people of Israel out of Egypt, at the end of four hundred and thirty-years (Exod. 12:41); of which was most exactly performed the self-same day in which that number of years was expired. The Greek word for *truth* (as some think), according to its etymology, implies not forgetting what one has promised.[160] God remembers whatever he has at any time said, and that so effectually, as to make every one of his promises good, although perhaps long after the making of them; yes, and after many appearances to the contrary. See it in Abraham. He receives a command to go out to a land which the Lord should show him, and a promise that it should be given to him and his (Gen. 12:7, 10). He goes; but meets with a great famine at his first coming there, which forced him to flee into Egypt for bread, because he was likely to starve there. Yet afterwards it proved "a land flowing with milk and honey," to his posterity. Another grand promise made to Abraham was that in his seed should be as the stars of heaven for multitude (Gen. 15:5) yet Isaac the son of promise was not born until a good while after; and being grown was like to have been offered up for a sacrifice at God's command. But the Lord spared him, and a wife is at length procured for him; yet for twenty year together after his

---

[158] Deus est veritas sine fallacia, bonitas sine malitia, felicitas sine miseria. Fulgent, lib. 1 ad monim.

[159] Diabolus semper fallax est, sed non semper mendax.

[160] Ἀληθεια ab α particular negetiva et λήθη oblivion.

marriage he has no children by her (Gen. 25:20 compared with 26). All this while how small appearance is there of a numerous seed? Neither did the posterity of Isaac begin to multiply for a long time after this: for all the souls of the house of Jacob which came into Egypt, were no more but threescore and ten (Gen. 46:27). In Egypt a course was taken by Pharaoh's tyranny to keep them from increasing. But behold the faithfulness and truth of God, who being mindful of his promise, caused such fruitfulness among them, notwithstanding all obstacles, that there were numbered in the second year after their coming out of Egypt, more than six hundred thousand fighting men, besides women and children, and the whole tribe of Levi.[161]

§7. Secondly, The accomplishing of all his threatenings, as it is written, "I the Lord have spoken it, it shall come to pass, and I will do it; I will not go back, neither will I spare, neither will I repent," (Ezek. 24:14). Accordingly when the seven angels appeared with the seven last plagues, they that stood on the sea of glass, said in their song, "Great and marvelous are thy works, Lord God Almighty, just and true are thy ways, thou King of Saints," (Rev. 15:1-3). And when the third of them poured out his vial on the rivers and fountains of waters, an angel out of the altar said, "Even so Lord God Almighty, true and righteous are thy judgments," (Rev. 16:4, 7). If it is objected that destruction was threatened to Nineveh at the end of forty days, but not then executed, the answer is at hand, their repentance prevented their ruin. For as some of God's promises are made with the condition of faith and perseverance; so his threatenings are denounced with the exception of repentance; which, though concealed for the most part, is always included, and sometimes expressed, as in that place of Jeremiah, "At what instant shall I speak concerning a nation and concerning a kingdom, to pluck up, and to pull down, and to destroy it: If that nation, against whom I have pronounced, turn from their evil, I will repent of

[161] Numbers 1:1 compared with chapter 2:32-33.

the evil that I thought to do to them," (Jer. 18:7-8). Be we admonished from here.

First, what to practice in reference to God, in other words, truth in our promises to and covenants with him, that so our returns may be answerable in kind to our receipts, "All his ways are mercy and truth," (Psa. 25:10) to usward; therefore all ours should be truth and faithfulness towards him. Three times we are happy, whatever our outward condition prove if we are able to profess in the sincerity of our hearty as they did in Psalm, the forty-fourth, "All this is come on us, yet have we not forgotten thee, neither have we dealt falsely in thy covenant." Our principal comfort flows from God's keeping his covenant of grace with us; it should therefore be our principal care to keep truth with him.

§8. Secondly, what to look for in reference to ourselves. In other words, an exact fulfilling of all promises and threatenings that are conditional according to their several conditions. Has the faithful and true Witness said, "He that believeth and is baptized shall be saved," but he that believes not shall be damned? Let no unbeliever then, while he continueth in that estate, expect salvation: neither any that believeth and walketh in Christ, fear damnation seeing he has truth itself engaged far his safety; and seeing "the faith of God's elect," (Titus 1:1-2) according to St. Paul's doctrine, should go hand in hand with the hope of eternal life, which God that cannot lie promised before the world began. Let all that wish well to Zion make full account that in due time, "The mountain of the Lord's house shall be established in the top of the mountains, and shall be exalted above the hills, and all nations shall flow into it," (Isa. 2:2); because it has been promised of old. Let them also know assuredly, that "the Lord will consume Antichrist with the spirit of his mouth, and destroy him with the brightness of his coming," (2 Thess. 2:8) because this commination stands on the file in holy scripture, and is not yet completely verified. Former ages have seen Antichrist Nascent, when the Bishop of Rome first usurped authority over all the churches; Antichrist Crescent, when he began to maintain the doctrine of adoring images, and praying to saints departed; Antichrist Regnant, when he exalted himself above kings and emperors, setting up his mitre above their crowns; yes, Antichrist Triumphant, when he once became Lord of the Roman Catholic faith, so as none might believe without danger more or less, or otherwise than he prescribed. To this observation made by one of our own learned countrymen,[162] let me add; we ourselves have seen him Antichrist Cadent, falling and warning ever since Luther, Calvin, Perkins and others were set on work by God to unmask him. And no doubt, if we do not, our posterity shall see him *Antichrist morient*, dying and giving up the ghost: for the Lord faithful and true has not only threatened his ruin, but foretold that his day is coming.

EXERCITATION IV.

Keeping mercy for thousands explained. Men exhorted to trust God with their posterity. Luther's last Will and Testament. Iniquity, transgression and sin, what. Six scripture expressions setting out the pardon of it. God's goodness in it. Faith and repentance the way to it. Pardon in the court of heaven, and of conscience. The equity and necessity of forgiving one another. We are to forgive as God for Christ's sake forgives us, viz., heartily, speedily, frequently, thoroughly. A twofold remembrance of injuries, in cautelam, et in vindictam.

§1. The sixth branch of divine goodness, is the Lord's keeping mercy for thousands; which phrase admits of various notions, worthy of diligent consideration.

First, keeping it as in a store-house. God is said to be "rich to all that call on him," (Rom. 10:12) and we read of the riches of his goodness. These riches are laid up with him, and kept as in a magazine, to be made use of on all occasions according to the emergent necessities of his people. Where it

---

[162] Dr. Crakanthorp in his *Vigilius dormitans* chapter 13. §24.

is, that we also read, of their "obtaining mercy, and finding grace to help in time of need," (Heb. 4:16).

Secondly, Keeping it for the present age, as well as having dispensed it formerly to predecessors. Our fathers were all liberally supplied out of God's forementioned treasury, as it is in Psalm 22:4-5, "Our fathers trusted in thee; they trusted, and thou didst deliver them; they cried to thee, and were delivered; they trusted in thee, and were not confounded." This should be no disheartening to us, as if his treasury were exhausted; but encourage us rather, as Paul's example did succeeding believers, "For this cause I obtained mercy (he said) that in me first Jesus Christ might show forth all long-suffering, for a pattern to them which should hereafter believe on him to life everlasting," (1 Tim. 1:16). Which is the next observable.

Thirdly. Keeping it for time to come, as well as dispensing it at present. God has mercy in hand, and mercy in store. We now say, as it is in the Lamentations, "It is of the Lord's mercy that we are not consumed, because his compassions fail not," (Lam. 3:22). The same will they have occasion to profess that shall come after us. God keeps mercy, and mercy keeps us; created goodness, indeed, being limited, may be justly suspected of penury. Esau might have somewhat to plead for his saying, "Hast thou but one blessing, my father?" But divine goodness is like an ocean without either bank or bottom. Our heavenly Father has blessings reserved, as well as bestowed; many more blessings than one, yes, for many more persons than one, as it *follows:*

Fourthly, keeping mercy for thousands, and that not of persons only, but, as it is in the Chaldee, *for thousands of generations.* "One generation goes," the preacher says, and "another generation comes; but the earth abideth forever," (eccl. 1:4). Not one of all these generations but coming and going tastes of mercy; and the whole earth, during the time of these revolutions, "are still full of the Lord's goodness," (Psalm 33:5). When the ark rested, Moses said, "Return, O Lord to many thousands of Israel," (Num. 10:36). He that charged his providence with the thousands of Israel, is ready to charge it with the thousands of England, both in this and after ages, if they do not apostatize him, and so, forsake their own mercy.

§2. Well may we therefore trust God with, our posterity, seeing he that has showed mercy to us, keeps mercy for them. As that fountain of light, the sun is not weary with shining; it gives us light, and keeps light for our antipodes. So this fountain of mercy is never tired with communicating goodness to one generation after another. Good parents in bad times are often troubled with great solicitude, when they think what will become of their children after them. Let such consider that they leave them in his hand, who is a God keeping mercy for thousands: as Luther did, who had this passage in his last will and testament. "Lord God, I thank thee for that thou hast been pleased to make me a poor and indigent mad on earth. I have neither house, nor land, nor money to leave behind me. Thou hast given me wife and children: I restore them to thee Lord, nourish, teach, and preserve them, as thou hast hitherto done me, O thou that art a Father of the fatherless, and a judge of the widows."[163] Let them remember how much mercy is entailed on the issue of believers, by virtue of these and the like places, "He will bless them that fear the Lord, both small and great. The Lord will increase you more and more, both you and. your children," (Psa. 115:13-14). "The just man walketh in his integrity; his children are blessed after him," (Prov. 20:7). And that Satan never can, God never will cut off this entail, unless either the children degenerate; or the parents, distrusting providence, make, use of some unlawful means for their promotion. In ease, "Woe to him," the prophet says, "that coveteth an evil covetousness to his house, that he might set his nest on high—Thou hast consulted shame to thy house—For the stone shall cry out of the wall, and the beam out of the timber shall answer it," (Hab. 2:9-11). If Jerboam of design to secure the kingdom, and settle the crown in his own line, will take

[163] Melch. Adam. Vit. *German. Theol.* page 134.

the practice of idolatry as a means to this end, "This thing becomes sin to the house of Jeroboam, even to cut it off, and to destroy it from off the face of the earth," (1 Kings 13:34). No wonder then, if when God's own peculiar people begin to distrust him, and by reason of unbelief take irregular courses for their advancement in the world, this very thing proves an obstruction to that mercy, and theirs might have otherwise been partaker of. Such as would be sure to find him a God showing and "keeping mercy to thousands," must be careful to be found in the number of those "that love him and keep: his commandments," (Exod. 20:6) as he himself informs us in the Decalogue.

§3. The seventh branch is, forgiving iniquity, transgression and sin, where the terms are multiplied to note the readiness of God to forgive our offences, how many whatsoever they are, though transgression is added to iniquity, and sin to transgression. How great whatsoever they are *Pescha*, which signifies *rebellious*, as well as *Chattaah*, which imports failings:[164] and of what kind whatsoever they are, whether original, *viz.*, the crookedness and perverseness of nature, intimated in *Avon*, the word used in that speech of David, "Behold I was shapen in iniquity," or actual expressed by the two other terms. To help our understanding in this, the Holy Spirit in Scripture is pleased to make use of various expressions very significant, when he speaks of God's pardoning sin, *viz.*,

I. Taking it away, as in that place of Hosea, where the church is directed to make her addresses on this wise, "Take with you words, and turn to the Lord, say to him, Take away all iniquity, and receive us graciously; so will we render the calves of our lips," (Hos. 14:2). Not as if when iniquity is forgiven it were presently to be taken out of the memory; but that which the saints desire, is to have it taken out of the conscience, that their hearts may accuse them for it no more. As a thorn in a hedge is a fence, but an offence in the midst of

[164] See Muis on Psa. 51:2.

a garden: so sin in the memory may do well to keep us from relapsing, but is a grievance in the conscience. This made Augustine after assurance of forgiveness, when he had made confession of his former abberrations, bless God that he could now call them to mind without being affrighted at the consideration of them.[165]

II. Casting of our sins behind his back. So in Hezekiah's song, "Thou hast in love to my soul," said he, "delivered it from the pit of corruption; for thou hast cast all my sins behind thy back," (Isa. 38:17). This God does with a purpose never to view them more *oculo vindice*, so as to take vengeance for them, though *oculo judice*, he cannot but by reason of his omniscience see and discern them. All the while David's sins were before his own face, and he making a penitent confession of them as in the fifty first psalm, "I acknowledged my transgressions and my sin is ever before me," (Psa. 51:3). They were cast behind the back of God, as the prophet Nathan assured him, saying, "The Lord has put away thy sin, thou shalt not die," (2 Sam. 12:13).

III. Scattering them as a cloud, or as a mist. So the Geneva translation has it in that cheering passage of Isaiah, "I have put away thy transgressions like a cloud, and thy sins as a mist," (Isa. 44:22). Sin is that which interposes itself between the soul and the light of God's countenance: but whether it is a slender mist or a thick cloud, an infirmity or a rebellion, the sun of righteousness eyes by faith, can and will dispel it, so as to make it vanish.

§4. IV. Covering or hiding them. So in the Psalm, "Blessed is he whose transgression is, forgiven, whose sin is covered," (Psa. 32:1). Men never punish hidden sins, because the law takes notice of none, but such only as come to light, by breaking out in words or actions.[166] God is according to

---

[165] Quid retribuam domino quod recolit haec memoria mea, etc. anima mea non metuit inde? August. *Confess*. lib. 2. c. 7.

[166] Si texit peccata Deus noluit advertere; Si noluit advertere noluit animadvertere; Si noluit animadyertere voluit punire. August, in loc.

cover and hide those sins as it were out of his sight, for which he never intends to inflict punishment.

V. Throwing them into the depth of the sea. So in Micah's prophecy, "Who is a God like to thee that pardoneth, *etc.* he will subdue our iniquities, and thou wilt cast all our sins into the depths of the sea," (Micah 7:18-19). Alluding perhaps to what befell Pharaoh and his host in the Red Sea, which drowned the greatest Egyptian commanders, as well as the meanest common soldier. The vast ocean overflows both the lowest sands and the highest rocks: that of God's pardoning grace removes both the smaller prevarication and the grosser abominations of all such as art truly penitent believers.

VI. Blotting them out as in David's petition, "Have mercy on me, O God, according to thy loving kindness; according to the multitude of thy tender mercies blot out my transgressions," (Psa. 5:1). In which he alludes to the custom of creditors, "Who use to set down what everyone oweth," and when debts are either forgiven, or paid, to blot them out. Our sins are called *debts* in the Lord's Prayer. Christ as our surety has given satisfaction to divine justice for them; when this is once apprehended and applied by a lively faith, God issues out a pardon, drawing as it were, the lines of Christ's cross over the lines of his debt-book; so as he may still see the sum we were indebted in, but sees it cancelled, never to be exacted more.

§5. We are then advertised from here in the first place, to acknowledge the singular goodness of God to us in this particular, of forgiving our iniquity, transgression and sin. David in the place last cited speaks of it as a special evidence of loving kindness and tender mercies. The apostles creed, having premised the articles concerning Christ, by whom all blessings were procurred for the catholic church, when it comes to recite them, names forgiveness of sins in the first place, as the choicest privilege on this side heaven. And in that compendious prayer, which our Savior taught us, there is a remarkable connection of two petitions by a conjunctive particle, not to be found in any of the former. *Give, us this day our daily bread, and forgive us our trespasses.* To show that as our daily sins make us unworthy of daily bread, so there is no sweetness in them until the other is pardoned. Bread and all other outward mercies a man may receive from an angry God: pardon of sin never comes, but from favor and special love, yes riches of grace, as Paul expresses it, speaking of Christ, "In whom we have redemption through his blood, the forgiveness of sins according to the riches of his grace," (Eph. 1:7).

§6. In the second, to believe and repent, that we may be found in the number of those to whom this choice blessing is imparted. Scripture tells us, men must be "turned from darkness to light, from the power of Satan to God, that they may receive forgiveness of sins, and an inheritance among them that are sanctified, by faith that is in Christ," (Acts 25:18). Also that "God has exalted him with his right hand to be a Prince and a Savior, to give repentance to Israel and forgiveness of sins." Observe the method, repentance first, and *then* forgiveness. God does not bestow his distinguishing favors on all men promiscuously. Pardoning mercy does indeed come from him with ease (he is called "a God ready to pardon" (Neh. 9:17)) but does not drop from him at unawares, that I may allude to what Seneca said of his liberal man.[167] He will know on whom he bestows his forgiveness. Unbelieving, unrepenting sinners never obtained it; faithful penitents never yet went without it. They may perhaps not be so sensible of it in times of temptation and of desertion: but, to make use of a known distinction, where there is a double forgiveness, one in the high court of heaven, of which the Lord speaks in his answer to Solomon's prayer, "Then will I hear from heaven and forgive their sins," (2 Chron. 7:14). All authentic pardons are coined there; the stamping of them is a part of prerogative royal; (and it is no less than high treason in the Pope to have his mint of indulgences going at Rome) another in the court of conscience, spoken of in the epistle to the Hebrews, "the

[167] Sinum habet facilem, sed non perforatum. de benefic.

worshippers once purged should have had no more conscience of sins:" (Heb. 10:2) it may safely be asserted, that forgiveness is certainly passed in the court of heaven, whenever Christ is received by faith; according to that, "be it known to you, that through this man, meaning Christ, is preached to you the forgiveness of sins; and by him all that believe are justified from all things, from which they could not be justified by the law of Moses." Yet may there for some space of time after this, not determinable by any man, be lacking a seal on earth to this pardon; and the believer continue not so fully acquitted in the court of his own conscience, as to be assured of forgiveness, until the Lord has taught, him by experience to see and acknowledge, that assurance of pardon is a free gift of his, as well as faith, or pardon itself.

§7. In the third place, "To be followers of God as dear children, tender-hearted, forgiving one another, even as God for Christ's sake has forgiven us," (Eph. 5:1 and 4:32)." We *should*,

First, forgive one another. The equity and necessity in which are both exceedingly pressed by our Savior, to the end we might not look at it either as unreasonable, or as arbitrary. The former is by his parable in the eighteenth of Matthew. "The wrongs we suffer compared to the sins we commit, are but as an hundred pence to ten thousand talents;" great odds both in number and weight, (Matthew 18:23 to the end), for number, ten thousand to one hundred; and for weight, the one sort are talents, the other pence. What more equal than that we who have so many talents forgiven us, should be ready to forgive so few pence? The latter in an express declaration annexed to the Lord 's Prayer. "If ye forgive men their trespasses, your heavenly Father will also forgive you; but if ye forgive not men their trespasses, neither will your Father forgive your trespasses," (Matthew 6:14-15). Where it follows, that persons addicted to revenge, so often as they repeat that petition, "Forgive us our trespasses, as we forgive them that trespass against us," do in effect make a dreadful imprecation against themselves, and fetch down a curse from heaven instead of a blessing. For he that says with his tongue, *Lord, I pray thee forgive me, as I forgive others*; but meanwhile says in his heart, *I cannot, I will not forgive such a one*, he not by consequence says to God, *Do not forgive me*? He pronounces himself unworthy of pardon, and in effect subscribe to the sentence of his own condemnation? Yet alas! how common a sin is revenge! As the heart in the natural body is the first member that lives, and the last that dies; so revenge in the heart is a lust that soonest appears in children, and is often longest though it is healed in the regenerate. Molanus tells us that the Christians of old, in Augustine's time, were accustomed to beat on their breasts in deep sense of their sins,[168] at the Nobis in the beginning of the forementioned petition, "forgive us;" well may the most of men now-a-days beat their breasts for grief, and hang down their heads for shame at the *Nos* in the latter clause, as we forgive. For how few are there that do it aright? Seeing *that*,

§8. *Secondly*, we should forgive others, as God for Christ's sake has forgiven us, in other *words*,

First, heartily without dissembling. Christ denounces a terrible threatening against such, "as do not from their hearts forgive everyone his brother," (Matthew 18:35). It is not a making a fair show in outward carriages, not binding up, as it were, the broken bones of peace, with good looks and sweet words, that God accepts, if the heart is full of wormwood and gall. Joab kissed, and stabbed, Judas kissed and betrayed. Hail Master, said the one to Christ. Art thou well my brother? said the other to Amasa. How hateful is such dissimulation to God and man? Forgiveness is a fruit of love; My little children, St. John says, let us not love, so say I, let us not forgive "in word and tongue, but in deed and in truth," (1 John 3:18).

Secondly, speedily without delay. Be like God, ready to

---

[168] Augustini seculo ad vocen Nobis quilibet Christianus pectus suum tundebat. Jo. Molanus. *Theol. practicæ compend.* page 211.

pardon.[169] As in bestowing, he doubles his benefit that gives betimes: so in pardoning, he "forgives twice that forgives with speed;" his forgiveness receives a double welcome, and shall have a double reward. It is not for Christians to harbor animosities in the course of their lives; and think to solve it by saying we forgive all the world, when they lie on their death beds; that may be applied to pardoning, which divines usually say of repenting, *True forgiveness is never too late, but late forgiveness is seldom true*. Wherefore, "let not the sun go down on your wrath," (Eph. 4:26) as Paul advises the Ephesians. If that which was but a mote at first, be watered and cherished with the fresh suspicions of some few days, it will turn to a beam, and go near to put out the eye of love.[170]

Thirdly, Frequently without stint or limitation. God "multiplieth pardon," (Isa. 55:7); so should we. "When ye stand praying, forgive," (Mark 11:25) Christ says, and Paul bids us "Pray continually," (1 Thess. 5:17). We should therefore be inclined to forgive continually; and to make actual performance whenever there is an opportunity. Peter thought he had offered fair when he asked, "How oft shall my brother sin against me, and I forgive him?" (Matthew 18:21-22) adding until seven times, as making account that surely that was often enough. But our Savior makes nothing of that number; would by no means have him stay there, "Jesus saith to him, I say not to thee until seven times, but until seventy times seven," putting a certain definite number for an indefinite, and by this intending to teach that his followers should forgive *toties quoties*, so often as they shall be trespassed against.

§9. *Fourthly*, thoroughly, as without excepting, so without remembering any offence. God excepts not any of our sins, when he affords pardoning grace. But "if we confess, he is faithful and just to forgive us our sins, and to cleanse us from all unrighteousness," (1 John 1:9). Should he reserve but one

---

[169] Neh. 9:17. Bis dat, qui cite.

[170] Ira festuca est, odium trabes. August.

unforgiven, that one would sink our souls to hell. It is our duty to imitate him herein. Forgive, Christ says, "If ye have aught against any," (Mark 11:25). Whoever the person, and whatever the thing is, you must forgive. One of the Evangelists sets down the petition this way, in our Savior's form of prayer. "Forgive us our sins, for we also forgive every one that is indebted to us," (Luke 11:4). It must then be performed without excepting any either person or offence. As also without remembering any, God so forgives our sins as not to keep a register of them. "I even I am he, saith the Lord, that blotteth out thy transgressions for mine own sake, and will not remember thy sins," (Isa. 63:25). Yet with us what more frequent then saying, I forgive such a man, such a wrong; but shall never forget it or him? A distinction that did not come out of Christ's school, but Satan's mint. Paul was of a different spirit: witness that remarkable passage of his to the Galatians, "Brethren, I beseech you be as I am, for I am as ye are; ye have not injured me at all."[171] Where he seems to desire that every member of the Church in Galatia would be to him as an alter ego, another self, seeing he was affected as another self to each of them. But had they not injured him? Yes, very much, in preferring the false apostles before him, questioning his doctrine, yes, becoming his enemies, and that for telling them the truth; yet behold him professing here, "Ye have not injured me at all," because these wrongs were as no wrongs in his estimation, it was not his purpose to impute them; he speaks as one that had really forgotten them by reason of his resolution to forgive them. There is, I confess, a kind of remembrance not inconsistent with true forgiveness, when prudent men remember offences and offenders *in cautelam*, so as to beware for the future of exposing themselves to the like injuries; but Christians ought not to remember *in vindictum*, so as to revenge themselves on the delinquents for wrongs done in time past, I say to revenge; for otherwise a Christian may seek to right himself in a legal way, yes, and to bring offenders

[171] Galatians 4:12. Vide Bezam and Grotium in loc.

to condign punishment, still retaining a charitable mind towards them: even as God, though he have forgiven justified persons, may notwithstanding and often chastises them with his fatherly corrections.

EXERCITATION V.

The latter clauses of Exodus 24:7 so translated and expounded as to contain an eighth branch of divine goodness, viz. Clemency in correcting. Equity in visiting iniquities of the fathers on the children. Clemency in stopping at the third and fourth generation. A lesson for Magistrates. A speech of our Queen Elizabeth. God's proclamation in Exod. 24. Improved by Moses in Numbers 14.

§1. The following clauses have somewhat more of difficulty in them than any of the former, as being variously rendered and expounded by interpreters. The most read as we do, "That will by no means clear the guilty, visiting, *etc.*" But among these that do agree in the translation, there is some difference about the meaning of the words. The major part of that combination applies them wholly to the justice of God in taking vengeance on obstinate sinners. Some few (in which Mr. Ainsworth is one) respecting the scope of the whole context, which is to set forth the goodness of God, consider this also as relating to that. His words are these. "This his justice on the wicked is a part of his goodness towards his people," as it is said, "The just shall rejoice, when he sees the vengeance. He shall wash his feet in the blood of the wicked," (Psa. 58:10). A gloss that may receive confirmation from certain passages in the hundred and thirty sixth Psalm where the destruction of opposite princes is recorded as an evidence of God's mercy to his church. "He slew famous kings, for his mercy endureth for ever. Sihon king of the Amorites, for his mercy endureth forever. And Og the king of Bashan, for his mercy endureth for ever," (Psa. 146:18-20). As also from that in the first of Nahum, "The Lord is good, a strong hold in the day of trouble: and he knoweth them that trust in him: but with an overflowing flood he will make an utter end of the place of it," (Neh. 1:7-8) that is, the oppressing city Nineveh, and darkness shall pursue his enemies.

§2. But the learned critic Ludovicus de Dieu, considering that in other places, by name Zech. 5:3 the word *Nakah* signifies to make void, and to cut off, by altering the translation of these words, puts them into a posture of looking directly at the goodness of God, and not with an oblique glance. He renders them this way, "Evacuating, cutting off or destroying, he will not evacuate, cut off, or destroy; visiting the iniquities of the fathers on the children, to the third and fourth generation,"[172] making this the sense, "So great is God's goodness, that even when he is angry and punisheth, yet he will not utterly, overthrow: he visiteth indeed the sins of the fathers on the children, but it is to the third and fourth generation only, not for ever." Now according to this interpretation (which for ought I know may well be received) the expressions import an eighth branch of divine goodness, in other words, clemency in correcting, here set forth by a general declaration, and by a particular instance.

First, by a general declaration in these words, *venakkeh lo ienakkeh*, destroying he will not destroy, that is not altogether, not so destroy as to make a full end, according to the expression in Jeremiah. (Jer. 46:28). So in the same forms of speech, *delivering you have not delivered*, that is, say our translators, *neither have you delivered this people at all*. Redeeming he cannot redeem; that is, they say, none of them can by any means redeem his brother. (Exo. 5:22; Psa. 49:7). Proportionably here, *destroying he will not destroy*, that is, God will not at all, he will not by any means utterly destroy his people, however he may correct and chasten for some time. Suitable to this is that in Amos' prophecy, "Behold the eyes of

---

[172] Evacuando non evacuabit, succidendo non succidet. Lad. de Dieu. *Animadvers.* in Exod. pages 81-82.

the Lord God are on the sinful kingdom; and I will destroy it from off the face of the earth, saving that I will not utterly destroy the house of Jacob, saith the Lord," (Amos 9:8).

§3. This sense is exceedingly favored by a parallel place in Jeremiah, "I am with thee, saith the Lord, to save thee. Though I make a full end of all nations whither I have scattered thee, yet will I not make a full end of thee; but I will correct thee in measure," (Jer. 30:11). Then follows, *venakkeh lo anakkeca*, which Pagnin renders, "And destroying I will not destroy thee." It may further, and yet more strongly be confirmed by a passage in the fourteenth of Numbers. The hand of faith having once fastened on God, will not readily let go its hold. Moses had taken fast hold of that discovery, which the Lord was pleased to make of himself in this place of Exodus, and accordingly on occasion improves it, by pleading with him for Israel's preservation from a total ruin, which was then deserved and threatened; making use to that end of those very terms the discovery was made in, and among others of those now under debate, as most argumentative in the sense contended for. It is as if he had said, "Wilt thou, O Lord, (Num. 14:17-18) bring an utter destruction on this whole people? What shall then become of that goodness of thine which it pleased thee to proclaim to thy servant in Sinai? If thou beest resolved to punish them, yet remember what thou hast said, destroying he will not destroy. If their iniquities must be visited on their children, O let it not be for ever, Lord, but only to the third and fourth generation, as thou hast spoken." Where from the words in that other sense, which is commonly received, Moses could not possibly have drawn so strong a plea. For if God will by no means clear the guilty; all Israel having at that time contracted a deep and deadly guilt, what inference could be made from there, but that all Israel were of necessity to perish?

§4. *Secondly*, By a particular instance contained in the last clause, "Visiting the iniquities of the fathers on the children, and on the children's children, to the third and fourth generation." For the clearer explication in which, it will be requisite to demonstrate that God in so doing exercises both equity, and clemency, lest either should be doubted of. Concerning the former; although by an express law magistrates are forbidden to put children to death for their parent's sins;[173] yet God, who is author of life and death, has reserved to himself a liberty of so doing, whenever it pleases him, by reason of his supreme dominion over all: and therefore for him to inflict inferior temporal punishments in that case, cannot but be accounted just. The rather if we take into consideration that children may be accounted part of the parents themselves: for as a man's wife is himself divided, so his children are himself multiplied, However they are undoubtedly part of their parent's goods, and so esteemed. When God had once said concerning Job, "Behold all that he has is in thy power," (Job 1:12). Satan by virtue of that commission slew not his cattle and servants only, but his sons and daughters. And when he had determined concerning Achan, "Let him and all that he has be burnt with fire," (Josh. 7:15, 24-25) the Israelites in obedience to that command burnt his children, together with his other substance.

§5. As to the latter, God's visiting on this wise will be found an act of clemency, as well as of equity, if it is *considered,*

First, That it is but to the third and fourth generation, not to all generations, and forever, according to the Psalmist's expostulation, *Wilt thou be angry with us for ever? wilt thou draw out thine anger to all generations?* (Psa. 85:5). Not to do this is mercy, witness that in Nehemiah, "For thy great mercies sake thou didst not utterly consume them, nor forsake them: for you are a gracious and merciful God," (Neh. 9:31).

Secondly, That all sorts of sinners are not punished, but only or mainly such as are guilty of the most heinous provocations; chiefly idolaters and worshippers of false gods. For the second commandment (which is the first place of

[173] Deut. 24:16, compared with 2 Kings 14:6. Vide Grotium de *jure belli et pacis*. Lib. 2, c. page 21. sect. 14.

Scripture in which we meet with this expression) has it this way, *I the Lord thy God am a jealous God, visiting the iniquities of the fathers on the children, to the third and fourth generation of them that hate me.*[174] That is, of them that manifest their hatred of me by committing spiritual adultery with idols, which, as some affirm is the most proper and only notion of that phrase throughout the Scripture.

Thirdly, That it is seldom done, but where children tread in their father's steps, and art guilty of the same sins with their progenitors. Then no wonder if what we find in Isaiah's prophecy be accomplished to the full, "Behold, it is written before me; I will not keep silence, but will recompense, even recompense into their bosom your iniquities, and the iniquities of your fathers together, saith the Lord, which have burnt incense on the mountains, and blasphemed me on the hills: therefore will I measure their former work into their bosom," (Isa. 65:6-7).

Fourthly, that it is never done but with merciful intentions; namely, to restrain men from sin on this ground, because their children, whom they affect so dearly are like to smart for it. He is a truly miserable heir that inherits his father's sins with his lands: the one will quickly eat out all, and more than all the comfort he can expect from the other. Now there is scarce any penalty more grievous in Chrysostom's[175] opinion, than for a man to see misery brought on his offspring, and that for his sake.

§6. Rulers should imitate God in this, by not dealing against malefactors to the utmost of rigor, but exercising clemency in their corrections: not writing all their laws in blood, as Draco of old is said to have done; not dismembering where a Band-Aid will suffice, nor applying scorpions where a rod will serve the turn. Humanity is a manlike, crusty a

---

[174] Deum odisse in sacris literis peculariter illi dicunter qui falsos Deos colunt; ita ut neget Maimonides alio sensu id loquendi genus reperiri. Grotius in *explicat. decalogi.*

[175] Ου λυπάσά μάλλον.

diabolical principle. In wrath God always remembers mercy, so should they of whom it is written, *I have said ye are gods.* The sword of his justice is always furbished with the oil of loving kindness; so should theirs. Our Queen Elizabeth is reported to have professed that next to the scriptures she knew no book which had done her so much good, as the often reading of Seneca's treatise *de Clementia.*[176]

§7. To shut up this so long discourse with a review of Moses' example touched on before in the third paragraph; Look as some kind of artificers after long poring on a piece of black work, finding a dimness in their sight, are accustomed to take an emerald, or some other green thing, by the virtue in which their eyes may be refreshed and their spirits cheered. So believers, when puzzled and dulled with the consideration of sad events, should for their spiritual relief make use of this glorious proclamation made by God himself concerning his goodness and the several, branches of it; which are all cheering to faith. Moses did so in the fourteenth of Numbers. The spies were then newly returned with their dismal report; the people fallen into their two epidemical diseases, rebelling and murmuring, excepting only Caleb and Joshua. On this God being highly provoked threatens to disinherit them, verse 12, to kill them all as one man, verse 15. It was now time for Moses, who loved them as his own soul to bestir himself, to become their advocate, and beg pardon on their behalf, as he does in the 17th, 18th, and 19th verses, grounding his plea on two topics; the former, God's power, in these words, "I beseech thee let the power of my Lord be great." Let it be, that is, be manifested, and appear to be great. But what has power to do with pardon? Much in every way. Forgiveness is an act of potency as well as of clemency. We know that in all civil states, pardoning such as the law has sentenced, is a prerogative belonging to the Supreme Power. His second topic is God's truth engaging him to make good what had formerly been proclaimed by himself concerning his goodness

176 Dr. Hackwel on Psa. 101, page 28.

in Moses' hearing. To an active believer such as Moses approved himself in his whole course, every revelation of God is like a clear and distinct voice uttered in an arched vault, which resounds again and again. "God has spoken once, David says, twice have I heard this, that power belongeth to God," (Psa. 62:11). Accordingly Moses, as he heard this admirable discovery of divine goodness, when the Lord first uttered it on mount Sinai. So now he hears it over again, and on this signal occasion makes a due improvement of it, by founding his plea for Israel on it, "According as thou hast spoken, saying, The Lord is long-suffering and of great mercy, forgiving iniquity and transgression," *etc.*

EXERCITATION VI.

Job 11:7-9, expounded of divine Greatness. Three reasons of that exposition, with the resolution of a question about it. The height of God's universal, unaccountable, omnipotent Sovereignty proved and improved.

§1. Zophar in Job, being about (as I now am) to set forth the greatness of God, premises this interrogation, "Canst thou by searching find out God?" (Job 11:7) to imply the truth of what is elsewhere clearly expressed by the prophet David, "Great is the Lord, and greatly to be praised; and his greatness is unsearchable," (Psa. 145:3). It could not otherwise be his. For as one says well, "Non esset Dew magnus, si non esset major captu nostro." Such is the shallowness of man's understanding, that God should not be really great if he were no greater than our capacities. The description he makes of it follows in these words. "It is as high as heaven, what canst thou do? deeper than hell, what canst thou know? The measure of it is longer than the earth, and broader than the sea," (Job 11:8-9). Where by height Zophar seems to understand the omnipotent sovereignty, by depth the omniscient wisdom, by length the everlasting duration, by breadth the omnipresent immensity of God. The grounds of this interpretation are chiefly three.

First, the dimensions here enumerated are those by which we are accustomed to estimate the greatness of things: and I find all the forementioned attributes spoken of as branches of divine greatness in other places. Omnipotent sovereignty, "great is the Lord, and of great power" (Psa. 147:5). Omniscient understanding. "God is greater than our heart, and knoweth all things," (1 John 3:20). Everlasting duration, "behold, God is great and we know him not, neither can the number of his years be searched out," (Job 36:26). Omnipresent immensity, "great is our God above all gods. Who is able to build him a house, seeing the heaven and heaven of heavens cannot contain him?" (2 Chron. 2:5-6).

Secondly, each particular dimension is elsewhere applied to these very attributes, though some with more clearness than others. Height to God's sovereignty, "he that is higher than the highest regardeth, and there be higher than they," (Eccl. 6:8). Depth to his omniscience, "O the depth of the riches both of the wisdom and knowledge of God!" (Rom. 11:33). Length to his eternity, "He asked life, and thou gavest it to him; even length of days for ever and ever," (Psa. 21:4). Which Calvin and the Chaldee paraphrase, apply to Christ, understanding by this the eternal duration of his kingdom. Lastly, breadth to his omnipresence, but covertly in that of Isaiah, "the glorious Lord will be to us a place of broad rivers and streams;" (Isa. 33:21) to signify that protection and safety, which his presence with his church in every place affords to all the members of it, like a broad river encompassing a fenced town on every side.

Thirdly, I think there is somewhat expressed in Zophar's speech which as to the two former particulars, tends to this interpretation. For having said, *It is as high as heaven*, he presently adds, *What canst thou do?* meaning perhaps, *what are your weak abilities to his omnipotence?* He in regard of his sovereign power can do all things; *but you, alas! what can you do?* and after affirming, *It is deeper than hell*, he subjoins, *what can you know?* as if he had said, *what are your shallow apprehensions to the depth of his thoughts*? He in regard of his omniscient understanding knows all things, *but you poor man what can you know*?

§2. If it is asked, why I expound all these clauses of God, seeing the particles it and of it (It is high as heaven, the measure of it) seem to relate to somewhat else. My answer is, that expositors differ much about this very thing, and according to their several apprehensions translate the words after a different manner. The vulgar Latin and our English translations carry all to Almighty God, who was mentioned in the verse before, *canst thou find out the Almighty*? reading it this way, "he is higher than heaven, what art thou able to do? His length exceeds the length of the earth, *etc*." Others considering that diverse words in the original text being feminine will not agree in construction with *Eloah* and *Shaddai*, by which God is there expressed, have therefore looked back to the sixth verse for an antecedent, where they meet with wisdom and expound all of it, inserting the word *Sapientia* into their Latin translations, as Oecolampadius and Junius do. But for my part, there is I conceive a word nearer hand, which will serve the turn better, and that is *perfection*. "Canst thou find out the Almighty to perfection?" It, that is, the perfection of God is as high as heaven, *etc*. And in this I join with Castellio, whose translation is fully squared to this sense; for so he reads the place, "Tune Dei intima pervestiges, aut ipsam adeo perfectionem omnipotentis invenias? Qmæ cum coelum altitudine adaequet, quid ages? *etc*." Now I interpret the words, as before, because however they be read, whether God, or wisdom, or perfection be taken for the antecedent, it comes to one and the same issue, for the wisdom of God is himself; and his perfection comprehends not wisdom only, but all his other excellencies whatever; insomuch as Lessius entitled his book concerning the attributes, *de perfection-ibus divinis*. The way so cleared, I now proceed without further interruption to single out the particular dimensions, and discourse of them in their order.

§3. Seeing all divine perfections far transcend human

capacities, the safest way, as I humbly conceive, for us to make a due estimate concerning the height of God's sovereignty is to compare it with that of earthly potentates, which is within the compass and reach of our understandings. Verily it is not without cause that St. Paul describes him "the blessed and only potentate, the King of kings and Lord of lords; (1 Tim. 6:15) that Moses, Melchisedec and Abram, entitle him "the most high God" (Gen. 14:5, 18-20, 22) four times in one chapter. For on searching it the name will appear that his sovereignty excels that of the high and mighty ones on earth in point of extensiveness, of unaccountableness, and of almightiness.

I. In point of extensiveness, "His kingdom filleth over all," (Psa. 103:19). The whole earth and sea, which make but one globe, is to the universe but as a little central point; but the mightiest potentate has no more but his share in that little. Where Seneca brings in his wise and virtuous man with this censure and sarcasm in his mouth. "Is this that point, which so many nations of the world do so strive to divide among themselves by fire and sword? O how ridiculous are the bounds of mortal men! All that in which they sail to and fro, manage their wars, and set up their petty kingdoms is but a point."[177] Where the sovereignty of God extends itself to the whole earth and sea, yes to heaven; and the heaven of heavens, giving laws not only to the visible host of sun, moon, and stars, but also to the invisible host of angels, who are said to "excel in strength, and to do his commandments, hearkening to the voice of his word," (Psa. 103:20). Yes there is not a devil in hell that can go beyond the length of his chain, for even those legions of darkness are, though much against their wills, subjected to the empire of the Father of lights. Yes, where the dominion of worldly potentates reaches but to the outward

---

[177] Hoc est illud punctum quod inter tot gentes ferro & igni dividitur? O quam ridiculi sunt mortalium termini! Punctum est istud in quo navigatis, in quo bellatis, in quo regna disponitis minima, etc. Senec. *Natural*, quaest. lib. 1. in *Praefatione*.

man, and their laws cannot directly oblige the conscience, so as to bring on it a guilt binding over the soul to death, his do. And in this respect St. James tells us that, "there is one lawgiver," one, and but one, "who is able to save and to destroy," (James 4:12) The style which Paul gives earthly governors is "masters according to the flesh;" (Eph. 6:5), but Moses calls God, "the God of the spirits of all flesh;" (Num. 27:16), to imply that however there are many, who lord it sufficiently over the flesh and outward man, there is no lord of our spirits but God alone, who only "is greater than our hearts," (1 John 3:20) as St. John speaks. This made the good emperor Maximilian the second say, "That whosoever assumed to himself a power over the consciences of men, set himself down in the throne of God."[178] His son Rodolphus who succeeded him in the empire resolved to walk in his father's steps, yet was once unhappily worked on by the subtlety of the Jesuits to give way to the passing of an edict, for shutting up the protestant churches during some time.[179] But that very day news was brought him, that Alba Regia, the chief city he had in Hungary was taken by the Turks. Where in great astonishment he is reported to have said, "I expected that some such mischief as this should befall me; seeing this day I began to usurp the government belonging to God, which is of consciences."[180]

§4. II. In point of unaccountableness. The greatest princes on earth do, or should govern by laws, to the making in which others concur as well as they. But our God is a law to himself. He only can write on his imperial edicts, "My reason for it is my will."[181] Yet because of the holiness of his nature, his will is always most just; so as he never enacted any thing, but what is in itself equal and reasonable, although perhaps to

---

[178] *History of the Bohemian Persecutions*, English in 8vo., chapter 30,§2.

[179] Ibid. chapter 40, §1.

[180] Expectabam tale quid postquam hodie Dei regimen, quod est conscientiarum, usurpare coeperam. Joh. Læt. *compen. hist.* page 666.

[181] Stat pro ratione voluntas.

our shallow understanding it may appear otherwise. As to our eyes turrets and steeples how upright whatsoever, if their height is exceeding great, often seem crooked, and look as if they stood awry; which should deter us from censuring any of his decrees or dispensations, as some great but unhallowed wits are accustomed to do; of whom Luther makes this sober and sad complaint, "They require that God act *jure humano*, according to what the sons of men do commonly account right and just, or otherwise, that he would cease to be God. Tell not them of the secrets of his Sovereign Majesty; let him render a reason of his being God, if he speak, do, or will anything, but what appears equal to men. Proud flesh cannot vouchsafe the God of heaven so much honor as to believe anything to be good or right; which is spoken or acted above what the Codex of Justinian, or the fifth book of Aristotle's Ethicks defines to be just.[182]

I confess indeed that God often condescends in his holy word to give men a reason of some proceedings, and to clear them up to our understandings: but it is more than he needs to do, more than we ought to expect in all cases. It will therefore be our wisdom to forbear playing the critics on his decrees and administrations: considering that he alone is ἀνείθυνος καί ἀνυωεύθυνος, unaccountable, not to be called in question for any of his doings: and always remembering that of Paul, "Nay but, O man, who art thou that repliest against God? Has not the potter power over the clay?" (Rom. 9:20-21). Together with that of Job, "God is greater then man: why dost thou strive against him? for he gives not account of any of his matters," (Job 33:12-13).

§5. Thirdly, in point of Almightiness. In the princes of this world Ἐξξυσία and Δύναμις, authority and power are often severed, their authority may be great, when their power to manage it is but small. David was king, yet could not act as he desired, for the sons of Zeruiah were too strong for him. But in God they always go hand in hand for the accomplishing

---

[182] Luther de servo arbitrio, c. page 173.

of what his wisdom has designed. Therefore I called it Omnipotent Sovereignty. "I know," Job says, "that thou canst do every thing, and that no thought can be withholden from thee," (Job 43:2) meaning that God cannot be hindered in the execution, or bringing to pass of whatever he has in the thoughts and purposes of his heart. The angel to Mary, "With God nothing shall be impossible," (Luke 1:37). Paul to the Ephesians, "He is able to do exceeding abundantly above all that we ask or think. (Eph. 3:20). Other scriptures may seem opposite to these, but are not. "God that cannot lie," (Titus 1:2) "He cannot deny himself," (2 Tim. 2:13) St. Paul says. For answer to these and the like instances, we must distinguish of impossibles. They are of two sorts, *impossibiliaa naturæ*, and *impossibilia natura.*[183] First there are diverse things impossible indeed to nature, such as in the ordinary course of secondary causes cannot be done, which yet to God are most feaseable; for example, working of miracles, giving sight to such as were born blind, raising up children to Abraham out of the very stones in the street. Secondly, Some other things are impossible not to nature only, but in nature; and that either in reference to the nature of God, when they are such as argue imperfection in the doer, as to sin, and to die: or in respect to the nature of the things themselves, when they are such as imply contradiction, as for a creature to be made independent. The former of these God himself cannot do; not through lack, but through height and abundance of power.[184] He cannot sin, lie, or deny himself, and that because he is omnipotent; it is for impotent creatures to be liable to such kind of imperfections as these are. Neither can he do the latter: yet is it not through any defect of power in God, that such things cannot be done, but through want of capacity in the things which are simply impossible. So then, when we ascribe almightiness to God, the meaning is, that where ever divine understanding can be a

---

[183] Voetius, *Dispage Theol.* part. i., page 409.

[184] Si ista posset Deus, non esset omnipotens. Magna in Deo potential est non posse mentiri. August. Lib. i. de *Symbol.* c. page i.

principle of direction, and divine will a principle of injunction, there divine power can show itself an able principle of execution. Or in plainer terms, that God can do whatever he will and the only reason why things that do either argue imperfection, or imply contradiction fall not within the compass of his power, is because they are such, as for lack of goodness or entity cannot become objects of his will.

§6. Now if the perfection of God is so very high in regard of his omnipotent sovereignty, think of your own lowness, O man, (or rather, *O worm*, and no man) and be confounded within yourself, on comparing your servile condition by nature with his sovereignty; your imbecility with his omnipotence. Adam indeed, so long as he stood, was a universal monarch, having dominion both over himself, and over the creatures: but every man since the fall, is a slave born, a servant to diverse lusts and pleasures: neither is there any way for getting out of this estate, but getting into Christ, who restores all such as close with him, to a spiritual sovereignty, "Making them kings to God and his father; (Rev. 1:6) and "upholding them with his royal Spirit, (Psa. 51:11) as some read that in the psalm. Until then what are whole nations of men, but to speak in the prophet's language, "as the drops of a bucket," (Isa. 40:15) which in their fall are so licked up by the dust of the earth as they are no more discernable; or as the small dust of the balance, which is of no moment at all towards turning of the beam one way or other? And if nations are so inconsiderable, what shall we say of particular persons? I will suppose a mighty prince, but an unbeliever, described your highness, or your majesty at every word; and be bold to present him on this occasion with Zophar's interrogatory, "What canst thou?" When God leaves you to yourself, how impotent are your best abilities, as to the things of a better world? Seeing they are such as no natural man "can either receive, for they are foolishness to him, and must be spiritually discerned;" (1 Cor. 2:14) or close with when they are discovered. For the "carnal mind is enmity against God, it is not subject to the law of God, nor indeed can be," (Rom. 8:7).

May these and the like considerations work so kindly on us, as Canute's not being able to set bounds to the ocean did on him. It is a history worth the remembering. This Canute was one of the ancient kings of England,[185] who really, to refute the flatterers by whom he was told that all things were at his command, caused his royal pavilion to be set on the sands, when the tide was coming in, then said to the sea, "Thou belongest to my dominion, and this earth which my throne standeth on, is mine. I charge thee therefore not to flow in on my ground, nor to wet the feet of thy sovereign lord." But in vain, for the tide kept its course, and came up to his feet, without doing him any reverence. On which he removed further off and said, "Be it known to all men in the world that the power of princes is but a vain empty thing, and that none fully deserveth the name of a sovereign lord, but he at whose beck heaven and earth yield their obedience, who can say to the sea, hitherto shalt thou come but no further; and here shall thy proud waves be stayed," (Phil. 4:13). It is also reported that after this he never put on his crown more.

O that all the sons of men would accordingly learn from this branch of divine greatness never to boast more of their own abilities! but to throw down all their crowns at the feet of Christ, who, though omnipotence be incommunicable, leaves on such as receive him by faith, some impressions and footsteps of it. For where divine Almightiness stands in two things especially, in other words, in God's being able to do all things that are regularly possible, and his not being able to do any sinful thing; there are some prints of both on Christians, "I can do all things," (1 John 3:9) St. Paul says, "through Christ that strengthened me." And "whosoever is born of God," St. John says, "cannot sin, because he is born of God."

EXERCITATION VII.

The depth of Divine Omniscience seen in discerning the deep things of man,

---

[185] *Cambden Britannia* out of H. Huntington.

yes, of Satan, yes, of God. Our ignorance discovered and acknowledged. The longitude of God's perfection stated, eternity proper to him. Not assumed by, or ascribed to, men without blasphemy.

§1. The second dimension is the depth of God's, omniscience, which appears in that he is able to sound and fathom the deepest things, whether of man, or of Satan, or of the divine essence and *will*,

First, there are "deep things of men." Their words are deep:" (Prov. 18:4) and again, "The words of a man's mouth are as deep waters." Their hearts and counsels are much more. "Both the inward thoughts of every one of them, and the heart is deep," (Psa. 64:6). So David said of the church's enemies. "Counsel in the heart of man is like a deep water. (Prov. 20:5). So Solomon said of wise sages, who are therefore compared by a learned writer to coffers with double bottoms, which when others look into, being opened, they do not see all they hold on the sudden and at once.[186] But these are no depths to God, to whom David said, "There is not a word in my tongue, but lo, O Lord, thou knowest it altogether," (Psa. 139:4). And elsewhere, "The Lord searcheth all hearts, and understandeth all the imaginations of the thoughts," (1 Chron. 28:9). Neither is it the least act of God's goodness to mankind, that he is pleased to reserve the searching of hearts to himself, as part of his own prerogative royal, because if men were able to dive into one another's thoughts, there would be no quiet in the world; no peaceable living one by another, in regard of that hidden hypocrisy and malice which lurks in the most.

§2. *Secondly*. "Deep things of Satan," spoken of in the Revelation, "As many as have not this doctrine, and which have not known the depths of Satan, as they speak," (Rev. 2:24). Seducers are accustomed to boast of their mysterious tenets, and to speak of them as great depths, not to be fathomed by common Christians. Christ in that epistle of his to the church of Thyatira, makes use of their own term, depths

[186] Sir Walter Raleigh's *History*, book v. page 359.

as they speak; but so as to brand them for depths of Satan fetched from hell, where they perhaps held them forth as new truths, glorious lights and revelations from above. In this way popery is a mystery, but a mystery of *iniquity*, as Paul describes it, and Socinianism a depth, but a depth of *Satan*. There is not a serpentine winding or turning in any of those corrupt opinions, which pester and poison the church of Christ at this day, but God sees and knows it, how hard whatsoever it is for his servants to discover and refute. To these may be added, all those other hellish designs which go under other names in the scripture, as "the wiles of the devil, and his devices," (Eph. 6:11; 2 Cor. 2:11) all which dark secrets are not in the dark to divine understanding. And he that now sees them all will one day reckon with Satan for them, yes, and sink him so much the deeper into hell, by how much his depths have done more mischief on earth.

I say into hell, where he shall have those agents and factors by whom he now carries on his cursed work, for his cursed companions to eternity, according to that in the Apocalypse, "The devil that deceived them was cast into the lake of fire and brimstone, where the beast and the false prophet are; and shall be tormented day and night for ever and ever," (Rev. 20:10)

§3. *Thirdly*, Deep things of God, of the divine essence and will, concerning which the apostle says, "The Spirit searcheth all things, yes the deep things of God," (1 Cor. 2:10). Things which the clearest understandings of men and angels entertain with amazement. We cannot but bewray our inability to understand when we treat of one in three, and three in one, such a mysterious gulf is the trinity. So when we discourse either of the personal union, or the acts of Christ as the God-man. And no wonder, seeing we meet with such secrets and depths even in God's revealed will. The greatest divines have acknowledged many things hard to be understood; yes, diverse knots that cannot be untied, until there either come further light into this world, or we be translated into a better. Such as every modest Christian will be ready to say of, as the learned Cajetan did concerning the reason of that difference, which in the Hebrew text is observable betwixt the title of Psalm one hundred and twenty first, and those other Psalms of degrees, *Reservo Spiritui Sancto*, I reserve the solution of this and that doubt to the Holy Spirit. For to Him and the other divine persons such things are no riddles; though to us they be dark and enigmatical, yes, perhaps unsearchable. Although we ever and later meet with cause of crying out as St. Paul once did, "How unsearchable are his judgments, and his ways past finding out?" (Rom. 11:33). Yet let us always remember and believe that of St. James, "known to God are all his works from the beginning of the world," (Acts 15:18).

§4. Well may the prudent consideration of what has been said concerning the depth of Divine Omniscience put the wisest of men in mind of their ignorance; keep them from leaning to their own understanding; and give them just occasion to think of an answer to Zophar's question, *What canst thou know*? If the secrets of nature do so puzzle you, what can you know concerning those much greater secrets of grace and glory? Of which Luther very excellently, "Philosophy receives them not, faith doth. The authority of Scripture is greater by far than the capacity of our wit; and the Holy Spirit than Aristotle."[187] Well may the depth of divine understanding (which the Psalmist says is infinite, "Great is the Lord, and of great power, his understanding infinite," Psa. 148:5.) cause us to reflect on the shallowness, the finiteness, yes, the folly of our own. For if 'the foolishness of God is wiser than men, (1 Cor. 1:25), yes, as the Apostle tells us it is, what is his wisdom? And if "the wisdom of this world be foolishness with God" (1 Cor. 3:19), what is its folly? No wonder if one learned man wrote a book of the vanity of sciences,[188] others of the nullity,

[187] Quid si philosophia, hæc non capit? fides tamen capit, major est verbi Dei authoritas, quam nostri ingenii capacitas. Major Spage Sanctus quam Aritotele. Luther *de captivit. Babyonies.*

[188] Cornel. Agrip.

quod nihil scitur. If the wise heathen professed, the only thing he knew was this, that he did not know anything at all.[189] If friar Paul of Venice, the judicious author of that excellent history of the Council of Trent, was accustomed to say,[190] "the more we study, the more we see how little or little or nothing we understand yes, if more knowing men than any of these abounded in acknowledgements of their own ignorance, Asaph, "So foolish was I and ignorant; I was as a beast before thee," (Psa. 73:22). Agur, "Surely I am more brutish than any man, and have not the understanding of a man. I neither learned wisdom, nor have the knowledge of the holy," (Prov. 30:23). So true is that of our great apostle, "If any man think that he knows any thing, he knows nothing yet as he ought to know," (1 Cor. 8:2).

§5. Next follows the third dimension, which is longitude, in this expression, "The measure of it is longer than the earth." For the better stating in which let it be considered, that where the word here translated *measure* relates not to extension only, but also to duration, and the earth has a double longitude, one of space, the other of continuance; which the scripture takes special notice of in other texts, as in that of Ecclesiastes, "One generation passeth away, and another generation comes: but the earth abideth for ever," (Eccl. 1:4) I conceive the latter may here be alluded to, *viz.* the earth's long continuance, as in some low proportion fit to resemble that everlasting duration of God, which cannot be adequately represented by any creature. Sure I am by the Ancient of days in Daniel the eternal Jehovah is described (Dan. 7:9, 13), by length of days in wisdom's right hand (Prov. 3:16), (of which it is in the Proverbs,) many interpreters understand the blessings of eternity; and this very place of Job is expounded by Gregory in this sense. His words are, *Terra*

---

[189] Anton. Verderius. Franc. Zanch. M. D. Hoc unum scio. Socrates.

[190] Quo magis studiis incumbimus eo magis nos videre quam nihil scimus, Apage Jo. Bevoricium. *Epist. quæst*. page 26.

longior, quia creaturæ modum perennitate suæ æternitatis excedit.[191]

All creatures had an original, all but some few shall have a dissolution. Of the Creator, and of him only is that of the Psalmist verified, "From everlasting to everlasting you are God," (Psa. 90:2). He gave beginning to all things, but he was himself without beginning;[192] is the end for which all things were made, but himself without end. The best of men, alas! are but of yesterday, and know not where they shall be tomorrow, according to that of Bildad, "We are but of yesterday, and know nothing, because our days on earth are a shadow," (Job 8:9). His being God from everlasting to everlasting, should encourage us to walk "in the way everlasting" (Psa. 139, last), having this "everlasting consolation and good hope through grace," (2 Thes. 2:16), that he will "save us with an everlasting salvation; (Isa. 45:17) because he lacks neither power to effect it, for his "strength is everlasting;" (Isa. 26:4) nor will, for his mercy is so too, as David testifies, "The mercy of the Lord is from everlasting to everlasting on them that fear him," (Psa. 103:17).

§6. The more to blame were some overweening sons of Adam for daring to assume to themselves, and ascribe to other persons and things this incommunicable perfection of God. Of old the heathenish people of Rome were accustomed to style their emperors, yes and their city Eternal. Concerning which practice of theirs, two ancient writers, Jerome and Prosper interpret those names of blasphemy mentioned in the Revelation. (Rev. 13:1, 5). They accounted such no less than blasphemers as called Rome the Eternal City, and saluted the emperor of it by the title of your Eternity.[193] A thing usually done among them. Yes, this Calenture has taken the brains of

---

[191] Greg. *Moral.* lib. x. c. page 7.

[192] Principium fine principio, finis sine fine.

[193] In fronte purpuratæ meretricis scriptum est nomen blasphemiæ, id est Romæ AEternæ. Hierom. Ad *Algusiam* quæst. AEterna cum dicitur quæ temporalis est, itique nomen est blasphemiæ.—Cum supplices dicunt, Altaribus vestries, Perennitati vestræ, &c. Prosp. De prædic. Et promiss. In *Dimid*, temp. c. page 7.

some even among the Christian emperors: so exceedingly contagious are words and examples that contain blasphemy in them. Ammianus Marcellinus reporteth of Constantius an Arian Prince, that being puffed up by the ostentation of his flatterers,[194] and the prosperous success of his affairs, he was come to that height of insolence as to presume he should never die, and in his writings to style himself Our Eternity. His words are these, *Immunem se deinde fore ab omni mortalitatis incommodo fidenter existimans, confestim & justitia declinavit ita intemperanter, ut (æternitatem meam) aliqioties subjeceret ipse dictando.* Yes, Justinian himself feared not to say concerning some of his edicts, *nostra murit æternitas.*[195]

EXERCITATION VIII.

Divine immensity shadowed out by the breadth of the sea. Divine Omnipresence cleared and vindicated. The proposal of it as an antidote against sinning in secret. Five practical corollaries from the greatness of God in general.

§1. The fourth dimension is still behind in that clause, "broader than the sea." It may be thought to relate to divine omnipresence, and immensity; which is, though not set forth to the life, yet some way shadowed out by the breadth: of the sea. In that the vast ocean stretches its arms far and near, (so we call them arms of the sea) to the embracing of certain shores, very much distant each from other; and is in that respect in a manner omnipresent with the several parts of the earth, to which it is united in one globe. So, and much more than so, the immensity of God's essence is such as to render him actually, and at all times present with every creature in the upper and lower world; for which cause he is said "to fill the heaven and earth," (Jer. 23:24). To a certain philosopher,

---

[194] Ammian. Marcel, innitio, lib. 5.
[195] Vide Contem. *politic.* lib. 7 c. page 4 §3.

who asked one of our profession, *Where is God?* the Christian answered, *Let me first understand from you where he is not,*[196] to intimate his being present everywhere. Which he is, not only by his power and providence, as some would confine it, but also by his essence, according to the true meaning of that which Paul said at Athens concerning God, "He is not far from every one of us. For in him we live and move, and have our being," (Acts 17:27, 28). He did not say (as Chrysostom observed) By him we live and move, but in him;[197] to note the intimacy of his presence, and that with all sorts of things, whether they are such as have life, or motion without life, or barely being without motion. Yes, where ever they are, whether in heaven or earth, or hell, as the Psalmist expressly, "If I ascend up into heaven, you are there; if I make my bed in hell, behold you are there; if I take the wings of the morning, and dwell in the uttermost parts of the sea; even there shall thy hand lead me. (Psa. 139:8-9). To which accords that of Seneca, "Turn thyself what way thou wilt, thou shall there see him meeting thee. There is not any thing void of him, He filleth whatever he has made."[198]

§2. This truth having been so fully acknowledged by a wise heathen, it will argue but too much weakness in any Christian to stumble (as some notwithstanding have done) at this sorry cavil against it. It seems unworthy of God, say they, to afford his presence with all things, even the least and filthiest. Neither do we see how he can possibly do it without receiving some defilement from them. For if God were not lessened by creating the meanest thing, then surely he is not by affording his presence to them after they were made. As for defilement, there can be no fear of that. Can the sun shine on dung-hills, and worse places, without being by this defiled? and shall not God's essence, which is infinitely purer than the

---

[196] Apud John Gerhard, in *Exeges.* page 797, in quarto.

[197] Chrys. *homil.* 38. in *Act Apost.*

[198] Quocunque te flexeris, ibi illum videbis occurrentem tibi. Nihil ab illo vacat. Opus suum ipse implet. Senec. *De Benefic.* lib. 4 c. page 8.

light, preserve itself from contracting filth from anything it comes near to! The soul of man united to a sickly and leprous body, does notwithstanding retain its purity. Much more God in the forementioned case. Be we therefore careful, in spite of all heretical cavils firmly to believe the truth of divine omnipresence and immensity, for the clearing up in which to our understandings, divines have invented various comparisons; two in which I shall mention. One out of Augustine, "The whole world," he says, "is so in God, as a little sponge in a vast ocean. The sea besides its encompassing the sponge on every side, doth also thoroughly penetrate, moisten, and sustain the whole substance within, and every part of it."[199] There is another out of Lessius. He compares the world to a crystal ball hanging in the light of the sun.[200] In which case the light would intimately pierce the whole ball, and also extend itself far and near, round about it. Such and so intimate is God's presence with every creature in every place.

§3. The contemplation in which should be effectual for the preventing of all sins, especially such as are usually committed in secret, on this grand presumption, which the prophet denounces a curse against the subjects of, saying "Wo to them that seek deep to hide their counsel from the Lord, and their works are in the dark, and they say, who seeth us? and who knoweth us?" (Isa. 29:15). A presumption that there is none by to take notice of them. Suppose it were so; yet men are bound to reverence themselves. The advice of Ausonius is excellent, "when you are about to act anything unseemly, be afraid of thyself, although there be no other witness."[201] But so it is not, for conscience is by; concerning which Lactantius produces an admirable quote out of Seneca, "O thou mad man! what will it profit thee to have none conscious of thy crime, so long as thou hast a conscience that is?"[202] But that you will say

[199] Augustin, *Confess.* lib. 7 c. page 5.

[200] Lessius *de Prefectonibus divinis* lib. 1. c. page3. §20.

[201] Turpe quid ausurus te sine teste time.

[202] Demens, quid prodest non habere conscium habenti conscientiam?

is part of yourself. True Therefore I add, *God is by*; of whom the apostle emphatically says, "If our heart condemn us, God is greater than our heart, and knoweth all things," (1 John 3:20). *Conscience* we are accustomed to say, is a thousand witnesses; and let it be considered here, that *God* is as a thousand consciences, both, for intimacy of presence, and perspicacity in discerning. It is worth observing how the mention of God's immensity is brought in by the prophet in that forecited place of Jeremiah, where the whole verse runs this way, "can any hide himself in secret places, that I shall not see him, saith the Lord? Do not I fill heaven and earth, saith the Lord?" (Jer. 23:24). Our most secret sins are, in reference to God, no more secret, in regard of his omnipresence, than if committed in the most open light. Witness that in Moses' prayer, "Thou hast set our iniquities before thee, our secret sins in the light of thy, countenance," (Psa. 90:8). Jacob once said of Bethel, "Surely the Lord is in this place, and I knew it not; how fearful is it?" (Gen. 28:16). Let every place be a Bethel to you, O watchful Christian, a place of fear, and in some sense a house of God, be it market, or shop, or field; be sure the Lord is in that place, not present only, but looking on; nor only looking, but weighing and pondering, whatever you do there in all the circumstances and aggravations of it, as Solomon testifies, "The ways of man are before the eyes of the Lord, and he pondereth all his goings," (Prov. 5:21).

§4. Having already made improvement of the several branches, let me now for a conclusion draw certain corollaries from the greatness of God in general; in number *five*,

First, "Let him be greatly praised for this, by all mankind." It is the Psalmist's inference, "great is the Lord, and greatly to be praised," (Psa. 145:3). The world is accustomed to commend greatness both in persons and things. Great princes have had panegyrical orations made in their praise, as Trajan by Pliny; great cities, as grand Cairo; great monuments, (as the Colossus) are greatly extolled by writers and travelers. How much more should the great God? Whom the prophet accordingly magnifies, saying, "Behold, the nations are as a drop of a bucket, and are counted as the small dust of the balance; behold he taketh up the isles, as a very little thing. And Lebanon is not sufficient to burn, nor the beasts of it sufficient for a burnt-offering. All nations before him are as nothing, and they are counted to him less than nothing and vanity," (Isa. 40:14-17). The drop of a bucket is nothing to the whole ocean, nor the dust of the balance to the whole earth; no more is the whole earth with all the inhabitants of it to God. In so much as if he were to be sacrificed to proportionably to his greatness, all the beasts in Lebanon would not suffice for a burnt-offerings nor all the wood of it for a fire, nor all men in the world for a priest to offer it.

§5. *Secondly*, let him be greatly confided in by all his people. That of St. John, "Ye are of God, little children; and greater is he that is in you, than he that is in the world," (1 John 4:4), should be made use of by the saints as a precious receipt against the most deadly poison that can at any time be administered to them. The church indeed is very often put on renewing Jehosaphat's complaint, and crying out, "We have no might against this great company" (perhaps both of wicked men, and wicked spirits) that comes against us; neither know we what to do," (2 Chron. 20:12). But so long as she can add, as he there does, "Our eyes are on thee;" (Titus 2:13). This contemplation of her great God and Savior may support her against the fear of them all. *The devil is mighty, I confess it,* said Luther,[203] *but he will never be Almighty, as my God and Savior is.* On these grounds a believing Christian, living up to his principles, may well say, "Show me a danger greater than my God, a destroyer, greater than my Savior, I will then fear it and him. Until then pardon me if I do not let my confidence go. What? Though Jacob is small, (as the prophet speaks, "By whom shall Jacob arise? for he is small," Amos 7:5) Yet arise he shall in spite of opposition, and that because Jacob's God is great.

---

[203] Esto diabolus magnipotens nunquam erit omnipotens.

Thirdly, Let the world learn to seek after interest in him. *Many*, Solomon says, "Many seek the ruler's favor," (Prov. 29:26). And the is reason good, because he is able to protect the persons, and reward the services of his followers. Behold here a ruler indeed, whose favor was never sought in vain, if sought in time; one that can protect from hell, and bestow heaven;[204] yes that which is the heaven of heaven, the fruition of himself. Being great with great men is a thing much affected by some, although in experience it often becomes not a burden only, but a mischief: where the love and favor of the great God, and our Savior always proves, (shall I say beneficial? that is too little) it proves, and that always beatifical.

Fourthly, Let such as have obtained interest from him look for great things from him. To Baruch it was once said, "Seekest thou great things for thyself? seek them not," (Jer. 45:5) because he sought them in the creatures; but if we seek them from and in the great Creator, we may lawfully seek great things, neither shall our doing so be attended with disappointment. "For open thy mouth wide (*the Lord says*) and I will fill it," (Psa. 81:10). We are accustomed either not to open our mouths at all, or not wide enough; and therefore it is that most of us continue so empty. "Ye have not, because ye ask not;" (James 4:2) so the apostle: let me say, you ask *perhaps*, and yet have but little, because you do not expect much. O consider, as Samuel once spoke of the men of Israel, "how great things God has already done for you" (1 Sam. 12:24), that so your experiments may be your encouragement, to expect yet greater: remembering that of our blessed Savior to Nathaniel, "Believest thou? thou shalt see greater things than these," (John 1:50). He in whom you trust, O believers, is a great God, and loves to do all things like himself. Therefore look for great things from him, great assistances, great enlargements, great deliverances, yes the forgiving of great sins, and the obtaining of great salvation.

---

[204] Dulcis inexpertis cultura potentis amici; expertus metuit. Horat.

§7. *Fifthly*, let such as have received great things from God, maintain a certain greatness of spirit suitable to their interest in him. I do not mean a haughty spirit, swelled with pride, for that is altogether unsuitable to a saving interest in God, "who beholds the proud afar off but an humble spirit greatened by continual converse with the great God; who by raising up his servant's hearts to the contemplation and fruition of higher objects, makes them too big for this world. It is reported of Moses, that "when he was come to years," of according to the original, "when he was waxed great," (Heb. 11:24-27) (in spirit perhaps, as well as in stature) he overlooked the preferments, pleasures, and riches of the world, which are all there intimated, yes, the menaces of it too. For it is there also said, "He feared not the wrath of the king, but endured, as seeing him who is invisible." His converting with the great God, had made all these appear to him as petty things.[205] To a soul truly great no worldly matter has any true greatness in it: as if one would take a station in heaven, whatever is here below would appear but small in his sight by reason of its distance. It is accounted by some a great matter to have the frowns and ill word of a great man. But St. John, whose conversation was in heaven, made nothing of it. Speaking of Diotrephes' malignancy and reproachful speeches he phrases it this way, "prating against us with malicious words?"[206] The term properly signifies trifling. Though Diotrephes were a great prelate, and his words very malicious; yet the apostle's spirit was raised so far above them, that with him all were but trifles, and by him condemned as such.

---

[205] Animo magno nil magnum.

[206] 3 John verse 10. διὰ τοῦτο, ἐὰν ἔλθω, ὑπομνήσω αὐτοῦ τὰ ἔργα ἃ ποιεῖ λόγοις πονηροῖς φλυαρῶν ἡμᾶς, καὶ μὴ ἀρκούμενος ἐπὶ τούτοις οὔτε αὐτὸς ἐπιδέχεται τοὺς ἀδελφοὺς καὶ τοὺς βουλομένους κωλύει καὶ ἐκ τῆς ἐκκλησίας ἐκβάλλει.

APHORISM V.

The goodness and greatness of God are both abundantly manifested by his decrees of Election and Preterition, together with his works of Creation and Providence.

EXERCITATION I.

How predestination comes to be treated of here. Election described from the nature, antiquity, objects, products and cause of it. Rom. 11:33, 2 Tim. 1:9, with Tit. 1:2, Eph. 1:4, with Matt. 25:34 opened. Of acts supposing their objects. Of acceptance of persons, what it is, and that predestination does not import it. Acts 13:48 expounded and vindicated. Whether one elect may become a reprobate? The negative maintained, and 1 Cor. 9:24-26 cleared. Eph. 5:11 enlightened. Concerning the good pleasure of God's will and the counsel of it.

§1. I do not dare wholly wave the doctrine of predestination, (no not in this treatise of principles) after I had duly pondered that grave admonition of Ambrose, or according to others of Prosper, "Such things as God would have kept secret must not be pried into by us; nor such denied as he has openly declared: lest we be found in the former attempt unlawfully curious, in the latter damnably unthankful."[207] And also laid to heart the endeavors, not of foreigners only, but of certain late English writers to possess their readers with vehement and strong prejudices against the long-received truth in those points. One of them tells us, "It is sacrilegious to grant that God has from eternity elected a certain number of men personally to salvation, whom he purposeth to bring thereunto infallibly, *etc.*"[208] Elsewhere

---

[207] Quæ Deus occulta esse voluit, non sunt scrutanda; quæ autem manifesta fecit non sunt neganda: ne in illis illicit curiosi, in istis damnabiliter inveniamur in grati. *De vocat.* Gent. c. page 7.

[208] I.G. Red. *Redeem.* page 243, lin. 7. Ibid. pag. 278, lin. 46.

styling it, that capital error of personal election and reprobation. Another speaking of preterition, or negative reprobation, has these words. "This is one of the σοφὰ φάρμακα, which have been infamously invented to disguise and palliate the frightful rigidness of their doctrine."[209] Not long after he calls it canting, (pretends the lamentable distinction as it is there by him described) to be no more than a trick insufficient to buoy up a sinking cause, and in another book of his the dream of absolute preterition.[210] Meanwhile where, alas! is the reverence and submission due to Scripture, that only card and compass by which we are to sail in this ocean, that only clue by the help in which this labyrinth is to be traversed? It directly opposeth *Electi* and *Reliqui*, the elect and such as were passed by, in that saying, "the election has obtained, and the rest were blinded."[211] In it we read of a book of life containing the names of all those whom God has chosen, and of others whose names were not written in that book, (Rev. 13:8, 21, 26, 27, *cf.* 15). Of some whom the Lord knows for his, (2 Tim. 2:19) and others to whom he will say, I never knew you. (Matt. 7:23). Of Christ's sheep given to him by the Father, and of such persons as were not his sheep, nor accordingly so given to him. (John 10:26, 28, 29). This, I hope, is no canting; there is neither error nor trick in all this; but to proceed.

§2. Election (as to our purpose which concerns the choice of men only, not of angels) is that secret unsearchable decree of God, in which he did from everlasting single out of the rest of mankind a definite number of particular persons, ordaining them infallibly to the attainment of holiness here, and happiness hereafter, according to the counsel and good pleasure of his will. Which description offers to the reader's consideration, as things material, and not unfit to be treated

---

[209] T.P. *Divine philanthropy defended*, c. 4. §2.

[210] *Divine purity defended*, page 97.

[211] Rom. 11:7. τί οὖν; ὃ ἐπιζητεῖ Ἰσραήλ, τοῦτο οὐκ ἐπέτυχεν, ἡ δὲ ἐκλογὴ ἐπέτυχεν· οἱ δὲ λοιποὶ ἐπωρώθησαν.

of, provided it is soberly done, the nature, antiquity, object, products and cause of election.

First, the nature of it. It is a secret unsearchable decree of God. The two principal emanations of God's will respecting intellectual features, are his *decrees*, and his *commands*. They differ, as in various other things, so in point of perspicuity. The commands are plain; he that runs may read his duty in them; the decrees abstruse. Our destinies cannot be so easily read, as our duties may. And where diverse secret things may yet be discovered on diligent search, according to that Proverb of Solomon, "Counsel in the heart of man is like deep water: but a man of understanding will draw it out," (Prov. 20:5). The Decrees of God are so secret, as to be with unsearchable. Where the Apostle says, "O the depth of the riches both of the wisdom and knowledge of God! How unsearchable are his judgments and his ways past finding out?" (Rom. 11:33) where by *judgments* it is, as I conceive, most proper to understand the Decrees of his will; by ways,[212] the administrations of his providence in order to the execution of those decrees. Some innovators there are indeed, who have so modeled the mysterious doctrine of predestination, as to leave little of nothing of mystery in it. Our remonstrants think themselves able to wade, where our Apostle was past his depth, and forced to cry out, ῷ βαθος! Their way pretends to give a clear reason why one is elected, another reprobated, one converted, another not; but for my part I had much rather with St. Paul be still ignorant than overlearned, (that I say not oversaucy) with Arminius and his followers.

§3. *Secondly*, the antiquity. It is from everlasting, an eternal decree. So Paul, "According as he has chosen us in him before the foundation of the world," (Eph. 1:4). This expression notes eternity. The kingdom we are elected to is said to have been prepared ἀπὸ καταβολῆς from the foundation. "Come ye blessed of my Father, inherit the kingdom prepared for you from the foundation of the world

[212] Κείματα from Κείμω whence cerno, decerno, & decretum.

(Matt. 25:34); in reference to the third heavens, that place where the kingdom is to be set up and inherited, which was in the beginning of time created by "the builder and maker of it," (Heb. 11:10) as God is described. But the decree by which we were designed thereunto, to have been πρὸ καταβολῆς, before the foundation of the world. That is, from everlasting; as may be further gathered from other phrases in the writings of our apostle; this by name, "Who has saved us, and called us with a holy calling, not according to our works, but according to his own purpose and grace, which was given us in Christ Jesus, before the world began," (2 Tim. 1:9). This both Erasmus and Calvin interpret of predestination. Compare we it with another speech of the same apostle to Titus, "In hope of eternal life, which God that cannot lie, promised before the world began." The meaning in which will no longer be obscure, if it is considered that the first-born of election was Christ himself (who applied to himself that which God said of old by the prophet Isaiah, "Behold my servant whom I have chosen, my beloved in whom my soul is well-pleased," Matt. 12:18). That certain persons were from eternity given to Christ, whom the Father had constituted head of all his elect, to be his members, and by him brought to eternal blessedness according to what we read in St. John's Gospel, "Thou hast given him power over all flesh, that he should give eternal life to as many as thou hast given him," (John 17:2). That in this transaction there passed promises from the Father to the Son in the behalf of himself and all his members. And that this is the grace which was given us in Christ Jesus, these the promises of eternal life before the world began, spoken of in the forecited places to Timothy and Titus: on the latter in which I meet with the same gloss from a reverend Scotish writer, whose name and words are here presented in the margin.[213] I shall add no more concerning the antiquity of this

[213] Promisit vitam æternam, non tantum initio mundi prædicando eam primis parentibus in paradiso, sed etiam paciscendo de ea ante conditum mundum cum Filio designato mediatore nostro in foedere redemptionis.

decree, save only a brief saying of Augustine, *Intra mundum facti sumus, & ante mundum electi sumus.*[214] We were made within the world, but chosen before it.

§4. *Thirdly*, The object of election is a definite number of particular persons singled out of the rest of mankind. We learn from St. Luke (Luke 18:7) the elect cry to God day and night: And St. John in his Apocalypse tells us what one of their principal cries is, "They cried, with a loud voice, saying, How long, O Lord, holy and true, dost thou not judge and avenge our blood?" (Rev. 6:10-11). As also what answer they had from heaven, "It was said to them that they should rest yet for a little season until their fellow-servants and their brethren that should be killed as they were, should be fulfilled." From the collation of which texts it may be inferred that their number is set, and shall in due time be completed; for that is the thing related to in the word πληρῴσονται shall be fulfilled. It is then a definite number, and that of particular persons, whose "names are elsewhere said to be written in the book of life," (Luke 10:20, Phil. 4:3). Names in scripture being often put for persons; as in the Acts, "the number of names together were about one hundred and twenty:" and in the Revelation, "In the earth-quake were slain of men seven thousand;" (Rev. 11:13. Ὀνόματα ἀνθρώπων.), it is in the original, names of men. They certainly shoot beside the mark, who so confidently teach that predestination is terminated not on persons, but qualifications; and that not this or that man in particular is elected or reprobated, but only in general, whosoever believes and perseveres belongs to election; whosoever continues in unbelief, to reprobation; and that so as the same person may be today under the one, and tomorrow under the other decree, according to the change of his qualifications. But if so, it would not in likelihood have been said, "The foundation of God standeth sure having this seal, The Lord knoweth them who are his," (2 Tim. 2:19 Ἔγνω

David Dickson *Exposit. Analytic.* in Tit. i. 2.

[214] August. l. *de Prædistin. et grat.* c. page 5.

κύριος τους ὄντας αυτοῦ.) Nor the Romans, "I will have mercy on whom I will have mercy." And again, "He has mercy on whom he will have mercy, and whom he will he hardeneth," (Rom. 9:15, 18) (which dearly relates to persons, not to qualifications) but rather, what sort he will.

§5. Against what has been said in this and the former paragraph there are two principal objections; in which neither is to be waved, lest it should be thought unanswerable. The first is borrowed from philosophy, and runs this way. Acts suppose the being of their objects; the decrees of God are divine acts, and therefore could not pass on men's particular persons before the world was, because there were then none in being. I answer that where the acts of God are either immanent abiding within, or transient passing from him, and terminated on somewhat without himself; his transient acts do either suppose, or produce the being of their objects; suppose it, as his rewarding and punishing, produce it, as his creating acts. But those that are immanent (of which rank his decrees are) do not necessarily require the pre-existence of their objects *in esse reali* in a way of reality; for it sufficeth that they have it *in esse cognito*, in the foreknowledge of God. Jesus Christ our Mediator is described a "Lamb foreordained before the foundation of the world (1 Pet. 1:19-20); yet had he no existence as such until after his incarnation. God who had designed Josiah to special services, called him by his name, and foretold what should be done by him, full three hundred and thirty years before he did it.[215] So elsewhere, Cyrus is named, and has a service allotted him in the foreknowledge of God one hundred and forty years before he was born.[216] It is reported by Procopius that when Misdates king of Persia was dead without issue, but had left his wife with child, the Persian nobility set the crown on the queen's head before she quickened, by it acknowledging her issue that should be for

[215] I Kings 13:3 vid. Junium et Piscat. in locum.
[216] See Scultetus on Isa. 45, page 623 fin.

their lawful sovereign.[217] So that Sapores (which was afterwards the child's name) began his reign before his life. If such acts when done by men seem not irrational, why should any think it strange for the only wise God, to set the crown of election on the head of certain persons, while as yet they have no being, save only in the womb of his decree?

§6. The other objection is taken from such places of scripture as deny God to be an accepter of persons, which they say he must needs be, if considering mankind in an equal condition he chose some to life, and passed by others.

In order to the solution of it here, I shall first distinguish between acceptation and acceptance of persons. We find them both mentioned by St. Peter as it were with one breath, in that short saying of his, ("Of a truth I perceive that God is no respecter of persons: but in every nation he that feareth him and worketh righteousness is accepted with him," Acts 10:34-35) the one as attributable to him, the other as not, were it not for his acceptation of persons, woe, and nothing but woe to the sons of men. It is the joy of their hearts to consider that there are certain "men of his good will,"[218] as some read that in the angel's song; and to remember that the church is by her head and husband called *Hephzibah*, that is *my delight is in her*; because the members of it are, as Paul speaks, "accepted in the beloved," (Eph. 1:6). Next declare the true notion of *Prosopolepsie* or acceptance of persons in scripture dialect.

Besides the prime importance of these words πρόσωπον in Greek, and *Persona* in Latin for an individual intelligent substance, (so, "The gift bestowed on us by the means of many persons" (2 Cor. 1:11), is the blessing of recovery granted on the prayers of various men and women) they have a secondary importance, and are sometimes put to signify a vizard, property or counterfeit resemblance assumed by any such individual. So in Seneca, *Nemo potest personam din*

[217] Procopius.
[218] ἀνθρώποις εὐδοκίας Luke 2:14.

ferre, that is, none can play the hypocrite long; and in the epigramatist a gray haired man having put on a black periwig to conceal his age, is told of it this way, —*Inveniet proserpina canum, Personam capiti detrahet illa tuo.* Now because these vizards and properties are things external, not at all belonging to the essence of the party assuming them, here it comes to pass that these words at the next remove signify such relations, accommodations and accomplishments as being external to the essence of a man as also to the merit of his cause, ought not to incline a judge to pronounce a sentence on his behalf, or in the distribution of justice to regard him above others to whom such helps are wanting. He who is swayed in judicial proceedings by such outward things is in the scripture said to be an accepter of persons.[219] So in Leviticus, "Ye shall do no unrighteousness in judgment: thou shalt not respect the person of the poor, nor honor the person of the mighty; but in righteousness thou shalt judge thy neighbour," (Lev. 18:15). And in the New Testament these two terms δικαιοκρισίας, righteous judgment, and προσωποληµψία, accepting of persons, are directly opposed. (Rom. 2:5 compared with verse 11). Divines have received it for a maxim. That acceptance of persons is not found *in gratuitis*, in acts of bounty, in which the donor is at liberty to dispose his free gifts as pleases himself, but in *debitis* in acts of justice and right, in which there lies an obligation on him that distributes to give every man his due.[220] On this they conclude that in divine predestination Almighty God, who is no debtor to any of his creatures, and who acts in it not as a judge, but as a sovereign Lord and liberal benefactor, chooses some and passes by others, as without injustice or wrong to any, so without any show of that which the scripture properly calls acceptance of persons, because he was not moved by any

[219] Thom. Secunda secundæ. q. 62. artic 1. in conclus. Ad personam refertur quæcunque condition non faciens ad causam.

[220] Thom. *prima secundæ* qu. 98. art. 4. in *respage ad secundum*. Pererius super Rom. 2. page 157. in 4to.

external thing in doing so.

If any reader think it is not safe to credit this on my single testimony, behold in the footnote further security, to which it were easy to add much more if need were.[221]

§7. Fourthly, The products of divine election are chiefly two. First, holiness here. God is said "to have blessed us with all spiritual blessings in Christ, according as he has chosen us in him before the foundation of the world, that we should be holy," (Eph. 1:3-4). Where spiritual blessings are pointed at as the streams, and election as the fountain where they flow. It as the root, and holiness as the fruit. So elsewhere, "We are bound to give thanks always to God for you, brethren, beloved of the Lord, because God has from the beginning chosen you to salvation, through sanctification of the spirit, and belief of the truth," (2 Thes. 2:13). Here we find not only sanctification in general, but faith which is the flower of holiness derived from election. The same apostle calls it, "The faith of God's elect," (Tit. 1:1). And St. Luke in Acts, speaking of the success which St. Paul's preaching had among the Gentiles, says expressly, "As many as were ordained to eternal life believed." (Acts 13:48).

A text which the soundest divines look at, as a most pregnant place to prove a causal influence of divine

[221] Potest Deus absque vitiosa personarum acceptione non modo ex duobus hominibus prorsus æqualibus unum eligere ad vis tam æternam alio præterito; sed etiam illum eligere quem præscivit pluribus et gravioribus peccatis implicandum, illo relicto quem prævidit pauciora et leviora admissurum. Bannes in lam. Thomæ quæst. 23. artic. 51.

Injusta personarum acceptio locum non habet ubi quis ex mera liberalitate de suo dat inaequaliter aequalibus; sed ubi in dispensatione rerum debitarum quis uni faveat prae altero ex respectu ad aliquam personae circumstantiam quae est extra causam meriti. Jam vero Deus eligens ad regnum gloriae unum præ alio non agit ex debito justitiae, sed ex dono munificentiae; neque respicit nobilitatem, divitias, ingeniuni, aut aliam qualitatem quamcunque, (unde προσωποληµψία nomen invenit) sed liberalitatem et bonitatem suam juxta illud Matthaei 20. Licet mihi quod volo facere de meo. Davenantius in *disserto de Praedestin. et Reprobat*. c. page 3. page 133.

predestination on the work of saving faith. Others, I know there are, (and they not a few, nor inconsiderable) who have strongly endeavored to turn the edge and strength of this place another way, by rendering the word Τεταγμένοι, not (as we do) ordained, but disposed, or well-affected to eternal life; to whose corrupt gloss, I oppose the following considerations.

First, If it were to be so read, then all that heard the apostle's sermon there recorded, even all and every one without exception should have believed, seeing there is not a man in the world, and therefore none in that congregation who was not disposed, and well affected to the reward of eternal life (the will of man being necessarily carried to the desire of blessedness, which none are so brutish as not to affect) for that to which these are said to be Τεταγμένοι, is not conversion, but life eternal.

Secondly, disposedness in their sense does not always precede faith, nor faith always follow it. When Saul was in the full career of his persecuting madness against the saints, what disposedness was there in him to conversion, unless fury is a disposition to faith? Yet then did he first believe. In that young man who came to our Savior, of whom it is testified, "That he was not far from the kingdom of God," which of their dispositions was wanting? Yet he went away sorrowful, and did not believe.

Thirdly, Faith itself is the first saving disposition that any man has, became it first lays hold on Christ, and of life by him; insomuch as none is formally disposed to eternal life until he has believed.

Fourthly, St. Luke nowhere uses Τατειν and τάσσωθαι, either in his Gospel, or in the Acts for disposedness, but for ordination and constitution diverse times, therefore our reading here, "As many as were ordained to eternal life," is to be retained.

§8. But the learned Grotius will by no means allow of this interpretation. They (he says) who apply this text to predestination, *nihil vident*, see nothing at all. Yet by his favor, a man that saw as far into the mysteries of divinity, as also into the idioms of the Greek tongue, as Grotius himself (be it spoken without disparagement to his great learning). Chrysostom I mean, applies it so in his commentary on the place. And his Αφωρισμένοι τῳ Θεω, by which Τεταγμένοι is expounded, Erasmus translates *Proefiniti a Deo, Presdestinated o God.*[222] Three things are alleged by Grotius, for the overthrowing of this sense; but all in vain. His first plea is, that it is not usual for all of a city, a congregation that are predestinated, to believe at one and the same time; therefore that which we assert is not likely to be the meaning here. For answer, I acknowledge it is not usual; no more is it to have three thousand inhabitants of one city brought in to God on one day. But what if God willing to glorify his gospel, and the power of converting grace, as he called three thousand Jews in one day, by Peter's ministry, Acts the second; so here by St. Paul's, at his first solemn undertaking to preach to the Gentiles, Acts 18, were pleased to work on as many in that congregation as did belong to the election of grace? Shall any many dare to prescribe, and plead custom to the contrary? His second argument runs this way. All that truly believe are not predestinated to life. Therefore that for which we contend is not to be thought a proper sense. Answer. This reason is founded on a grand mistake, *viz.* That faith is common to all, whether elect, or non-elect, although Paul describes it, "the faith of God's elect," as before; and Christ tells the Jews, "Ye believe not, because ye are not of my sheep," (John 10:26). He argues in the third place, from St. Luke's unacquaintedness with the secrets of God. It was not in his power to tell who of that company were elected, who not; therefore by his τεταγμὲνοι, he must not be conceived to have understood such as were in that sense ordained to eternal life. I answer, although the penman did not, the inditer, *viz.* the Holy Spirit, did exactly know whose names were written in the book of

[222] Οσὄι ἧσαν τεταγμενοι εις ζωην ἀιωνιον. Τοι εσιν ἀφωρισμενοι τῶ Θεῶ. Chrys. *Hom.* 20. in *Act. Apost.* [IX.10, 12].

life, and whose were not. Now, he it was that in the history of the Acts, suggested and dictated to his secretary both matter and words.

§9. The second product of election is happiness hereafter. Accordingly the objects of this decree, are those whom "God has not appointed to wrath, but to obtain salvation by our Lord Jesus Christ," (1 Thes. 5:9). Salvation is that which they are said to be chosen to (2 Thes. 2:13); and that in which their names are written, called, "The book of life," (Phil. 4:3). For as in military affairs, commanders, have their muster-rolls, in which are contained, the names of all the soldiers whom they have listed, where the phrase of *conscribere milites*; and in commonwealths there are registers kept in which are recorded the names of such as are chosen to offices of trust and other preferments, where the title of *Patres conscripti* ascribed to the senators of Rome. So the scripture condescending to our capacities, and speaking of God after the manner of men, attributes to him a book of life, in which it supposes a legible writing and registering the names of all those persons whom he has irreversibly predestinated to life everlasting. I say irreversibly, for if that of Stoics be true, *In sapientum decretis nulla est litura*, in the decrees of wise men there will be no blotting and blurring; how much more may it be asserted concerning those eternal decrees of the only wise God? If it became Pilate to say, "What I have written I have written," (John 19:22), it would certainly misbecome the great God to blot so much as one name out of the Lamb's book of life written by himself before the world was. We may take it for granted that this book will not admit of any *deleatur*, or of any expurgatory index, whatever some pretend to the contrary, whose arguments have been elsewhere sufficiently answered.[223] I shall only here propound and endeavor to satisfy another objection, in which no mention is there made. Paul knew himself to be "a chosen vessel" (Acts 9:15), for

---

[223] See my *Tactica Sacra.* lib. 3. c. page 2. & 9, 10, 11. et sequent.

Ananias had told him so from Christ's own month: yet speaks of himself as of one in some danger, at least in some possibility of becoming a reprobate, in these words, "I keep under my body, and bring it into subjection: lest that by any means, when I have preached to others, I myself should be a castaway," (1 Cor. 9:27) or, as other translations have it, a reprobate. *Ergo*, The decree of election is not irreversible.

Response. To prepare the way for a full answer; let it be considered, 1. That the places cited in the objection are not fitly opposed; because the former is not necessarily to be understood of election to salvation, but may probably be limited to Paul's being chosen an Apostle; neither is the latter infallibly meant of that reprobation, which is contradistinctive to the said election, but of somewhat else. Yes although it is true, and may strongly be inferred from other texts, that Paul knew his own election to life eternal, the reprobation spoken of in the end of the verse is not be taken in the most rigid sense, but in a milder. 2. That our Apostle, (according to his custom in various epistles) was in the end of this chapter fallen on the use of terms agonistical, borrowed from the Olympic and other Grecian games in that age; as appears in the foregoing verses. "Know ye not that they who run in a race, *etc*. Every man that striveth for the mastery, *etc*. I so run, not as uncertainly. So fight I, not as one that beateth the air," (1 Cor. 9:24-26). And that in the last verse he has no less than four allusions to these exercises. One in ὑπωπιάζω to cuffing, in which the combatants were accustomed with their blows to make one another livid under their eyes; so did he by acts of mortification beat himself as it were black and blue. A second in δολαγωγῶ to the exercise of wrestling, in which, the antagonists mutually strove to cast each other to the ground, and to keep them under. So he, the better to subdue his body of sin, was careful to keep down his body of flesh, which if pampered, is apt to rebel. A third in κηρίξας. We read in the second epistle to Timothy, chapter second verse fifth, of their striving lawfully, that is, according to the rules and laws, prescribed for that game respectively, in which they were to strive for the mastery. The officer by whom these laws were propounded to the combatants was called κήρυξ, Paul in allusion there says, of himself κήρυξας, because in the discharge of his apostolical office he had acquainted them with the rules and laws of Christianity. A fourth in, ἀδοκιμος, unapproved, a term of disgrace put on those whom such as were to judge and pass sentence on the combatants disallowed. Where those whom the judges rewarded were called ἐυδομοι, approved ones. 3. That this unapprovedness may either relate to God himself, or to, good men. If to God the supreme judge, then whosoever carries himself amiss in any particular course of living, offends the Lord, falls, under his fatherly displeasure, and is as to this would certainly have put an end to altercations, and silenced disputes in these points; but that corrupt reason is extremely talkative, and the wisdom of flesh direct enmity against God (Rom. 8:7), and therefore such as will never yield until its corruption be removed; for enmity cannot be reconciled, the enemies may. Where that excellent speech of Melancthon, worthy to be had in. every lasting remembrance, *Dulcescet nostra de predestinatione sententia, ubi impiæ rationis judicium Spiritus Dei stultificaverit. Then and there only will our doctrine of predestination have a sweet relish, when and where the Spirit of God shall have befooled the conceits of wicked reason.* That which Paul celebrates as the true cause of our election *is*,

1. The good pleasure of God's will,[224] according to which he disposes both of persons and things arbitrarily, as himself likes best. And in this our reason would better acquiesce were it thoroughly defecated by grace; that of Christ, which never had any corruption in it, fully did; as appears by that famous address of his to God the Father, "I thank thee, O Father, Lord of heaven and earth, because thou hast hid these things from the wise and prudent, and hast

---

[224] Ευδοκια θελήματος.

revealed them, to babes. Even so, Father, for so it seemed good in thy sight."[225]

2. The counsel of his will.[226] Although God may be said to act arbitrarily, yet he never does anything unadvisedly, but according to the counsel of his will, which is always rational, though our shallow reason in this state of degeneracy and mortality be not able to fathom the depth of its contrivements, and on this ready to cavil at, and call in question the equity of them. Such as do so, (if any such shall cast an eye on these papers) must give me leave to say to them, as one of our ancient writers did to their forefathers, "The apostle (*he says*) having discoursed of these mysteries acknowledgeth their depth, and adoreth the wisdom of God in them. *Dignare et tu ista nescire. Concede Deo potentiam sui. Nequaquam te indiget defensore*. Be thou also willing to be ignorant of such things. Leave God himself in the modelling of his decrees and dispensations. He will be sure to do it so, as not to stand in need of any apology or defence of thine."[227] To which let me add a saying of Luther, and with it conclude this exercitation. "Reason (*he says*) you are a fool, and does not understand the matters of God. Therefore be not obstreperous, but hold your prating, make not yourself a judge of these things, but attend to the word of God and believe."[228]

EXERCITATION II.

Preterition described. The term defended. Eph. 1:4 compared with Revelation 17:8, Eph. 1:9 and Rom. 9:13 expounded. God not bound to any creature except by promise. The parable in Matt. 20 urged. The three consequents of negative reprobation. Dr. Davenant's animadversions against Mr. Hoard's book recommended. The goodness of God manifested

---

[225] Matt. 11:25-26. Ουτως εγὲνετε ευδοκια ἐμωραθὲν συ.

[226] Βῳλη τῶ θελὴ̣ματος.

[227] Hieron. in *epistola ad Ctesiphontem.*

[228] Tu, Ratio stulta es, non sapis qua sunt Dei. Itaque ne obstrepas mihi, sed tace non judicat, sed audi verbum Dei et crede.

in Election, as in a most free, peculiar, ancient, leading, and standing favor.

§1. Having so fully discoursed of election, (by which the decree of preterition is to be measured) there will be less need of enlarging much on that. Take only this description of it; after a brief explication in which, I intend, if God will, to proceed to other concernments. Preterition or negative reprobation is an eternal decree of God purposing within himself to deny to the non-elect that peculiar love of his, by which election is accompanied, as also that special grace which infallibly brings to glory: of which negations, permission of sin, obduration in sin, and damnation for sin, are direct consequents. This description carries in the face of it a clear reason, why the thing described goes under the name of negative reprobation, because it stands mainly in the denial of those free favors which it pleases God to bestow on his elect. As for the term of pretention, we neither are, nor ought to be ashamed of it, (however some bold writers have jeered it,) because it is very significant, and has been made use of by their betters. Prosper by name, and that both in verse and prose. For in one of his poems he records this as a Pelagian tenet. *Quod gratia Christi Nullum omnino hominem de cunctis qui generantur, Prætereat.* That of all mankind the grace of Christ passes by none. And in his treatise *de Vocatione Gentium* he begins the thirteenth chapter of his first book with this saying, *Quod, si aliquos Salvantis gratia præterierit, etc.* If saving grace has passed by any, it is to be referred to the unsearchable judgments of God, and those ways of his which are past finding out by us in this life. This premised, let us take a transient view of the chief particulars in the description.

§2. It is first an eternal decree, coeternal with that of election; for the very choosing of some to salvation implies a passing by of such as were not chosen. Let the reader compare that passage in Ephesians 1:4.[229] "He has chosen us before the foundation of the world," with that parenthesis Revelation 17:8, "whose names were not written in the book of life from the foundation of the world."

Secondly, A decree which God purposed in himself. We read in one place of "the purpose of God according to election," and in another of "God's good pleasure, which he has purposed in himself."[230] The like may be said of preterition. His good pleasure is the sole fountain of both. The root of both is within himself, and not in anything without him; as has been well observed by Calvin.

Thirdly, the eternal purpose of God was to deny the non-elect that peculiar love, by which his election is accompanied, in which respect he is said to hate them. "Jacob have I loved, but Esau have I hated," (Rom. 9:13). A term by which some divides are willing to understand no more, than his not being willing to bestow everlasting happiness on them; because hatred in scripture is often put to signify a less degree of love. We may not believe that Leah was odious to her husband; yet the text says, "God saw that Leah was hated," which is certainly to be expounded out of the verse foregoing, where it is said of "Jacob that he loved Rachel more than Leah," (Gen. 29:30-31). He loved Leah perhaps less than he ought, surely less than he did her sister, and in that respect is said to have hated her. That to the Romans concerning Esau, some interpret in proportion to what is there said concerning Leah, and among the rest Aquinas. "God (*he says*) loveth all men in as much as he willeth some good to all; but in as much as he does not will to all men the chief good, *viz.* eternal life, he is said to hate and to reprobate them."[231]

---

[229] Agnoscendum est secreti hujus profunditatem nobis in hac vita patere non posse.

[230] Rom. 9:11; Eph. 1:9. Deus in negotio predest instichis non egreditur extra seipsum.

[231] In quantum quibusdam non vult hoc bonum, quod est vita æterna, dicitur eos habere odio vel reprobare. Tho. *part 1. qu. 23. art.* 3 ad 4[um.]

§3. *Fourthly*, his purpose was to deny to the non-elect that special grace, which brings infallibly to glory, those on whom God bestows it. No creature can challenge effectual grace at the hands of God, as a due debt either to his nature, or to his labor. There are many that speak and write of God saucily, as if he were bound to give this and that and the other grace, even where they can produce no promise by which he has made himself a debtor. I cannot but commend the zeal of Peter Lombard against such men. To me (*he says*)[232] this word he ought, or he is bound seems to have much poison in it; and cannot be properly applied to God, who is no debtor' to us, save only in those cases in which he has passed some promise. Sure I am, our Savior tells his disciples plainly, "It is given to you to know the mysteries of the kingdom of heaven, but to them it is not given," Matthew 13:11. And the householder in the parable stops the mouths of those murmurers that repined, as expecting more from him than it was his pleasure to give, with the sole consideration of its being his will to have it so. "Friend, I do thee no wrong. Take what is thine, I will give to this last even as to thee. Is it not lawful for me to do what I will with mine own?" (Matt. 20:10, 13-15).

Fifthly, The consequents of the forementioned denials, are, 1. Permission of sin, particularly of unbelief. John 10:20. "Ye believe not, because ye are not of my sheep." 2. Obduration in sin. Romans 9:18. "He has mercy on whom he will have mercy, and whom he will, he hardeneth." 3. Condemnation for sin. Rev. 20:15. "Whosoever was not found written in the book of life, was cast into the lake of fire." This last is that which by divines is usually described positive reprobation, and is clearly distinguishable from the negative, in that the one is an act of punitive justice respecting sin committed and continued in: but the other an absolute decree of God's most free and sovereign will, without respect to any

---

[232] Ut mihi videtur hoc verbum Debet venenum habet—nec Deo proprie competit, qui non est debitor nobis, nisi forte ex promise. Lib. 1. sententiarum *Dist*. 43.

disposition in the creature. I call them consequents, not effects; because, though negative reprobation is antecedent to them all, it is not the proper cause of them. This difference between the decrees Aquinas long since took notice of.[233] "Election (*he says*) is a proper cause both of that glory which the elect look for hereafter, and of that grace, which here they enjoy. Where reprobation is not the cause of the present sins of the non-elect, though it is of God's forsaking them; but their sin proceeds from the parties themselves so passed by and forsaken." But I am under a promise of brevity, and therefore shall add no more, but only advise the English reader, who is desirous of further information in these deep points, to procure and peruse that excellent piece of the profound Dr. Davenant printed at Cambridge, anno 1641. under this title, *Animadversions* written by the right Reverend John Bishop of Salisbury, on a treatise entitled, *God's love to mankind*: where he will not only meet with the doctrine of Predestination modestly handled, but also with ample satisfaction to most of those wicked cavils which flesh and blood have been accustomed to suggest against it.

§4. Having so finished that preamble, which the daring heterodoxy of some modern writers put me on a necessity of, I proceed to the making good of two assertions, tending to clear the former part of our present aphorism, *viz.* That the goodness of God is abundantly manifested in his decree of our election; and his greatness no less in that of preterition. In order to a demonstration of the former, I desire to have it considered, how free, how peculiar, how ancient, how leading, how lasting a favor election is.

First, A free favor. (Rom. 11:5). It is therefore called election of grace; and spoken of as tending "to the praise of the glory of free grace," (Eph. 1:6). The Lamb's book of life (so named, because the Lamb Jesus stands there enrolled in the head of it, as the head of all the elect, and the Captain of that

[233] Thom. *part 1. quæst.* 23. Artic. 3 ad 2um.

salvation to which they are chosen) is a book of love. "Behold my servant whom I have chosen, my beloved, in whom my soul is well pleased," (Matt. 12:18). It was so said of Christ, and may be applied to all the elect in their measure. Here Paul describes his Thessalonians, "Brethren beloved of the Lord, because God had chosen them to salvation (2 Thes. 2:13) and God expresses the election of Jacob, by Jacob have I loved, to show that free love on God's part is the fountain of this favor. We love persons or things, because they are lovely. God loves them first, after makes them lovely, then loves them more for being so. The cause of our love is in the objects of God's, in himself: we are predestinated "after the counsel of his own will," not after the good inclinations of ours. (Eph. 1:1).

Secondly, a peculiar favor. Rarity much enhances a benefit.[234] Immunities and privileges are therefore much valued and stood on, because they are not common to many, and are therefore more rejoiced in, because but few partake of them. There were but eight persons saved from the deluge of waters in Noah's time, who is accordingly said to have found grace in the eyes of the Lord, (Gen. 6:8) in that he and his were preserved when all the world beside perished. And in regard the deluge of fire that came upon Sodom and Gommorrah swept away all the other inhabitants but Lot only, and his nearest relations were exempted from it. God is said to have magnified his mercy toward them, as Lot acknowledged, saying, "Behold thy servant has found grace in thy sight, and thou hast magnified thy mercy which thou hast showed to me," (Gen. 19:19). We should all have perished in the deluge of fiery indignation, had not God elected some few whom "he has not appointed to wrath but to obtain salvation by our Lord Jesus Christ," (1 Thes. 5:9). They are but few, as Scripture tells us again and again, "Many are called, but few chosen," (Matt. 20:16, 22:14). The goodness of God is therefore to be more acknowledged in so peculiar a favor.

§5. *Thirdly*, an ancient favour. Old things, if evil, are so

---

[234] Τὸ απανιον τιμιον. Plato. Privilegium gaudet paucitate.

much the worse for that; old leaven is to be purged out, (1 Cor. 5:7), and the old man to be put off. (Eph. 4:22). But every good thing is commended by its antiquity. One said well that old wood is best to burn, old friends best to trust, and old books best to read.[235] What price do scholars put on an ancient manuscript? Doubtless the oldest of all manuscripts, is the book of life. And the writing of our names in it are the first-born of all God's favors. If God so value the first-fruits of our services, as he does; how careful should we be to magnify the first-fruits of his goodness? If old charters be of so great esteem as they are in the world, how great an estimate should we set on the most ancient *Magna Charta* of our election, having this seal, the Lord knows who are his. (2 Tim. 2:19).

Fourthly, a leading favor. Those are the most valuable blessings that have influence on, various others, which they draw infallibly after them. Such is election. Paul makes it the first link of his golden chain, and shows how introductive it is of all the rest, "whom God did predestinate, them he also called; and whom he called, them he also justified; and whom he justified, them he also glorified," (Rom. 8:30). Here is a chain which God lets down from heaven that by it he may draw up his elect there.[236] The first link of it is predestination, taken in a restrained sense for the election of grace. The next, effectual vocation; into this the former has a causal influence according to what the Lord once said by his prophet Jeremiah, chap. 31:3. "I have loved thee with an everlasting love, therefore, with loving kindness, have I drawn thee." Election having once pitched on a man, it will find him out, and call him home, whereever he is. Zaccheus out of cursed Jericho; Abraham out of idolatrous Ur of the Chaldeans; Nicodemus and Paul out of the college of the Pharisees, Christ's sworn

---

[235] Sir Fr. Bacon.

[236] Quatuor annuli sunt unius catenæ, qua e coelo demissa Pater in coelum trahit electos. Primus est, Predestinatio ad vitam in Christo. Secundus, vocation efficax ad Christum; tertius, justification per Christum; quartus, glorification cum christo. Zanch. *Tom. 7. col.* 177.

enemies; Dionysius and Damaris, out of superstitious Athens. In what dunghill whatsoever God's jewels are hid, election will both find them out there, and bring them there.

The third link is justification; the dependance of it on election may be gathered from that passage in the same chapter to the Romans, "who shall lay any thing to the charge of God's elect? It is God that justifies," (Rom. 8:33). As also from the vision in Zechariah, where Joshua the high priest representing the people, appeared clothed with filthy garments (Zech. 3:3-4) in sign of guilt by them contracted, until God had commanded, saying, "Take away the filthy garments from him. Behold, I have caused thine iniquity to pass from thee," (Zech. 3:5). Where there was a fair mitre put on his head and he clothed with change of garments, in reference to their change of condition from guilt to free justification; the spring in which is hinted at in that speech, the Lord said to Satan, "the Lord rebuke thee, O Satan, even the Lord that has chosen Jerusalem rebuke thee," (Zech. 3:2) The fourth and last is glorification, that takes in both beginnings of glory in sanctification (of which Paul in his second to the Corinthians third Chapter and last verse), "we all with open face beholding as in a glass the glory of the Lord, are changed into the same image from glory to glory, even as by the spirit of the Lord:" and of which he tells us elsewhere, that all the graces of which it consists proceed from this prime grace of election (saying, "God has blessed us with all spiritual blessings in Christ, according as he has chosen us in him"—Eph. 1:3-4.) and the consummation of glory in heaven; the foundation in which is by our Savior clearly laid in the Father's giving us to him by election at first, "This, he says, is the Father's will which has sent me, that of all which has given me I should lose nothing, but should raise it up again at the last day," (John 6:39). So true is that of a modern writer, "election depends on God alone, all other blessings on election."[237]

---

[237] Cætera pendent ab electione, *Electio a Deo. Heins. Hom.* In John 17:9. page

Fifthly, A standing favour. The favours of men may be suddenly changed to frowns; as those of King Ahasuerus towards Haman were: who but he over night in the King's esteem? next day he will not endure the sight of him. But God's are immutable. All the blessings of the covenant of grace are sure mercies, according to that by the prophet Isaiah, "I will make an everlasting covenant with you, even the sure mercies of David;" (Isa. 55:3). Election in a special manner. Our apostle accordingly intimates in one place, that "the purpose of God according to election must stand:" (Rom. 9:11) and affirms in another, that "this foundation of God stands sure, having this seal, the Lord knows who are his," (2 Tim. 2:19). In which few words, we have no fewer than three grounds of its stability; a foundation, a seal, and a science. Election is the Foundation of God; a firm foundation that stands sure. With us things founded on a rock, have great stability, "the rock of ages," (Isa. 26:4) as he is called, even God himself, his good pleasure and counsel is that on which our election is founded. With us, writings once sealed receive a confirmation thereby, and become unrepealable. God has set his seal to this decree. With us, knowledge or science is of things certain and unalterable, not as opinion, which being of things only probable may be changed. The seal here is, The Lord knows who are his. No wonder then if the Lord be for ever found to make good that which he said by his apostle, "God has not cast away his people whom he foreknew." If having named election in the foregoing verse, he presently subjoins, the gifts (Rom. 11:2) and calling of God are without repentance. (Rom. 11:29).

EXERCITATION III.

An Introduction to Romans 9. Most part of that chapter expounded, together with various; passages in chapter 10, and 11, for proof of these two conclusions. 1. That Paul in Rom. 9 does on occasion propound and

46.

prosecute the doctrine of predestination. 2. That he derives the decree of preterition from the sovereign greatness of God. An inference showing how useful the said doctrine is to sober minds.

§1. For a full proof of our second assertion, That the greatness of God is abundantly manifested by his decree of preterition, we must of necessity have recourse to the ninth chapter of Paul's epistle to the Romans, as to the proper seat of that argument; although diverse from abroad and, some at home by foreign interpretations, forced glosses and strained paraphrases have endeavored to carry the sense quite another way; against the poison of whose endeavors our people may perhaps stand in need of an antidote.

It shall be my care, by divine assistance, (which is always needful, especially in the debating of such mysteries) to present them with one, and in as calm a way as may be, without provoking, however without reproaching such as are contrary minded, to demonstrate these two conclusions, *viz.* That Paul in the ninth of the Romans does on occasion propound, and prosecute the doctrine of predestination. And that he plainly derives the decree of pretefition from the sovereign greatness of God. But before we enter on so great a depth (which I do with fear and trembling) let it be observed that our apostle from the end of the eight, to the beginning of his twelfth chapter, continues a profound complicate discourse wholly about the main concerns of his countrymen the Jews; and that the best help we have for enlightening certain clauses in the ninth; ought to be brought from passages in the tenth and eleventh chapters. The neglect in which, I verily think, has occasioned the miscarriages of so many in their interpretations of that scripture. I hope to improve the observation to good purpose.

§2. Concerning the former of our conclusions, there will be no need of going far to seek the occasion of Paul's falling on this doctrine. He had carefully and continually preached faith in Christ, as the only way of salvation, in opposition to all others. This, however embraced by diverse

Gentiles, could by no means find entertainment with the Jews. Be pleased to compare chapter 9:31-33. "Israel which followed after the law of righteousness, has not obtained to the law of righteousness. Wherefore? because they sought it not by faith, but as it were by the works of the law: for they stumbled at that stumbling stone. As it is written, Behold I lay in Sion a stumbling-stone, and rock of offence and whosoever believes on him, shall not be ashamed," with chapter ten, verses 2-4, "I bear them record that they have a zeal of God, but not according to knowledge. For they being ignorant of God's righteousness, and going about to establish their own righteousness, have not submitted themselves to the righteousness of God. For Christ is the end of the law for righteousness to every one that believeth." This their stumbling at Christ, as they generally did, caused a great stumble in the thoughts of considering men, who could not but stand amazed to see that where God had set up but one only way to be laid hold on, for the attainment of blessedness, his own only people in the eye of the world, should almost universally decline that, and venture their souls on another. Yet this they did, even they who are here so magnificently described, chapter 9, verses 4-5. "Who were Israelites; to whom pertained the adoption, and the glory, and the covenants, and the giving of the law, and the service of God, and the promises: Whose were the the fathers, and of whom as concerning the flesh Christ came, who is over all, God blessed for evermore, Amen." On this some were apt to cry out, "All is undone, the word of God itself has taken no effect. The promise of Abraham is fallen to the ground. All sermons and other ordinances have been but as so much rain on rocks that glides off and leaves no impression." Our apostle to recover them out of these dumps, leads them by degrees into the knowledge of divine predestination, as the root of all this: giving them first to understand, that all who bore the name of Israelites, and enjoyed the ordinances, were not indeed such children of God, as belonged to the election of grace, and therefore did not close with Christ in the use of them; as some few did, on whom the word of grace was effectual, and in whom (as few as they were) God's promise to Abraham was preserved. As for those to whom his gospel was hid, they were as he elsewhere tells the Corinthians, (2 Cor. 4:3) a sort of lost men and women. For this see chapter 9:6-8, "Not as though the word of God has taken none effect. For they are not all Israel, which are of Israel. Neither because they are the seed of Abraham are they all children. But in Isaac shall thy seed be called." That is, "They which are the children of the flesh, these are not the children of God; but the children of the promise are counted for the seed." Where the elect people of God (who only are accounted the spiritual seed, and who only in the conclusion will concur to constitute Christ mystical) are described children of the promise, perhaps in reference to that grace and promise of eternal life, given to them in Christ Jesus before the world began, to which I have spoken before in this *Aphorism, Exercitation first, Paragraph third.* However in allusion to the birth of Isaac, who was produced above the power of nature, by virtue of a promise declaring God's will and pleasure to have it so; for the elect in the respective hours of their conversion, are all of them "born again not of blood, nor of the will of the flesh, nor of the will of man, but of God. (John 1:13). Who of his own will begetteth them with the word of truth, that they should be a kind of first fruits of his creatures," (James 1:18)

§3. Having in this way given a more obscure intimation of some few elect ones complying with the gospel, although most part of the Jews were recusants as to that interest; he goes on to profess it more openly in the beginning of the eleventh chapter, "God has not cast away his people which he foreknew," verse second, the infallible meaning in which may be gathered from that in Peter, "Elect according to the foreknowledge of God the Father," (1 Pet. 1:2). And more plainly yet in verse seventh and eighth of the same chapter, "The election has obtained, and the rest were blinded; according as it is written, God has given them the spirit of slumber, eyes that they should not see, and ears that they should not hear to this day." But to return to our ninth chapter. Who can advisedly read that passage in his discourse about Jacob and Esau, "That the purpose of God according to election might stand," and consult the circumstances of it (*viz.* the children not yet being born, nor having done good or evil; as also a choice no way founded on him that willeth, or on him that runeth, but on God alone who showeth mercy,) and not reflect on that election by me describeed in the first *Exercitation* under this *Aphorism*, §2? Add on this those apostolical distributions of men into those on whom the Lord will have mercy, and those whom he will harden in verse eighteenth, that is in other terms, elect and reprobate. Also, into vessels of mercy, and vessels of wrath, verses 22-23. What if God willing to show his wrath, and to make his power known, endured with much long-suffering the vessels of wrath fitted to destruction, and that he might make known the riches of his glory on the vessels of mercy, which he had afore prepared to glory? Where I desire to have it punctually observed that the vessels of wrath are only said to be fitted to destruction, without naming by whom, God, Satan, or themselves; where on the other side God himself is expressly said to have prepared his chosen vessels of mercy to glory. Which was purposely done, (as I humbly conceive) to intimate a remarkable difference between election and preterition; in that election is a proper cause not only of salvation itself, but of all the graces which have any causal tendency thereunto; and therefore God is said to prepare his elect to glory.[238] Where negative reprobation is no proper cause, either of damnation itself, or of the sin that brings it, but an antecedent only; wherefore the non-elect are indeed said to be fitted to that destruction which their sins in the

[238] Electio non est causa tantum salutis sed et omnium eorum quae causæ rationem habent ad salutem. Reprobatio vero neque damnationis, neque peccati quod meretur danmationem est proprie causa sed antecedens tantum. Ames. *medul*, l. 1. c. 25. *thes*. 40.

conclusion bring on them, but not by God. I call it a remarkable difference, because where it is once rightly apprehended and truly believed, it suffices to stop the mouth of one of those greatest calumnies and odiums which are usually cast on our doctrine of predestination, *viz.* that God made various of his creatures on purpose to damn them: a thing which the rhetoric of our adversaries is accustomed to blow up to the highest pitch of aggravation. But is as soon blown away by such as can tell them in the words of the excellent Dr. Davenant, "It is true that the elect are severally created to the end and intent that they may be glorified together with their head Christ Jesus; but for the non-elect we cannot truly say that they are created to the end they may be tormented with the devil and his angels. For we may then say, God makes such a thing for such an end, when he gives the thing a nature and qualities fitted for such an end," (*e.g.* that he made the sun to enlighten the world, because he filled him with light). "Now no man is created by God with a nature and quality fitting him to damnation. Yes, neither in the state of his innocency, nor in the state of the fall and his corruption doth he receive any thing from God which is a proper and fit means of bringing him to his damnation. And therefore damnation is not the end of any man's creation."[239]

§4. We have seen our apostle propounding the doctrine of predestination in this his discourse; see how he prosecutes the same more ways than one.

1. By producing certain instances. The persons he instanceth in, if not as solemn examples, yet, as types and figures are at least, of election Isaac and Jacob; of reprobation, Ishmael and Esau. It is the grand privilege of God's elect to have his covenant established with them in special manner. The Messias, saith the angel in Daniel, "was cut off, but not for himself; and he shall confirm the covenant with many," (Dan. 9:26-27). The word is *larabbim* with those excellent ones, by whom Piscator understands the elect, those "Many whom

[239] B. Daven. *Animadversions* on God's love to mankind; page 89.

God's righteous servant is said to justify," Isaiah 53:11, where we meet with the same word. If so, who more fit to figure out them than our father Isaac concerning whom the Lord said to Abraham, "I will establish my covenant with him for an everlasting covenant, and with his seed after him," (Gen. 17:19). Again, the description of all those "who are written in heaven," (Heb. 12:23) that is, of the elect, is the general assembly, and church of the first-born. If so, who more fit to typify them than Jacob, a man of all others most famous for procuring a *primogeniture* in an extraordinary way? As for reprobation, the objects in which are cast-a-ways, well might Ishmael stand for a figure of them, because of him Sarah said to her husband, "Cast out this bond-woman and her son, for the son of the bond-woman shall not be heir with my son, even with Isaac," (Gen. 21: 10, 12). And her word was ratified by God himself, saying to Abraham, "In all that Sarah has said to thee, hearken to her voice, for in Isaac shall thy seed be called." As also Esau, who here fails under two sad characters; one of God's hatred, than which nothing more dreadful, "Jacob have I loved, but Esau have I hated," verse 13, the other of servitude, verse 12. "The elder shall serve the younger." Concerning which Mr. Ainsworth has these words, "Servitude came in with a curse and figureth reprobation, Gen ix. 25. John 8:54ff. Gal. 4:30-31. Therefore here the prophet teaches that God loved Jacob, and hated Esau, and the apostle gathers the doctrine of election and reprobation," Romans 9:10-13. So he gives that interpretation.[240]

§5. The main exception, which our adversaries here have been accustomed to take at this and the like expositions, arises this way. Jacob and Esau are considerable in a double capacity, the one *personal*, as they were this and that individual member of mankind; the other *patriarchal*, as they were heads of several nations, Jacob of the Israelites, Esau of the Edomites or Idumeans. They suppose we cannot safely apply the oracle delivered to Rebecca, to their persons, seeing Malachi long

[240] Ainsworth on Genesis 25:23.

since expounded it of their posterity in these words, "Was not Esau Jacob's brother?" (Mal. 1:2-3) the Lord says, "yet I loved Jacob, and I hated Esau, and laid his mountains and his heritage waste for the dragons of the wilderness," *etc.*

My conceptions concerning this matter (which as I would not impose on any, far be such presumption from me, so I would, have no reader condemn, until he have considered them) are as follows. According to their double capacity, the answer of God to Rebecca about them seems to have had a double aspect: one to their posterity regarding temporal things especially, of which Malachi speaks, another to their persons eyeing chiefly their spiritual concernments; and of that Paul treats in Romans 9 as the context imports. Nor can this be wondered at by such as consider how usual it has been with God, as to discover himself by degrees (witness that in Deuteronomy, "The Lord came from Sinai, and rose up from Seir to them, he shined forth from mount Paran," Deut. 33:2) so to reserve more spiritual discoveries for gospel times.

§3. Where it is further objected that "the elder's serving the younger" was never verified in the person of Easu, who did never servilely submit to Jacob; I answer. 1. He that should go about to prove that negative, would find a hard task; but suppose it proved, yet in point of right Esau as having sold his birth-right became servant to him that bought it. For in this respect it is said to Cain the elder brother, concerning Abel, "Unto thee shall be his desire, and thou shalt rule over him," (Gen. 4:7). 2. In point of fact, time was when Esau became a very humble suppliant to Jacob for a mess of pottage. "Feed me, I pray thee, with that same red pottage, for I am faint," (Gen. 25:30). Now, "The borrower," Solomon says, "is a servant to the lender," (Prov. 22:7). How much more he that craves to him that gives? Besides if the word *serve* is taken in a large sense, Esau *served* Jacob well-nigh all his life long, and brough him much nearer to God by vexing him. *Non obsequendo, sed persequendo*, as one says, not by obeying, but by opposing. Which put me in mind of that story in Bromiardus concerning an apprentice that had served a hard master, by whom he had been often sore beaten. These blows the Lord had made a means of the man's conversion; on which lying on his death bed, and his master striding by, catched fast hold on his hands and kissed them, saying, "*Hic manus perduxerunt me ad paradisum*," these hands have helped to bring me to heaven. 3. The patriarchal capacity does not exclude, but comprehend the personal, for Jacob and his Israelites, Esau and his Edomites make a nation. In which respect, when "David put garrisons in Edom; (throughout all Edom put he garrisons, and all they of Edom became David's servants)," (2 Sam. 8:14) Esau himself in his offspring might not unfitly be said to have served Jacob in his. Lastly, If no more can be had than this bare acknowledgment that our exposition must be confined to their posterity, even that will go near to serve our turn, and to suit with the apostle's scope, if it is considered, how exceedingly fit the Israelites were to typify election, of whom God said, "You are a holy people to the Lord thy God, and the Lord has chosen thee to be a peculiar people to himself, above all the nations that are on the earth," (Deut. 14:2). The Edomites to figure out reprobates, seeing of them it is said by the prophet, "They shall call them the border of wickedness, and the people against whom the Lord has indignation for ever," (Mal. 1:4).

§7. II. By resolving certain *queries*. The first in which is, that in verse 14. "What shall we say then? Is there unrighteousness with God? God forbid." Had the doctrine of predestination which Paul taught, been the same with that of our modern heretical remonstrants, *viz.* God's electing on foresight of men's being in Christ by faith, and reprobating on foresight of their final unbelief and impenitency, there would then have been no occasion for the query; for reason how corrupt whatsoever would soon have closed with the equity of such decrees to render *par pari*, like to like. It is God's awarding *paribus imparia* unlike destinies to men of like conditions considered in the same lump, and doing this arbitrarily, according to the good pleasure and counsel of his own will, that sets it a crying out of iniquity in God's proceedings. But what does Paul answer? He abhors the thoughts of such a thing. God forbid, it is as if he had said, far be it from every one that pretends to a rational being, much more then every Christian to entertain the least thought of a possibility of injustice in any decree of God, whose will is the supreme rule of righteousness. The judgments of God (as Augustine has said truly of them) can neither be fully comprehended, nor justly reprehended of any.[241] Let me desire such as are so very apt to be cavilling at them, to swallow and digest by a serious consideration, those admonitions and reproofs which a late Belgick contra-remonstrant has handed to their fellows. "*Calceati Deum aditis,*" *etc.* You draw near (he says) with shoes on your feet to him that dwelleth in an unaccessible light, and presuming on certain axioms of crooked and distorbed reason, pass sentence on the decrees of God. We blame you in this regard especially, for intruding yourselves into things which ye have not seen, and giving answers about the secrets of heaven with so much confidence, as if ye sat at God's counsel-table. You examine his counsels by the rules of human proceedings; and if any thing concur that does not suit with your preconceived opinions about free will, expunge it quite out of the number of God's designs as unworthy of him."

Yes, our apostle not content with a bare expression of abhorrence, goes on to free the decrees of God from all iniquity, each by itself. Election, because it is an act of mere bounty and free grace, in performing in which God cannot possibly be unjust, as being under no law, but at absolute liberty to dispose of his free undeserved favors according to the good pleasure and counsel of his own will, to which

---

[241] Dei judicia nemo plene comprehendit, nemo juste reprehendit. August. *de Civit. Dei.* lib. 2. c. page 23. Isaaci Junii Antapologia in parænes. ad Remonstrantes. page 1, and 2. Freti aximatibus rationis oblique et distort.—Revocatis omnia Dei consilia sub humanam incudem, *etc.*

purpose that is cited out of Exodus. "For he saith to Moses, I will have mercy on whom I will have mercy, and I will have compassion on whom I will have compassion," and that inferred verse 16. "So then it," (that is the purpose of God according to election, of which before verse 11), "is not of him that willeth, nor of him that runneth, but of God that showeth mercy." As for reprobation rightly stated, no iniquity will be found in them, if the grand laws of the universe be duly heeded, which is that all creatures be subservient to their maker's glory according to the proverb. "The Lord has made all things for himself, yes even the wicked for the day of evil," (Prov. 16:4). Seeing the end of reprobating any is mainly this, that God may by it be exalted, as Paul tells us here verse 17 in the instance of Pharaoh. "For the scripture saith to Pharaoh, even for this same purpose have I raised thee up, that I might show my power in thee, and that my name might be declared throughout all the earth."

§8. The next query is that in verse 19. "Thou wilt say then to me, Why doth he yet find fault? for who has resisted his will?" He had said concerning God in the words immediately foregoing, "He has mercy on whom he will have mercy, and whom he will he hardens." Corrupt nature catching at the latter clause, is ready to impute to God himself, (as injustice before, so here) rigor and cruelty, for that notwithstanding his own willing in a sense the hard-heartedness of reprobates, he yet finds fault with them for it, yes, and *damns them* in the conclusion, although his will is irresistible. The substance of this cavil, namely what influence the will and providence of God has to men's induration, and how guilty themselves are of it, shall hereafter be made to appear (if the Lord will) in explication of the following *Aphorism*. Meanwhile, it is carefully to be observed how St. Paul, as provoked by the malapertness of men, who though conscious to themselves of their own hardening themselves, will be laying the blame on God, strikes in with his apostolical authority, and gives them this severe check, "Nay, but O man, who art thou that repliest against God?" *Qui ex adverso responsas*

Deo, as it is well rendered by Beza in reference to the continual and manifold bubblings up of carnal reason against divine dispensations and decrees, that which our English proverb calls *chopping logic* with God. A vice from which our very being men should suffice to wean us. So as the word, "O man," here seems to carry an emphasis in it which Augustine long ago observed in various passages of one and the same set of his sermons. "Ask me not an account (*he says*) of divine dispensations, why things are carried so and so, towards this and that person. I am a man of whom thou askest; thou that enquirest art a man. Let us both attend to the man that said, "O man! Who art thou that repliest against God?" Let man hear, lest man perish, for whose sake God himself became man. And again: mind it well who he is against whom thou repliest, and who thou thyself art that repliest against him. He is God, you are but a man." And yet again most fully.[242] "Thou askest a reason of this and that, I will tremble at the depth; thou arguest, let me wonder. Do thou dispute, I resolve to believe. I see the depth, but the bottom I cannot reach."

§9. His third way of prosecution is, by alleging certain testimonies out of Moses and the prophets. I shall only fix on one, namely that in Romans 9:27. Isaiah also cries concerning Israel, "Though the number of the children of Israel be as the sand of the sea, a remnant shall be saved." He who wishes may see this and the following verses expounded to our purpose by the learned *Ludovic de Dieu* of God's decrees, yes, (which is more Paul himself) interpreting the remnant of God's elect in Rom. 11:2-5, where the conclusion is, "Even so then at this present time also, there is a remnant according to the election of grace."

---

[242] Nolo a me quæras, etc. Audiat homo, ne pereat homo propter quem Deus factus est homo. Augustine, de verb. Apost, Serm. 7. and 11. Quis sit ille attende, quis sis tu attende. Ille Deus est, tu homo Serm. 22. *de verb. Apost.* Quæris tu rationem, ego expavescam altitudinem. Tu ratiocinare, ego miror. Tu disputa, ego credam. Altitudinem video, ad profundum non pervenio. ib. *Serm.* 22. prope finem.

And now, reader, I pray that you judge between us; and tell me after all this, that has been produced, whether a vehement agitator in these points, had any just cause to say as one did, "That to him who shall narrowly and attentively weigh and consider the tenor, and process of the apostle's discourse, Romans 9 from verse 6 to the end, it will be found as clear as the light at noon day, that there is *nec vola nec vestigium*, neither print nor footstep, neither little nor much of any such thing, as either election or reprobation in it."[243] Meaning (as he there expresses himself) a peremptory election and reprobation from eternity of a determinate number under a mere personal consideration.

§10. As for the proof of our second assertion, those words in verses 20-22. "Shall the thing formed, say to him that formed it, Why hast thou made me thus? Has not the potter power over the clay, of the same lump to make one vessel to honor, and another to dishonor? What if God willing to show his wrath, and to make his power known, endured with much long suffering the vessels of wrath fitted to destruction?" clearly hold forth to my apprehension the sovereign greatness and power of God, as the fountain of negative reprobation; and contain a direct allusion to that in Isaiah 45:9. "Woe to him that striveth with his Maker. Let the potsherd strive with the potsherds of the earth. Shall the clay say to him that fashioneth it, What makest thou? or thy work, He has no hands? Now if the prophet and apostle, or rather the Holy Spirit by them, do rightly infer the silence and submission of the clay from its relation to the potter; much more may the quiet submission of non-elect persons to the disposing will of God, be here concluded (as Lessius demonstrates) seeing mankind has much more dependence on the sovereign Lord of all, than a potter can challenge over any vessel whatever,"[244] and this notwithstanding they are not yet fully convinced of the reason of all God's proceedings with them. Such as still

---

[243] J.G. *Exposit. of Rom. 9* in his epistle to the reader. §3.

[244] See Lessius *de perfection.* ac ibus divinis l. 10. c. 3. §19.

expect that, and therefore fly in the face of God, for lack of satisfaction in this and that particular, must give me leave to send them to the morals of Gregory for the learning of better manners. "Man" (*he says*) "considering himself, holds his peace, and he that acknowledgeth himself but dust, is afraid to discuss the judgments of God. For him to seek a reason of God's secret decrees, is nothing else than to rise up proudly against the counsel of his will. Wherefore when the cause of any action of his is not discerned, it calls for our silence and humility; for the sense of flesh sufficeth not to pierce into the secrets of Majesty. So that he who sees not a reason of this or that divine dispensation, by considering his own infirmity, may see a clear reason why he sees it not."[245]

§11. But, say Gregory what he can, yes and Paul himself what he will, the fault is not likely to be mended so long as carnal minds have to do with these points. We are all by nature enemies in our minds, as our apostle tells the Colossians: yes, the carnal mind, or the wisdom of the flesh (as he speaks to the Romans) is enmity against God; for it is not subject to the law of God, neither indeed can be, (Rom. 8:7) where it is that one or other of the great masters of reason (as they would be accounted) although they be not unwilling to yield an independent sovereignty and arbitrary working to some men, as in the eastern parts of the world most do to their absolute monarchs as at this day, and the Roman Senate did of old to Augustus Caesar, witness Dion Cassius in his history, "the senate," he says, "freed him from all the necessity of law, so as he might do or not do what he list, as having both

[245] Semetipsum homo considerans tacet, et divina judicat discutere metuit, qui esse se pulverem agnoscit.—Rationem de occult Dei consilio quærere, nihil est aliud quam contra ejus consilium superbire. Cum ergo factorum causa non deprehenditur, restat ut sub factis illius cum humilitate taccatur: quia nequaquam sufficit sensus carnis, ut secreta penetret majestatis. Qui in factis Dei rationem non videt, infirmitatem suam considerans, cur non videat, rationem videt. Gregor. *Exposit. moral.* in Job 9. chapter 8.

himself and the law at his disposal;"[246] yet out of their deep enmity and malignity against God, deny him the like prerogative, and will therefore be always found opposing his decrees, and those most, that are most arbitrary. This has been the root of that notorious piece of opposition in laboring that the decrees of God should be wholly silenced, and either not studied, or if studied, not disputed, or if disputed, not preached of. Some such there were in Augustine's time, against whom he bends his discourse in the 14th, 15th and 16th chapters of his book, *De Bono perseverantiæ*. And some there are at this day that rank the points of predestination among fruitless and sapless speculations.

Holy Martin Bucer was of a far different judgment. He in one of his first lectures at Cambridge on the epistle to the Ephesians, after published by Tremellius. *Si hujus electionis, etc.*[247] If the memory and meditation of God's election were taken from us, good Lord, how should we resist the devil! For so often as Satan tempts my faith, which he is ever tempting of, then I always take myself and thoughts to free election, *etc.* A little after he asserts the doctrine of election as a principal ground not of solid comfort only but of solid piety, and of true love to God; in which regards he would by all means have it preached in *cœtu fidelium*, in the open congregation. Verily this famous university is likely to continue famous, so long as it continues orthodox. We may expect to share in the apostle's benediction, and hope that the grace of our Lord Jesus Christ, the love of God, and the fellowship of the Spirit will be with us, so long as we teach to the praise of the glory of free grace, the love of God in electing freely what persons he will; the

---

[246] Πασης αυτον της τως των νομων αναγκης απηλλαξαν, και αυτοτελης οντος και αυτοκρατωρ, και ἑαυτῶ και των νομων παντα τε οτα βωλοιτο ποιοιη, και τανθ' οσα αν μη βωλοιτο, μη ῳρατιη. Dion Cass. *Roman. hist.* lib. 53. page 516. in ant. edit. *Græc. Lat.*

[247] Si hujus electionis memoria & meditation nobis auferretur, Bone Deus! quomodo resisteremus Diabolo. Quoties enim disbolous tentat fidem nostrum, (nunquam autem non tentat) tunc semper ad electionem est nobis recurrendum.

grace of Christ in dying freely and with a special intention for those whom the Father had elected; and the communication of the Spirit in freely converting and finally preserving those whom the Father had so chosen, and for whom the Son so died. Sure I am, our blessed Savior once said to his disciples, "In this rejoice that your names are written in heaven," (Luke 10:20) and that nothing more inflames a Christian's love than a firm belief of his personal election from eternity, after he has been able to evidence the writing of his name in heaven, by the experience he has had of a heavenly calling, and a heavenly conversion. When the Spirit of God (whose proper work it is to assure, as it was the Father's to elect, and the Son's to redeem) has written the law of life in a Christian's heart, and therewith enabled him to know assuredly that his name is written in the book of life; he cannot then but melt with flames of holy affection, according to that most emphatic speech of Bernard, *God deserveth love from such as he has loved long before they could deserve it.*[248] And his love to God will be without end, who knows that God's love to him was without any beginning. I confess indeed that the book of life, like the tree of life in paradise, has a tree of knowledge growing hard by which cannot with safety be tasted of. There are some nice and needless questions started about it that might be spared, and should be forborn. But these high walls and sons of Anak should by no means prevail with us to play the unworthy spies, and bring up a bad report, or give way to any brought up by others on a land that flows with so much milk and honey as the doctrine of predestination doth. Surely for men to silence it, were to stop up those wells which the prophets and apostles, especially Paul, have dug in their writings for the refreshing of thirsty souls; yes to endeavor the cancelling of that first and great charter of our salvation.

EXERCITATION IV.

---

[248] Amat ille immerito, qui amatus est sine merito. Amat sine fine, qui sine principio se cognoscit amatum. Bern. *epist*. 107.

Creation what? Pythagoras and Trismegist. Hebrews 11:3. opened, Scripture Philosophy. Ex nihilo nihil fit, how true. Creature what? God's goodness in works of creation, particularly in the framing of Adam. The consultation on which, pattern after which, parts of which he was framed. Two histories, one of a Priest, the other of a Monk. The original of body and soul improved.

§1. The word *creation* has diverse acceptations. It is taken either largely, for the production anything remarkably good or evil; so magistrates in a Common-wealth, and graduates in a university are said to be created, God is said to create a clean heart," (Psa. 51:10) and we are called "his workmanship" (Eph. 2:10) created in Christ to good works; and for evil, Moses in Numbers speaking of the remarkable judgment inflicted on Korah and his accomplices, uses this expression, *Si creationem creaverit Deus*, if God created a creature: the *radix* is ברא and that either strictly, for the generation of living preatures in a natural way, of limited, with some restraint; so in Horace, *Fortes creantur fortibus et bonis*, and in Virgil, *Sulmone creatos quatuor hic juvenes.* (Where also, *procreare*,) or more strictly, for the making of a thing out of some pre-extent matter, but such as is naturally indisposed and unapt for that production, where in generation there is always *materia habilis et disposita*;) as when God created man of the dust of the earth, and woman of man's rib, or more strictly, for the production of a thing without any pre-existent matter at all, out of mere nothing; we are to speak of it in the two latter senses, for so it belongs to God alone, "Thus saith the Lord thy Redeemer, and he that formed thee from the womb, I am the Lord that makes all things, that stretcheth forth the heavens alone, that spreads abroad the earth by myself," (Isa. 44:24). Yes, so necessary was the confession of this truth with the utmost hazard to distinguish God from idols, that to the end the Jews, who were then captives in Babylon, might not be wholly to seek for a profession of their faith, they had this verse in the Hebrew Bible written then, and so still in Chaldee letters, *Thus shall ye say to them*, "The gods that have not made the heavens and the earth, even they shall perish from the earth, and from under these heavens," (Jer. 10:11). Not unsuitable of which is that of Pythagoras long since cited by Justin Martyr, "Whosoever would from hereforth challenge any deity to himself, must be able to show such a world as this, and to say in truth, this is of my making."[249] And that of Trismegist (a heathen too) in one of his books, "There are mainly three to be considered; God, the world, and man: the world made for man, and man for God."

§2. But we have a more sure word of prophecy, and to that let us take heed: It will show us, First, How we Christians "by faith understand that the worlds were framed by the word of God, so that things which are seen were not made of things which do appear," (Heb. 11:3). Well might a late writer conclude his discourse of creation with this epiphonema, *Quantum est quod nescimus!*[250] The truth is, it is but little that we can learn from philosophers, even concerning creation itself, (the only article of the creed which they speak fully too) unacquainted with Scripture. Which made Maximilian the first say, "that the heathens were to be heard not as singing nightingales, but as croaking frogs;"[251] And two great physicians take themselves to the study of Scripture for understanding the secrets of nature.[252] One Sennertus, who finds much fault with those who perverted the text of Moses, and interpreted him out of heathen writers, *ausu infelici* (he says) *et non tolerando* by an unhappy and intolerable undertaking. The other Vallesius, who in the preface to his Sacra Philosophia, tells us, where he had in the former part of

---

[249] Ἑι τις εροι Θεος ειμι παρεξ ενος, ὅτος οφελλει κοσμον ισον τοτω ςυσαι ειπειν εμος ὁτος. Just. Mart. *De Monartia Dei*. Δευτερον ὁ κοσμος, δια τιν ανθρωπον, ὁ δ᾽ ανθροπος δια τον Θέον. Trismegistus.

[250] Gilb. Voetius *Disput. Theol.* part 1. page 881.

[251] Audiendi sunt Ethnici, non tanquam Philomena, sed tanquam Ranæ.

[252] Apud Voetium ibid. page 680.

his life commented on all Aristotle's *Acromatics*, and many pieces both of Hippocrates and Galen, he was resolved to devote the remainder of his days to the study of the holy Scriptures, and to seek his philosophy out of them for time to come.[253] By *faith* we understand a Christian firmly believes those truths concerning the time and manner of the world's creation, because he has Scripture testimony for them. That the worlds were framed, speaking after the Jewish mode, (though there is indeed but one world,) in the plural number; for the Hebrews then were accustomed to mention a threefold, *viz.* an inferior, a middle, and a superior world, as Camero tells us. "Framed by the word of God,"[254] this place says. When Solomon was to build a magnificent temple, he needed many workmen, and they many tools. Not so God, who did all without any co-adjutor, any instrument, by the sole word of his command. "By the word of the Lord were the heavens made, and all the host of them by the breath of his mouth," (Psa. 33:6). "Let them praise the name of the Lord, for he commanded, and they were created," (Psa. 148:5). Art can work, if nature first afford it some complete matter: let an artificer have a stone, he can make a statue, otherwise not. Nature can work if there be a principle to work on, though incomplete; let there be seed, it can produce a plant, let there be spawn, a fish. But to work without pre-existent matter, so as to bring forth the first plant without seed, the first fish without a spawn,[255] yes the first principles of these, and all things else out of nothing, by his sole word, is proper to God. "So that things which are seen (as it follows here) were not made of things which do appear." That rule, *ex nihilo nihil sit*, holds *in natura constituta*, now that God has set nature in a course of working by secondary causes enabled to produce effects like themselves; but *in natura constituenda* it was

---

[253] Huic lectioni consecrari senectutem.—statui in his philosophari, *etc.* Vallesius.

[254] Cameron. Myrothec. page 228.

[255] Dr. Jackson's *Commentary on the Creed*, part 2d, chapter 2 §4. page 64.

otherwise, when God worked by his word of command, and is therefore called *Elohim* by Moses two and thirty times in his history of creation, as Mercer observes.

The Schoolmen for the most part express that which is here called, "Things that do not appear," by the term *nothing*, either simply nothing, or *no such thing*, as it appeared to be at first: yet when they speak of *non-ens*, they do not take the word *materially*, as if mere nothing were the matter of which any being were framed; but terminatively, as the term from which the Creator moved. For example, the angels, they say, and the souls of men, together with the essential forms of natural bodies, were not then educed *ex potentia materiæ*, (as they are since in the ordinary course of generation by particular agents,) but induced *in materiam* by God himself the universal cause, and had an immediate production by the Creator:[256] Where some other things, as the sun and man's body, had a mediate creation, as being produced *ex non-ente tali* from such things as of themselves could not have caused such effects, but by virtue of God's creative word. Dr. Hall has given us the true notion of this in a compendious saying of his, "God made something out of nothing, and of that something, all things."[257] So as if all things be run to their first original, they will be found to come up out of the womb of nothing, where nothing but Almightiness could have brought them.

§3. That although the creatures are now subject to vanity, yet the goodness of God did shine forth in their first production, and is still abundantly manifested in them. The creature, Paul says, speaking of its present state, "was made subject to vanity," (Rom. 8:20). Whatever thing had any being of itself, and was not for ever, but did receive a being in time, and that from God, is a creature, Daneus well says; by this excluding the divinity of Christ which was from everlasting, as the angels were not, but produced by God in time; and sins

[256] Vessii *Thes.* page 12.

[257] B. Hall *Contemplat.* of Creation.

of all sorts, because though God is someway an actor about, yet he is no author of them;[258] as also works of art, for which God enables men, but does not produce them. The vanity to which all such things are subject, is partly negative, a non-ability to serve man as they did before the fall; after it the Lord said to Adam, "Cursed is the ground for thy sake; in sorrow shalt thou eat of it all the days of thy life," (Gen. 3:17). Partly positive; where that of Solomon, "Behold, all is vanity and vexation of spirit," (Eccl. 1:14). Yet, if any shall here conclude, that it was so from the beginning, Moses will expressly confute him, by whom we are told, when God at the very end of his creation, "Saw every thing that he had made, and behold it was very good;" (Gen. 1:31) which to me is a demonstration that the angels were not then fallen. Yes, if any shall deny that the goodness of God is still visible in them, let that saying of the Psalmist stop his mouth, "The earth is full of the goodness of the Lord," (Psa. 33:5). What he predicates of the earth, I am not afraid to extend to the sea, and to all other parts of the universe, they are all at this day full of the goodness of the Lord; the sea especially, of which we Islanders are especially bound to take notice by way of rejoicing, and to glorify God for, according to these direct places, "Glorify ye the Lord, even the name of the Lord God of Israel, in the Isles of the sea," (Isa. 24:15). And in the Psalms, "The Lord reigneth, let the earth rejoice, let the multitude of the Isles be glad of it," (Psa. 97:1). Well may the earth rejoice in it, because if the Lord did not so reign as to set bounds to that (whose natural place, is above the earth, as Psalm 104 informs us,) it would all quickly be overflown. Well may the multitude of the Isles be glad of it: for what are they in regard of that ocean that surrounds them, but as so many nut shells in a great vessel of water; how suddenly drowned, if God did not reign so as to restrain that element?

§4. But I must not allow myself too much scope, I shall

[258] *Creatura est res omnis quæ neque a seipsa est neque semper fuit; sed ut aliquando et a Deo product est*. Daneus *Physic. Christ.* page 59.

therefore restrain my future discourse on this head to the sole creation of man, and show how goodness appeared in it. It is reported as the speech of Favorinus; that in the vast world of creatures, there is nothing truly great except the little world of man.[259] Surely, next to the knowledge of God, there is nothing of more concernment to us; and therefore let none wonder at me, who cannot go over all, for singling out his creation to be insisted on: concerning which I intend to show out of certain texts in Genesis, the consultation on which the pattern after which, and the parts of which he was made at first.

For the first, it is the manner of artificers to deliberate much, and to put themselves more than ordinary pains about their master-pieces. Man was to be the Master-piece of that visible world, and accordingly Moses speaking of God according to the manner of men, brings him in consulting about so prime a piece. God said, Let us make man: (Gen. 1:26) where most other things were made with a word speaking, "Let there be light, and there was light. Let the earth bring forth, and it was so," (Gen. 1:3, 24). Here the Creator calls as it were a solemn council of the sacred persons in Trinity, when he is about to proceed to the making of man. Which is to be taken notice of, both because other Scriptures use the plural number where man's creation is spoken of (as in Eccles. 12:1. Remember thy Creator: according to the original, Creators; and Job 35:10. Where is God my maker? Hebrew, *makers*); and because it should restrain us from deriding any man's deformity, for fear of our reproaching his Maker. To which purpose that history is very remarkable. An Emperor of Germany came on a Lord's Day morning unattended to a poor country Church, where, pretending himself a soldier, he was present at Mass, which was said by the parish priest, a man so deformed, that he was, my author says, *Pœne portentum naturae*, almost a monster in nature. And as the Emperor wondered within himself, that God, (whose beauty and majesty is

---

[259] Nihil est in macrocosmo magnum praeter microcosmum.

infinite) would be served by so deformed a creature, it came to pass that the Priest reading the hundred Psalm, which was in the course of his Liturgy to be rehearsed on that day, pronounced the second verse of it, "Know ye that the Lord he is God, it is he that has made us and not we ourselves," in such a different tone and voice from that which he before used, that the Emperor apprehended it as a thing ordained by Almighty God to meet with and answer his present cogitation, and began to entertain so reverend an opinion of the Priest, that having informed himself after mass of his great virtue, he made him archbishop of Colen, much against the good man's will: who notwithstanding behaved himself in that great charge with singular commendation, and left a most sweet savour behind him.[260]

§5. For the second. The pattern after which man was made, is sometimes called *image* alone. So, "God created man in his own image, in the image of God created he him; (Gen. 1:27) sometimes likeness alone, "In the day that God created man, in the likeness of God made he him," (Gen. 5:1). Sometimes both, "Let us make man in our image, after our likeness:"[261] which makes a wise interpreter think that when they are joined, it is by hendiadys, and that the Holy Spirit means an image most like his own, *ad imaginem et si militudinem suam*, that is, *ad quam simillimam sui imaginem*. It is exceeding much for man's honor, that he is an epitome of the world, an abridgement of other creatures, partaking with the stones in being, with the stars in motion, with the plants in growing, with beasts in sense, and with angels in science. But his being made after God's image is far more. As great men are accustomed, they often erect a stately building, then cause their own picture to be hung up in it that spectators may know who was the chief founder of it: so when God had

[260] Fitz Herb. *of policy and religion*. Part l. pag. 54. out of *Guil. Malms*. l. 2. c. 10.

[261] Gen. 1:26. Mos est Hebræis duo substantive ita conjungere ut diuersæ res esse videantur, cum tamen alterum adjective et epitheti significationem habeat, Andr. Rivet, in *Gen. exercitation* 4.

created the fabric of this world, the last thing he did was the setting up his own picture in it, creating man after his own image. Now there is a threefold sense of this phrase: for the image of God is taken, first, in a large sense, and so it is applicable to all men in regard of the substance of their souls, which are invisible, incorporeal and intelligent, as God is. "Whoso sheddeth man's blood, by man shall his blood be shed, for in the image of God made he man," (Gen. 9:6). And again in James, "Therewith curse we men which are made after the similitude of God," (James 3:9). We read of the emperor Theodosius, that having exacted a new tribute from the people of Antioch,[262] there arose a commotion in which the people broke down the statue of the empress Placilla his late wife. He in a rage sent his forces against the city to sack it. One Macedonius a monk interceded thus. If the emperor is so much, and so justly offended that the image of his wife was so defaced, shall not the king of heaven (said the monk) be angry at him if he shall deliberately deface and break the image of God in so many men as are like to perish in this massacre. What a vast difference is there between reasonable creatures, and that brazen image? We for that image are easily able to set up one hundred, but the emperor with all his power is not able to restore so much as a hair of these men, if once he kill them. On which admonition Theodosius, it is said, forbore his design. Secondly, in a strict sense. So it is applicable only to Christ, who is "the image of the invisible God; the brightness of his glory, and express image of his person," (Col. 1:15; Heb. 1:3). For all the three things that go to make a perfect image, *viz.* likeness, derivation, and agreement in nature are concurrent here. The king's image is in his coin, and in his son, but after a different manner. In his coin there may be likeness and derivation, but not identity of nature, which is also added in his son. In saints there are the former; they are like to God in their qualities derived from him; but in Christ all three. Thirdly, in a middle sense, neither so largely as to extend to all

[262] See Theodor. *hist.* lib. 5. c. 21.

men, nor so strictly as to be restrained to Christ alone, but between both. So taken, it is nothing else but that conformity to God from which all men fell in the first Adam, and to which none but saints are restored by the second.

§6. For the third, the parts of which man consists, are body and soul; Moses at first speaks to both, "The Lord God (he says) formed man of the dust of the ground, and breathed into his nostrils the breath of life: and man became a living soul," (Gen. 2:7). God had before made spirits by themselves, and bodies by themselves, some celestial, others terrestrial; now on the sixth day for a conclusion of his works, he frames a creature consisting of a spirit and a body joined together, in whom he includes the choice perfections of all the former. One observes that God has joined all things in the world by certain Media.[263] The earth and water by slime; the air and water by vapours; exhalations are a middle between air and fire; quicksilver a middle between water and metals; coral between roots and stones, so man between beasts and angels. Manilius has comprehended much in few verses,[264]

—Quid mirum noscere mundum
Si possint homines, quibus est et mundus in ipsis,
Exemplumque Dei quisque est in imagine parva?

In English thus,

What wonder if men know the world
Since they themselves the world epitomize,
Yes every one a medal of God is?

Where he does in effect call his body μικροκοσμος, a little world, and his soul μικροθεος, a little God. In the pursuance of the former, the Stoics were accustomed to say,[265] that it was better being a fool in human shape, than being wise in the

---

[263] Weemse *Portraiture*, page 41.
[264] Manil. lib. 4. apud *Lips. Physiolog.* l. 3. dissert. 2.
[265] Charron *of wisdom*, page 16.

form of a beast. Yes Solomon himself in the twelfth of Ecclesiastes finds in his head both sun, moon, and stars. Well therefore may his head resemble the heavens where these lights are (as our eyes also are in our upper parts) without which the world would be a dungeon; his heart the fire, it being, kept hot by continual motion, and conveying natural heat to the whole body; his blood and other humors the water; his spirits the air; and his flesh and bones the earth. In prosecution of the latter, Tully a Platonist goes so far as to bid a man take notice that he is a God,[266] and some divines find a resemblance of the trinity in man's soul.[267] The understanding, will, and conscience, three faculties, but one soul; as Father, Son, and Holy Spirit, three persons, but one God: let us all meanwhile, "taste and see how good the Lord is" in preparing us such bodies, and infusing such souls into us: but withal so as to consider and improve the original of both.

§7. Seeing Adam's body had its original from the dust of the earth, the consideration of it should be an antidote against pride in all his posterity. Are you not the son of Adam? Was not he the son of dust? Was not that the son of nothing? When the Lord would humble Adam after the fall he put him in mind of his being dust. "In the sweat of thy face shalt thou eat thy bread, until thou return to the ground; for out of it wast thou taken: for dust you are, and to dust shalt thou return," (Gen. 3:19). And when Abraham would be low before God he describes himself dust and ashes, "Behold now I have taken on me to speak to the Lord, who am but dust and ashes. (Ecclus. 10:9). Why art thou proud, O dust and ashes?" Siracides says, and Bernard, *Cum sis humi limus, cur non es humilimus?* Why art not thou most humble, O man, seeing you are but the dust of the earth. As for the soul, that was purely from God, *Divinæ particula aurae*, as an ancient poet calls it, for God, Moses says, breathed into his nostrils the breath of life; and man became a living soul. This should render us restless

[266] Scito te Deum esse *etc*. Lib. de somn. Scipage

[267] Bonaventure *Amatorium*, page 60. 1. col. 2.

until that image after which Adam was made be renewed in us by regeneration. The relics of it found in men unconverted what are they but *magni nominis umbra*, the mere shadow of a great and glorious name. How unlike are natural men to God for all these? Our Queen Elizabeth once in her progress observing some pictures of hers hung up for signs to be very unlike her, caused them to be taken down and burnt. Burning must be the end of those that continue unlike to God, where such as are by converting grace changed into the same image (as Paul speaks—2 Cor. 3:18) from glory to glory, shall at length arrive at that perfection of glory, which is also the image of God, as David has it, "As for me, I shall behold thy face in righteousness, I shall be satisfied when I awake with thy likeness."

EXERCITATION V.

The same and other attributes of God declared from, his providential dispensations, the inter-changeableness in which largely discoursed of and applied from Ecclesiastes 7:14. *A gloss on* Isaiah chap. 66:10-11. *Cheerfulness a duty in six respects; crosses how to be considered.*

§1. The vicissitude of divine dispensations (which I am to treat of next) is exactly recorded by Solomon, saying, "In the day of prosperity be joyful, but in the day of adversity consider: God also has set the one over against the other, to the end that man should find nothing after him," (Eccl. 7:14). It is most clear here, that there is an intermixture of dispensations, adverse and prosperous, in the course of divine providence, and that we may see much of God therein. It will appear in six particulars.

There are times. I. In which things go very ill with a man in reference to his private affairs, yet well with the public, which keeps him from sinking into despondency. Mephibosheth was cheated by Ziba of half his lands, yet "let him take all, said he, for as much as my Lord the king is come again in peace to his own house," (2 Sam. 19:29-30). The woman of Sparta, of whom we read in Plutarch,[268] being told that all her five sons were slain in the battle, but with that the enemies were worsted, and her countrymen victors, uttered this heroic speech, *Lugeant ergo miseræ; Ego victrice patria beatam me esse judico. Let such as are miserable lament; I cannot but account myself happy now that my country has had the better.*

II. In which a man's personal comforts are multiplied, but the church's misery damps his mirth. Nehemiah was much in favor at the king of Persia's court, yet his countenance could not but be sad when he heard "that the city the place of his father's sepulchers lay waste, and the gates of it were consumed with fire," (Neh. 2:3). We read of Terentius,[269] an orthodox captain under Yalens an Arian Emperor, who having done some eminent service was desired by the Emperor, who intended him a just recompense, to ask of him what he would. He preferred a petition in behalf of the orthodox Christians, that they might have a Church allowed them by themselves to worship God in. Valens displeased, tore the petition and threw it away. He gathered up the scattered pieces, and professed that seeing he could not be heard in the cause of Christ, he would make no suit for his own advantage. That of Isaiah, "Rejoice ye with Jerusalem, *etc.* that ye may suck and be satisfied," (Isa. 66:10-11) is both preceptive and argumentative. Jerusalem is compared to a nursing mother, believers to her sucking children; if the nurse be in health, the child has cause to rejoice in that, and shall fare the better for it: if she is distempered, the child will go near to suck the disease from her.

§2. III. In which long prosperity follows after much adversity, as in Joseph's case. He had been envied, sold, imprisoned, "His feet were hurt in the stocks, the iron entered into his soul," (Psa. 105:18). Yet afterward Pharaoh give him his own ring, arrayed him in vestures of fine linen, puts a gold

---

[268] And. *Camerar. cent.* 3. page 174.

[269] Theodoret *lib.* 4. c. page 2. 8.

chain about his neck, makes him ride in the second chariot he had, caused the people to cry before him, bow the knee; and appointed him ruler over all the land of Egypt; in which height of honor he lived and died. (Gen. 41:42-43).

IV. In which adversity treads on the heels of long prosperity, as in Job's case. The candle of God had long shined on his head, and the secret of God been on his tabernacle. His children then were about him, he had washed his steps with butter, and the rock poured him out rivers of oil. His root was spread by the waters, and the dew lay all night on his branch. His glory was fresh in him, and his bow renowned in his hand, which are his own expressions. (Job 29:3-6, 19-20). But ere long, his servants are slain with the edge of the sword, his cattle taken away by the enemy; all his children killed at once with the fall of a house in which they were feasting, he himself afflicted in body, vexed in spirit, grieved by his comforters, in a word brought from the throne to the dunghill, so as to give just occasion to the proverb, *As poor as Job*.

V. In which crosses and comforts take it by turns, so that a man goes out of one into another, in a succession of vicissitudes. So it fared with Hezekiah. After his coming to the crown for diverse years, "the Lord was with him, and he prospered whithersoever he went forth." But in the fourteenth year of his reign, the tide of prosperity begins to turn. Sennacherib comes up against him with a most formidable host, and took his fenced cities. He takes himself to prayer, and the Lord delivers him by a miracle, sending an angel to destroy one hundred and eighty five thousand of his enemies in a night. But the next news we hear, is that Hezekiah was sick to death; yet he does not die, but had fifteen years added to his life, and was assured by a sign from heaven of his recovery. (2 Kings 20:2). Yet presently after all this, he receives a sad message there concerning the loss of all his treasure, and the woeful condition of all his posterity. See what a strange succession is here; after glorious victories, comes the loss of his fenced cities, and an alarm given to Jerusalem itself. After that miraculous deliverance, then a mortal sickness, then a cheering sign, but ere long a message of very sad concernment.

§3. VI. In which pleasure and sorrow, joy and grief are so interwoven one with another, as a man may seem happy and miserable both at once. Jacob is at once scared with the hearing of Esau's four hundred men, and cheered with the sight of a host of angels sent to guard him. He doth at once receive a hurt in the hollow of his thigh, and a blessing from the angel that wrestled with him. David at once is hated by Saul, and loved by Jonathan. Ahasuerus at once enjoys the glory of an absolute monarch, and is slighted by his own wife. Haman at once swims in an ocean of court delights, and is tormented for the want of Mordecai's knee. As on the one side, "Out of the strong comes sweetness:" (1 Pet. 4:14) when the spirit of glory and of God rest on a suffering saint, because he is a saint and a sufferer: so on the other, "Even in laughter the heart is sorrowful," (Prov. 14:13).

—Medio de fonte leporum
Surgit amari aliquid, quod in ipsis floribus angat.[270]

That is,

Some bitter thing from midst of sweetness breeds;
And that which vexes from the flowers proceeds.

§4. This God does for diverse good ends and purposes. I. As first to manifest his wisdom in compounding passages of providence, so as one shall qualify another: prosperity allay the sourness of adversity; and this assuage the swellings of that. As the painter's skill appears in tempering bright colors, and dark shadows; the cooks in mingling sweet and tart ingredients; the musicians in raising harmony out of discords; orators in making up curious sentences by a fit opposition of contrarities.[271]

---

[270] Lucret. 1.4.
[271] Librat in *Antithetis*.

II. To magnify his goodness. The frame of our spirits is such, that if prosperity were continued without interruption, we should be apt to swell and presume; if adversity without intermission, to sink and despair. Our weakness such, that we should never give a due estimate to blessings, were we not sometimes taught by experience what it is to be under pressures. We learn by sickness to prize health, and by restraint to value liberty. A calm is much more pleasing to us after a tempest; and the shining forth of the sun after an eclipse. It is therefore an act of much mercy in God so to intermingle favors and crosses, lest by a constant course of the former, we should grow wanton and effeminate, or by continuance of the latter sottish and stupid.

III. To keep up and maintain his respect in the world. God will be known to be the sovereign Lord of all persons and things; the great disposer of all affairs in such a way as seems best to himself, and therefore gives out blessings and crosses interchangeably, so as man shall be at no certainty what to expect, but live in a constant dependence on him, who keeps the disposal of prosperity and adversity in his own hands, to the end that man should find nothing certain but this, that there is a great uncertainty of future events. *Wherefore,*

§5. *First*, take notice here what we are to look for in our pilgrimage here, *viz.* vicissitudes and changes from one condition into another. If Solomon had nowhere said, "There is a time to weep, and a time to laugh," (Eccl. 3:4) experience would soon have forced us to acknowledge that our whole course is checkered with prosperity and adversity; that most of a Christian's drink in this life is *Oxymel*, most of his food, bitter-sweets. While Israel marched throughout the wilderness, the blackest night had a pillar of fire, and brightest day a pillar of cloud; so in this world, things never go so well with the Israel of God, but that they groan under some affliction; never so ill, but that they have some comfort afforded them.

Secondly, learn to maintain in ourselves a mixture of

affections suitable to this mixture of divine dispensations. "Rejoice with trembling," (Psa. 2:11). Leaven and honey were both excluded under the law, from offering by fire: (Lev. 2:11) leaven for its excessive sourness; honey for its excessive sweetness; to show (Ainsworth says) that in saints there should neither be extremity of grief, nor of pleasure, but a mediocrity. We should be careful in time of prosperity to fear affliction with a fear of expectation, though not of amazement; with such a fear as may cause preparation, but no discouragement. Look at a very fair day, as that which may prove a weather breeder, and usher in storms. On the other side, in time of adversity, hope for refreshment. The psalmist did so, "All thy waves are gone over me, yet the Lord will command his loving kindness."[272]

Thirdly, observe the difference that is between this present, and that other world. Dying Aristotle is reported to have said, "I rejoice that I am now going out of a world of contraries." This indeed is so. But that which dying men go into is without such mixture. All tears shall be wiped from the saint's eyes; and impenitent sinners shall have judgment without mercy; briefly in this militant church, as in the ark of old. "There is a rod and a pot of manna." Here on earth we have little manna without some rods, little welfare without some sharp affliction; few rods without some manna, not many afflictions without some measure of consolation: where in heaven there is nothing but manna, in hell nothing but rods, or scorpions rather.

IV. We should keep ourselves in a frame of cheerfulness, that we may be always prepared in the day of prosperity to rejoice. This will appear a duty to which we are *bound*,

I. Because God does not only approve and like it. (He loves a cheerful giver, so a cheerful thanksgiver and worshipper. (2 Cor. 9:7). Nehemiah was afraid to be seen sad

[272] Psal. 43:7, 8. Nemo confidant nimium secundis; nemo desperet meliora lapsus. Sen. *Trag*.

in the king's presence. (Neh. 2:2). Mordecai dared not go into the Court gates with his sack-cloth on, (Esth. 4:2), dejected looks, and the sack-cloth of an uncheerful carriage ill become the servant of the king, the followers of the court of heaven.) But also require and command it, "Serve the Lord with gladness," (Psa. 100:2). The Jews of old were commanded to rejoice in their solemn feasts: which were accordingly to be kept in the most cheerful seasons. (Deut. 16:14-15). The Passover at the first ripening of corn, Pentecost at the first reaping, and the feast of Tabernacles at the end of harvest.

II. Because Jesus Christ was "anointed to give us the oil of joy for mourning, and the garment of praise for the spirit of heaviness," (Isa. 61:3). He himself indeed was anointed with the oil of gladness above his fellows, but such as are received into fellowship with him, should, and shall, if the fault be not in themselves, partake with him in some degree of the same unction.

III. Because the spirit of Christ is a spirit of cheerfulness. His two first fruits mentioned, Gal. 5:22, are love and joy. Yes, when it is said, "Grieve not the holy Spirit of God,"[273] Heinsius thinks this to be part of the meaning. *Be cheerful after a holy manner. Let none offend that great guest, the Spirit of God by overmuch sadness.* And Drusius tells us in the preface to his Praeterita of a usual saying among the Hebrews, *Spiritum sanctum non residere super hominem mcesium,* that the Holy Spirit is not accustomed to reside on a sad spirited man.

IV. Because our adversary the devil, being a melancholy spirit himself, delights in our sadness. The prince of darkness loves to see the servants of God in a dark condition. He is gratified and gets advantage by our uncheerfullness. Therefore Paul writes to his Corinthians concerning the incestuous person, that on his repentance they would comfort him and prevent his being swallowed up with overmuch sorrow, lest Satan, he says, "should get an

[273] Ephes. 4:30. Sanctam hilaritatem admitte. Ne quis nimio mærore magnum illum hospitem offendat. Heins. *in locum.*

advantage of us, for we are not ignorant of his devices," (2 Cor. 2:7, 11).

V. Because if we look to ourselves, cheerfulness is advantageous both to our bodies, therefore compared to the best food, such as men use to have at feasts. "He that is of a merry heart has a continual feast," (Prov. 15:15) and the best physic too. "A merry heart doth good like a medicine: but a broken spirit drieth the bones," (Prov. 17:22); and also our spirits. Uncheerfullness makes the soul of a man drive heavily, as the chariots of Pharaoh did in the red sea; but the joy of the Lord oils the wheels. Cheerfulness supplies the joints of our hearts, and so renders them nimble and active in our holy performances. See Nehemiah 8:10.

VI. Because if we cast our eyes on others, the uncheerfullness of professors often brings a bad report on the profession; and makes the world ready to believe that Christians serve a bad master, or have but a hard service of it; where their rejoicing in the ways of the Lord would help to bring others in love with religion, see Acts 9:31 and Esther 8 the two last times.

§7. *Fifthly*, endure afflictions so as in the day of adversity duly to consider the nature, author, and ends of crosses.

I. The nature of those afflictions that befall men in Christ. They are not from vindicative Justice, (which is wholly removed from such by the mediation of him in whom they have believed,) and so not formally punishments: but from fatherly discipline, by which it comes to pass that although the matter be the same, there is as much difference between the sufferings of believers, and of ungodly persons out of Christ, as there is between the cords by which an executioner pinions his condemned malefactor,[274] and those by which the indulgent surgeon binds his patient; the one's design being to kill, the other's to cure. They are crosses indeed which believers undergo, but no curses, and have no such malignity

[274] Inter vincula carnificis et chirurgic. Cahmier. *Panstrat.*

in them as the world imagines.

II. The author, well might Eliphaz say, "Trouble springs not out of the ground," (Job 5:6) for it comes from heaven, and that out of love. "As many as I love," Christ says, "I rebuke and chasten," (Rev. 3:19). How bitter whatsoever the cup is, which I am to drink, and by whomsoever it is handed to me, the comfort is, it was of my heavenly father's mixing, who I am sure would not put any poisonous, although he do put some displeasing ingredients into it. I will therefore say, Christ enabling, as Christ himself did, "The cup which my Father has given me, shall I not drink it?" (John 18:11).

III. The ends, which are specially three. 1. The mortifying of our corruptions. "By this shall the iniquity of Jacob be purged, and this is all the fruit to take away his sin," (Isa. 27:9). All the harm which the fiery furnace did the young men in Daniel was to burn off their cords; our lusts are cords, cords of vanity in Scripture phrase; the fiery trial is sent on purpose to burn and consume them. Afflictions help to scour off this kind of rust. Adversity like winter-weather is of use to kill the vermin, which the summer of prosperity is accustomed to breed. 2. For the enlivening and quickening of our graces. "I spake to thee in thy prosperity and thou saidst, I will not hear," (Jer. 22:21). But elsewhere, "Lord in trouble have they visited thee; they poured out a prayer when thy chastening was on them," (Isa. 26:16). These two places compared show how apt prosperity is to make men Gallios, adversity to render them Zealots. As bruising makes aromatical spices to send out their savor; and collision fetches fire out of the flint, which was hid before; so pressures excite devotion. The cold water of persecution is often cast in the church's face to fetch her again when she is in a swoon. 3. For the furthering of our glory. Christ went from the cross to Paradise; so do Christians. "He was made perfect through sufferings;" (Heb. 2:10) so are they. "It became him to suffer, and to enter into his glory:" (Luke 24:26). It becomes them to tread in their master's steps. When the founder has cast his bell, he does not presently hang it up in the steeple, but first try it with his hammer, and beat on it on every side, to see if any flaw is in it. Christ does not presently after he has converted a man, convey him to heaven, but he suffers him first to be beaten on by manifold temptations, and after advances him to the crown spoken of Jam. 1:12.

"Blessed is the man that endureth temptations, for when he is tried he shall receive the crown of life which the Lord has promised to them that love him." For this crown the cross makes way; although no cross can merit it but that of Christ. Yet as law is said to work wrath occasionally, so "our light afflictions which are but for a moment, work for us a far more exceeding and eternal weight of glory," (2 Cor. 4:17).

APHORISM VI.

Providence extends itself, not only to all created beings, and to all human affairs, especially those that concern the church: but even to the sins of angels and men.

EXERCITATION I.

Introduction concerning the contents of this Aphorism. Providence over all created beings. Preservation of men to be ascribed to God himself, not to good men, yes not to good angels, in whom heart-searching and patience are wanting. Providence reaching to human affairs: economical, civil, military, moral and ecclesiastical. Anastasius' design frustrated. Rome and our nation instanced in. I. G. castigated.

§1. This Aphorism requires a clear demonstration of these propositions. 1. That divine providence extends itself to all created beings. 2. That it reaches to all human affairs. 3. That it is especially seen in such affairs as concern the church. And, 4. That although God is not the author of sin, yet his providence is an actor in it; to these when I shall have added an answer to objections, and from each proposition an inference, the whole will be completely handled.

The first proposition, with which I am to begin is, divine providence extends itself to all created beings. Well may we strike in with the Levites in that form of acknowledging God in which they went before the people, saying, "Thou even you are Lord alone. Thou hast made heaven, the heaven of heavens with all their host, the earth, and all things that are therein, the seas and all that is therein; and thou preservest them all," (Neh. 9:6). David brings it down a little lower, "Thy judgments are a great deep, O Lord, thou preservest man and beast," (Psa. 36:6). Job lower yet, "What shall I do to thee, O thou preserver of men," (Job 7:20). As God made all things by the word of his command. (Psa.

148:5). He commanded and they were created, so he "upholds them all in being by the word of his power," (Heb. 1:3). Heaven, earth, sea, man and beast, *especially* man are all under divine providence. It is not with God, as with carpenters and ship-wrights, who make houses for other men to dwell in, vessels for others to sail in, and therefore after they are made look after them no more; God who made all things for *himself*, looks to the preservation of all. It is accordingly said of Christ, "All things were created by him and for him, and by him all things consist," (Col. 1:16-17). The creatures are all as vessels, which if unhooped by the withdrawing of support, all the liquor that is in them, their several virtues, yes their several beings would run out, and they return to their first nothing. Schoolmen compare God to the sun, creatures to the air. The sun shines by his own nature, the air only by participation of light from the sun. So whatever good the creatures have, is by derivation from Jehovah, the fountain of being. Take away the light of the sun, the air ceases to shine, and so it is here. As things artificial are preserved in their being by the duration of such natural things as they consist of *v. g.* a house by the lasting of stones and timber: so things natural, which depend on God, by the continuance of that divine influence by which they were at first made.

§2. It is not in good men to preserve themselves or others. They derogate from God exceedingly that ascribe too much in this kind to any man, as some luxuriant French wits did to cardinal Richieleu: of whom they said, that God Almighty might put the Government of the world into his hands.[275] That France in God's and the cardinal's hands was too strong; that what the soul was to the body, the same was he to France.[276] *Si foret his nullus, Gallia nulla foret.* Yes one frivolous pamphleteer profanely and ridiculously called him, the fourth person in the Trinity. Yes, not in good angels themselves, "who though they be all ministering spirits, sent

---

[275] Howel's *Lustra Ludovici*, page 166.

[276] Idem in the proem to his *history of Lewis* 13 fol. 2.

forth to minister for them who shall be heirs of salvation?" (Heb. 1:14), yet are none of them governing spirits, appointed to provide for mankind the utmost rewards and punishments. They are wanting in two qualifications which should enable them hereunto; one is the knowledge of men's hearts where the truth of grace, or venom of sin lies: the other patience, in which no angel has enough to bear with men without destroying them for their continual provocations. Where in God there is a meeting of both these. See for the former, "Jerem. 15:9-10. The heart is deceitful above all things, and desperately wicked, who can know it? I the Lord search the heart; I try the reins, even to give every man according to his ways, and according to the fruit of his doing." And for the latter, Hosea 11:9, "I will not execute the fierceness of mine anger: I will not return to destroy Ephraim, for I am God and not man?" We may add and say, God, and not angels.

§3. The second proposition follows, *viz.* that Divine Providence reaches to all human affairs which we may for method's sake subdivide into *œconomical*, civil, military, moral, and ecclesiastical. Human affairs *are*,

I. Oeconomical, such as do belong to a family. For example, riches and poverty, preferment and debasement, which in Hannah's song are ascribed to the sole Providence of God. (1 Sam. 2:7-8). "The Lord (she said) makes poor, and makes rich: he bringeth low, and lifteth up. He raiseth up the poor out of the dust, and lifteth up the beggar from the dunghill," *etc.* yes, to instance in blessings highly prized by Christian families, grace and peace, which are the things prayed for by the apostles in most of their benedictions. We read of saints in Cesar's household, Phil. 4:22. Nero that monster of men, was Cesar then; he that had published a bloody law, that whosoever, professed himself Christian, should be apprehended as an enemy to mankind, and put to death: without any further defense.[277] Yet even in his house

[277] Quisquis Cristianum se esse confitetur, is tanquam generis humani hostis, sine ulterioresui defensione capite plectatur. Camerar. *Orat.* 1. c.

the Providence of God has so worked as to convert and preserve such men as were of grace; saints indeed, not only in his empire; and under his government, but in his family, and under his roof. As for peace, that of the Rabbins, although it is somewhat a quaint, yet may be an useful observation.[278] Take the first letter (they say) of God's name, out of the name of the man, and the last of the woman's name and there remains nothing but fire; implying that there is like to be nothing but the fire of contention and strife, jealousy and heart burnings between man and wife, where they do not come together in God's name. Where if wisdom make the match, as it doth when people marry in the Lord, happy are they who are so met. For "her ways are ways of pleasantness, and all her paths are peace," (Prov. 3:17).

II. Civil, such as belongs to kingdoms, republics, corporations, or to men as combined in such societies. Many are the contrivances of men to work themselves and others into places of government; but when all this is done, that of the Psalmist is most true, "Promotion comes neither from the east, nor from the west, nor from the south. But God is the judge: he pulleth down one, and setteth up another," (Psa. 75:6-7). And that of Daniel, "He changeth the times and the seasons; he removeth kings, and setteth up kings," (Dan. 2:21). Witness this history: Anastasius a Grecian emperor having no male issue to succeed him, was desirous to transfer the throne to one of his three nephews, whom he had bred up; and not being able to resolve which of them he should take, put the thing to lot in this way. He caused to be prepared three beds in the royal chamber, and made his crown to be hung within the tester of one of these beds, called the realm, being resolved to give it to him who by lot should place himself under it. This done, he sent for his nephews, and after he had magnificently

---

page 39, page 135.

[278] Take י the first letter of יהוה out of איש *Vir*, and ה out of אשה *Femina*, there remain אש *Ignis*. M. Gataker's *Serm.* on Eleazar's prayer, Gen. 24:12-14, page 8.

entertained them, commanded them to repose themselves, each, one choosing one of the beds prepared, for them.[279] The eldest accommodated himself according to his fancy, and hit on nothing; the second did the same. He then expected the youngest should go directly to the crowned bed; but he prayed the emperor that he might be permitted to lie with one of his brothers, and by this means not any of the three took the way of the empire, which was so easy to be had, that it was not above a pace distant. Anastasius, much amazed, well saw God would transfer the diadem from his race, as he did afterwards to Justin. Who can read and consider such examples without saying as he did?

Ludit in humanis Divina potentia rebus.

That is,

Divine power often dares
Desport itself in men's affairs.

Remember Daniel's four beasts, and the seven heads of that beast in the Revelations, conceived by interpreters to resemble the seven forms of government which Rome was to undergo successively; from a commonwealth to kings; from kings to consuls; from consuls to dictators; there to *decemvirs*; there to tribunes of the people; there to emperors; there to popes. Reflect on this nation of ours, which has been governed at first by Britains, then Saxons, then Danes, then Normans! one while in the way of a *heptarchy*, another while of a monarchy, and now of a republic; and, if you can, refuse to cry out, O the depth!

§4. III. Military, such as belong to the managing of wars. It is not for nothing that God is so often described, "Lord of hosts" in the Old Testament. We find him so called no less than one hundred and thirty times in two of the prophets, Isaiah and Jeremiah. Because in the ordering of

---

[279] Causinus' *Holy Court*, part 2. page 239.

martial affairs, he in a manner doth all. Captains, and superior officers may, and do consult, but God determines. They throw the dice, he appoints the chance; they set their men as it pleases them, he in the issue plays the game as it pleases him. Hear David in that Psalm of his which he made in the day that the Lord delivered Him from the hand of all his enemies, and from the hand of Saul, speaking of his own experiments, and celebrating God as assisting him both in the field, and at sieges, "By thee I have run through a troop; and by my God have I leaped over a wall," (Psa. 18:29) giving him strength, activity, skill," "It is God that girdeth me with strength. He makes my fee like hinds feet. He teacheth my hands to war, so that a bow of steel is broken by mine arms," (verses 32-34). Yes, success and victory, you have girded me with strength to the battle; you have subdued under me those that rose up against me. You have also given me the necks of mine enemies, that I might destroy them that hate me," (Verses 39-40). In the New Testament, we seldom or never meet with that title. That which comes nearest it is, *Lord God Almighty*; and this occurs twice in the Revelation, when mention is made of the victories which it pleases God to give to the reformed churches against antichrist and his adherents, once in these words, "We give thanks, O Lord God Almighty, which art, and wast, and art to come; because thou hast taken to thee thy great power, and hast reigned," (Rev. 11:17). And again in these, "Great and marvelous are thy works, Lord God Almighty, just and true are thy ways, thou king of saints," (Rev. 15:3).

IV. Moral, such as belong to good manners, or in more gospel terms, "To living soberly, righteously, and godly in this present world," (Titus 2:12). The two former I well know are pretended to by men unregenerate, yes, by heathens. Socrates (they say) lived so soberly, as not to be discomposed by any outward emergency, to show himself always the same man. Fabritius so righteously, as that it was commonly said of him, *To turn the sun out of its course would be found more easy than to turn him from the way of justice*. But for godliness, which is the third, it is hard if any should pretend to that without strong impressions from God in Christ, yet the Pelagians of old did, asserting those virtues which appeared in moral men, who had not received Christ Jesus the Lord, nor known what it was to walk in him, for true graces; for which very fault as St. Augustine tells us,[280] above all others, the Christian church most detested them. Yes, a Christian minister of late has in print dared to collect from that saying of Paul, "All men have not faith," an implication, "That men who act and quit themselves according to the true principles of that reason which God has planted in them, cannot but believe, and be partakers in the precious faith of the gospel."[281] But we have been taught, and must teach that it is not in the power of any inferior creature so to improve its faculties, as to raise up itself to a superior rank. No tree can make itself a beast, no beast a man, no man a saint by the bare improvement of his reason, where he comes to be a man. Moral principles prove to such as rely on them, and seek no further, mortal principles. We believe that of Prosper, "The whole life of an unbeliever is sin." Neither is there anything good, where the chief good is wanting,—but false virtue in the midst of the best manners.[282]

V. Ecclesiastical, such as belong to the church, and the legitimate members of it. In that song of loves, Psalm 45:9, "On thy right hand did stand the queen in gold of Ophir," is meant the church. Look as an indulgent prince, besides the common affection he bears, and protection he gives to all his subjects, has a peculiar respect to, and converse with his princes: so there is a peculiar providence of God towards his church; the handling in which at large I refer to the next *Exercitation*.

EXERCITATION II.

[280] August. contr. Julian. Pelag. l. 4. c. 3.

[281] J.G. Preface to the Reader before *Red. Redeemed*, fol. 6. a fine.

[282] Omnis infideliura vita peccatum est, et nihil est bonum, sine summo bono, ubi enim deest agnitio æternæ et incommutabilis voluntatis, falsa virtus est et in optimis moribus. Prosper *sent*. 106.

Deuteronomy, 11:12 opened. God's care over the Church proved from the provision he makes for inferior creatures. From Israel's conduct. From the experiments and acknowledgments of saints in all ages. Experiments of the Virgin Mary, Rochellers, Musculus, acknowledgments of Jacob, David, Psalmist, Augustine and Ursin. From God's causing things and acts of all sorts to co-operate to the good of the saints. Isa. 27:2-3 explained. The Church preserved from, in, and by dangers.

§1. Our third proportion is, that diving providence is seen more especially in such affairs as concern the church, and the members of it. In order to the clearing in which, I intend to insist on two places of Scripture. The first is that in Deuteronomy 11:12. Where Moses describing the land of Canaan, says of it this way, "A land which the Lord thy God careth for: the eyes of the Lord thy God are always on it, from the beginning of the year, even to the end of the year."[283] That land was then the only habitation of God's church, and besides, a lively type of the catholic church which was afterwards to be spread over the whole face of the earth, where it is that believers in all places were described inward Jews, and the circumcision. (Rom. 2 to the end; Phil. 3:3). This continual care of God over his church and the members of it *appears,*

1. From the provision made by him for inferior creatures. So our Savior argues, "Behold the fowls of the air: for they sow not, neither do they reap, nor gather into barns, yet your heavenly father feedeth them. Are ye not much better than they?" (Matt. 6:26). They have no caterers to bring in provision for them; no barns to fetch provision out of; yet want it not, but go cheerfully on, chirping continually, because God feeds them: and that sometimes in a way little less than miraculous, if that be true which is reported by some good writers, namely, that when the young ravens are

[283] Επισκοπεῖται. LXX hic.

forsaken of their dams and left bare, out of their own dung there arises a worm which creeps to their mouths, and becomes nourishment to them.[284]

§2. II. From the conduct of Israel after the flesh in former times. A breviate of that nation's story will presently let us understand how they were brought into that land, (in which this place in Deuteronomy speaks) and cared for there by a thousand providences. Time was when Joseph was raised up to be a nursing father to them, and that by a most remarkable dispensation. He had been formerly sold into Egypt, was imprisoned without cause, cast as Junius thinks, into that prison whereunto such were put as had most highly offended the king, to be sure into one "where his feet were hurt in the stocks, And he laid in irons," (Psa. 105:17-18). Had not his prison-house been so bad, it is likely he should not have had an opportunity to make himself known to the butler and baker of Pharaoh, who were his fellow prisoners. The butler being restored to his place according to Joseph's interpretation of his dream, forgets to acquaint Pharaoh with him until all other means had been used to quiet the king's mind, and none found effectual: then he speaks, and then is Joseph speedily advanced. Being so, he becomes a preserver of the church in his father, brethren, and their families. Afterwards when there was risen another generation that did not know Joseph; and the king of Egypt had set himself by force and art to extinguish Israel, the bush, although burning, was not consumed in the midst of the fire: their burdens were increased, yet their persons multiplied; and Moses ere long raised up to deliver them out of their bondage. A man preserved by the daughter of that Pharaoh, whom he was called to destroy, and by that means brought up at court, yes instructed there both in the art and government, and in all the learning of the Egyptians. Under his conduct God "did for them (as one prophet speaks) terrible things which they looked not for," (Isa. 64:3). Pulls them out of Pharaoh's heart

[284] B. Andrew's *Pattern of Catechetical doctrine*, page 60.

in spite of his heart, at their departure sends them away laden with the jewels and treasures of Egypt; makes a passage for them through the sea, and accompanies their hosts into the wilderness. There providence fetches them water out of a rock, than which nothing is drier; and bread from heaven, which is accustomed to grow out of the earth. There their food is manna and quails; a cloud and pillar of fire their guides; when this servant of God was dead, up steps Joshua in his room, brings them into and settles them in the promised land; which proved to them after their settlement by lot, "an habitation of righteousness, and mountain of holiness." A land flowing not only with temporal, but also with spiritual milk and honey, after Solomon had erected a magnificent temple for them, which was the wardrobe of those ceremonies by which God was then to be served. Then were they (as the Psalmist has it) "abundantly satisfied with the fatness of God's house, and made to drink of the river of his pleasures." But their sins having at length cast them out of that good land, and occasioned the burning of their temple, God left them not destitute of his help, but ordained for them various refreshments in the time of their captivity. This among others in Esther's time. King Ahasuerus under whom they then were in a state of captivity had his sleep taken from him, would spend the time not in this or that exercise, but in reading; of all books, calls for that of the Chronicles; of all places has that read to him which concerned a good service done by Mordecai a Jew; does not only take notice of it, but inquire what reward had been given him; understanding he had received none, causes Haman his favorite to be called; puts him on doing singular honor in the view of all men to this Mordecai, gives his wife queen Esther occasion of impleading this Haman, discovering his plot against all the Jews and preventing that massacre of them, which should speedily have been executed. Yes providence went on to work so happily in the hearts of those monarchs, who then held them captives, as not long after to proclaim their deliverance, and liberty for them to rebuild both Jerusalem and the temple; which they also attempted.

While the second temple was building by Herod not so magnificent as the former, yet in some respect more glorious: if Josephus misinform us not, for the space of almost ten years it never rained all that while in the day time, the providence of God so ordering it, lest the work should be interrupted.[285] Yes so remarkable was the power and greatness of God in assisting the builders then, that we find him in Haggai and Zechariah's prophecies, which were both written about that time, frequently described by that name, The Lord of Hosts, particularly five times in four verses of Haggai. "Thus saith the Lord of Hosts, yet once it is a little while, and I will shake the heavens, and the earth, and the sea, and the dry land; and I will shake all nations, and the desire of all nations shall come; and I will fill this house with glory, saith the Lord of Hosts. The silver is mine, and the gold is mine, saith the Lord of Hosts. The glory of this latter house shall be greater than of the former, saith the Lord of Hosts: and in this place will I give peace, saith the Lord of Hosts," (Hag. 2:6-9). That which raised the glory of this second above that of the first temple, was the personal presence of Jesus Christ in it. His coming, preaching, and suffering, so ripened the sins of this people, (who began again to degenerate after their return) as hot weather doth the corn, that ere long they and their temple became a prey to the Roman Eagle.

§3. III. From the experiments and acknowledgments of godly persons in several ages. The blessed Virgin Mary after her journey to Bethlehem, and lying in of her child there, may be probably thought to have been straitened in her means, as being but poor, and not to have sufficient for the maintenance of her child, herself and Joseph in the journey which they were to take presently after into Egypt.[286] See how God provides; hard before that, he sends the wise men from the east, and

[285] Nunquam interdiu ne interrumperetur ædificatio pluisse. Joseph. *Antiq. Judaic.* lib. 15. c. page 14.
[286] Chemnit harmon.

they bring costly presents with them, gold among others, which was certainly of no small use for defraying their ensuing charges. In the year 1573 when the Protestants were besieged in Rochelle by the French king's forces, God sent them in daily with the tide an infinite number of small fishes; such as before that time were never seen within that haven, and presently on the end of the siege retired again.[287] We read of Wolfangus Musculus, a late German divine, that having received by Luther's books, the light and sense of the gospel, he forsook his monastery and married; that after this he was so poor, as to let his wife go out to service, and betake himself to work with a weaver, who proved an Anabaptist. That during his abode there, he solaced himself with this distich,

Est Deus in cælo, qui providus omnia curat:
Credentes nusquam deseruisse potest.[288]

That is,

There is a God in heaven, who such as cleave
To his providence on earth, can never leave.

That the Anabaptist within a while turned him off, and he being then to seek for maintenance, was hired to work at Strasburg about the town ditch, which was then to be new cast and enlarged, and to have begun the next morning. That Bucer having notice of it, and of his parts, prevailed over night with the consul to give him a call to the work of the ministry, which he gladly embraced.

Suitable to these and the same experiments are the following acknowledgments. Jacob, "I am not worthy of the least of all thy mercies, and of all the truth which thou hast showed to thy servant: for with my staff I passed over this Jordan, and now I am become two bands," (Gen. 32:10). David, "Thou hast been my help; leave me not, neither forsake me, O

[287] *Collection* of French massacres, page 288.
[288] Melch. Adam. in *vit. Theol. Germ.* page 373.

God of my salvation. When my father and my mother forsake me, then the Lord will take me up," (Psa. 27:9-10). Another Psalmist, Psalm 71:5-7, "You are my hope, O Lord God: you are my trust from my youth. By thee have I been holden up from the womb. You are he that took me out of my mother's womb: my praise shall be continually of thee. I am a wonder to many; but you are my strong refuge." Augustine again and again to this purpose.[289] "The Lord has so looked after me, as if he had in a manner forgot the whole creation, to consider me and my ways. He so careth for every saint, as if he cared for none besides; so for all, as if he had but one to care for."[290] And Piscator in Ursin's life reports, that he, in other words Zacharius Ursinus was accustomed to say, *I had oft lain in the streets, had not the providence of God been my hostess, and afforded me a lodging. Nisi hospita fuisset divina providentia.*

§4. IV. From the effects of care ascribed to God, when Scripture speaks of him after the manner of men. For example, we men are by our cares made solicitous and thoughtful about the person or the thing cared for. So the Psalmist says of God, "I am poor and needy, and the Lord thinketh on me: you are my help and my deliverer, make no tarrying, O my God," (Psa. 40 ult.). We are rendered inquisitive what to do for them. So the Scripture brings in God, saying, "How shall I do for the daughter of my people?" (Jer. 9:7). "O Ephraim, What shall I do to thee," (Hos. 6:4). We are grieved if they miscarry. Of God it is said, his soul was grieved for the misery of Israel. (Judges 10:16). We are not content until we have taken a particular survey of whatever concerns them. So of God is said, "That he numbereth their hairs," (Matt. 10:30), "bottleth their tears," (Psa. 56:8) has a book of life for their names, (Luke 10:20) a book of providence for their members, (Psa. 139:16) and a book of remembrance for their discourses. (Mal.

[289] Sic gressus meos considerans, &c. veluti si totius creaturæ oblitus, tantum me solum consideres. August. *soliloq.* c. 14.
[290] Deus ita curat unumquemque nostrum tanquam solum curare; & its universos ut singulos. Id. *confess.* l. 3. c. 11.

3:16). Lastly, as men endeavor the good of such as they receive into their special care, and do what they can to make things operate to that end; so we know (*St. Paul says*) that "all things work together for good to them that love God; to them who are the called according to his purpose," (Rom. 8:28). Make me this assertion good, and the abundance of his care will be presently visible to any man. Now this may be done by showing how God makes use of things, and of acts of all sorts to this end.

§5. I. Of all sorts of things, whether they are natural, or artificial, necessary, or contingent, real, or imaginary. The reflexion of the sunbeams on water is a natural thing; if providence orders so, as the Moabites taking it for blood, conjecture a mutiny in the armies of the king of Israel and Judah, come up disorderly, and perish. (2 Kings 3:22-24). So this *deceptio visus* in them, worked for the church's deliverance. Those trumpets, pitchers, and lamps in the seventh of Judges were things artificial, no way able of themselves to produce such an effect, as the defeat of a huge host: yet the Lord so disposes of the sound of the trumpets, the breaking of the pitchers, and the burning of the lamps, as by them to strike a terror into the great army of Midian, and make them fly. That the fire should burn, and the sea keep its channel according to the order of nature, were necessary things: yet did providence so over-rule in the case of those three worthies in Daniel, that the fire, though it burnt up their accusers, should not so much as scorch them; and resembles in the Israelites' case, that the sea, though it swallowed up their enemies, the Egyptians, should afford a safe passage to the Hebrews. What more contingent than that Pharaoh's daughter should go with her maids to wash in the river at that very place where Moses was exposed? That seeing an infant, she should imagine it a Hebrew, be moved into pity towards it, adopt it for her own son, and light on the child's own mother to be its nurse? Yet on this did Israel's redemption much depend. There were such real alterations in the heavens, that the stars are said to have fought against Sisera in their orders. (Judges 5:20; 2 Kings 7:6-

7, *etc.*). Elsewhere an imaginary noise was so apprehended by the Syrians, as to make them fly, and leave their tents, whereon followed great plenty after a famine.

II. Acts of all sorts, whether voluntary, or involuntary, gracious or sinful. Augustus' taxing the Roman Empire, and requiring everyone to repair to his own city, was a voluntary act on his part to enrich himself: but ordered by providence to further ends: for hereby the Virgin Mary comes to Bethlehem, and Christ was there born in the place so long before prophesied of. Augustine was once out in his sermon much against his will; but providence disposed it to the conversion of a soul. The story is this: That holy man fell one day in the pulpit on a large discourse against the Manichees, contrary to his purpose and intention when he came there. At his return home spoke of it, asked Possidonius and others whether they did not observe it.[291] Their answer was, they did, and wondered. Where he said, God I believe has made "use of my oblivion and error to cure some one or other of the people." Two days after one Firmus a merchant comes to him, and falling down at his feet with, tears, confesses he had been nursed up for many years together in the heresy of the Manichees, but was that day by his sermon rightly informed, truly converted and made a catholic: which Augustine and others then hearing, "glorified and admired the profound counsel of God in converting souls when he will, and by whom he will, whether the preacher know of it or not."[292] How gracious acts, such as Obadiah's hiding and feeding the prophets, Ebed-melech's helping Jeremiah in and out of prison are subservient to providence in procuring the church's good, is easy to discern. It is so even in sinful acts themselves. Such was the Philistines invading the land of Palestine, yet there was a time when their doing it was so disposed of, as to be a

[291] Credo quod aliquem errantem in populo Dominus per nostrum oblivionem curare voluit. Possidonius in *vita August*.

[292] Profundum consilium Dei admirantes ac stupendtes glorificaverunt ejus nomen, qui cum voiuerit, & unde voluerit, & quomodo voluerit, per scientes, & per nescientes animarum operator salute. Idem. Ibid.

means of preserving David and his men. Saul was then ready to seize on his prey, but was diverted by this news, coming in that very nick of time. "Saul went on this side of the mountain, and David and his men on that side of the mountain: and David made haste to get away for fear of Saul, for Saul and his men compassed David and his men round about to take them. But there came a messenger to Saul, saying, haste thee, and come, for the Philistines have invaded the land: wherefore Saul returned from pursuing after David, *etc.*, (1 Sam. 23:26-28).

§6. The second text I have made choice of to insist on, is in the prophecy of Isaiah, chapter 27:2-3. "In that day sing ye to her; a vineyard of red wine. I the Lord do keep it, I will water it every moment: lest any hurt it, I will keep it night and day." The prophet had said before of this vineyard, that God "looking it should bring forth grapes, it brought forth wild grapes," (Isa. 5:2). But it being since purged, here he calls it a "vineyard of red wine," that is of the best, according to that in Solomon's proverbs, "Look not thou on the wine when it is red, when it gives its color in the cup, when it moves itself aright," (Prov. 23:31). So as we are here by it to understand a reformed church. Such at this day are the protestant churches come out of popery: for we may distinguish a fourfold face of the Christian visible church spoken of by divines. The first *fair*, in the apostle's time, she was then a virgin undefiled: the second *spotted*, in the succeeding age of fathers and heretics, in which traditions began to prevail, she was then a *wanton*: the third *deformed*, when popery overspread all; she was then a *whore*: the fourth *reformed*, since Luther's time: she is now a *mairon*, and may expect (so far as it shall be for her good, and her keeper's glory,) that continual irrigation, and constant custody, which is here spoken of. Such as wish and project (as some have done) the total and final ruin of the visible church, must effect it in a time that neither belongs to day nor night: for the Lord has here promised to keep it lest any hurt it, yes, to keep it night and day.

There is a three-fold preservation, which it, and the

members of it may look for from divine providence. One *from*, another *in*, and a third *by* dangers. First, from dangers, according to the promise in one of the psalms, "Because thou hast made the Lord who is my refuge, even the most high, thy habitation: there shall no evil befall thee, neither shall any plague come nigh thy dwelling," (Psa. 91:9-10). "Augustine had appointed to go to a certain town to visit the Christians there, and to give them a sermon or more. The day and place were known to his enemies, who set armed men to lie in wait for him by the way: which he was to pass, and kill him. As God would have it, the guide whom the people had sent with him to prevent his going out of the right way mistook, and led him into a by-path, yet brought him at last to his journey's end. Which when the people understood, as also the adversaries' disappointment, they adored the providence of God, and gave him thanks for that great deliverance."[293]

II. In dangers. So in Job 5:19-20. "He shall deliver thee in six troubles, yes in seven, there shall no evil touch thee. In famine he shall redeem thee from death; and in war from the power of the sword." In time of famine the widow of Sarepta's store was made to hold out. The providence of God was with Daniel in the lion's den, shutting up the mouths of those furious beasts: and with the men in the fiery furnace, giving a prohibition to the fire that it should not burn, when they were in the jaws of danger, yes of death. The church has always been a lily among thorns, yet flourishes still. This bush is yet far from a consumption, although it have seldom or never been out of the fire.

III. By danger, there is a preservation from greater evils by less. No poison but providence knows how to make an antidote; so Jonah was swallowed by a whale, and by that danger, kept alive. Joseph thrown into a pit, and afterwards sold into Egypt, and by these hazards brought to be a nursing father to the church. Chrysostom excellently, *Fides in periculis*

[293] Agnoscunt omnes miram Dei providentiam cui ut liberatori gratias meriot egerunt. Possidonius in *vita August.* chapter xii.

secura est, in securitate periclitatur.[294] Faith is endangered by security, but secure in the midst of danger, as Esther's was, when she said, "If I perish, I perish." God preserves us, not as we do fruits that are to last but for a year, in sugar; but as flesh for a long voyage, in salt, we must expect in this life much brine and pickle, because our heavenly father preserves us as those whom he resolves to keep forever, in and by dangers themselves. Paul's thorn in the flesh, which had much of danger and trouble in it, was given him on purpose to prevent pride, which was a greater evil. Lest I, he said, "should be exalted above measure through abundance of revelations, there was given me a thorn in the flesh, the messenger of Satan to buffet me, lest I should be exalted above measure," (2 Cor. 12:7). Elsewhere, having commemorated Alexander the copper-smith's withstanding and doing him much evil, (2 Tim. 4:14-15, 17-18), yes Nero's opening his mouth as a lion against him, and the Lord's delivering of him there, he concludes as more than a conqueror. "And the Lord shall deliver me from every evil work, and will preserve me to his heavenly kingdom; to whom be glory for ever and ever, Amen."

EXERCITATION III.

Hard heartedness made up of unteachableness in the understanding, untractableness in the will, unfaithfulness in the memory, insensibleness in the conscience, and unmoveableness in the affections. Metaphors to express it from the parts of man's body, stones and metals. A soft heart. Mischief, searedness, and virulency, attendants of hardness. God concurring thereunto by way of privation, negation, permission, presentation. Tradition to Satan. Delivering up to lusts and infliction.

§1. Our fourth proposition is still behind, *viz.*, divine providence is an actor even in sin itself. I shall single out hardness of heart, a sin common to all sorts of men, though in

---

[294] *Homil. xxvi.* Operis imperf. in Matt.

different degrees, intending to declare, I. What hard heartedness is. II. That it is a sin. III. That God is an actor in it. For the first. This word *heart* is of various acceptations in the scripture. Sometimes it signifies the understanding, as when it is said, "God gave Solomon largeness of heart, as the sand," (1 Kings 4:29). That is, he had an understanding full of notions, as the sea shore is full of grains of sand. Sometimes put for the will, as when Barnabas exhortsh the Christians of "Antioch to cleave to the Lord with purpose of heart," (Acts 11:23), that is, with the full bent and inclination of their wills. For as to know is an act of the understanding, so to cleave is an act of the will. Sometimes for the memory, as when the blessed Virgin is said "to have laid up all our Savior's sayings in her heart," (Luke 2:51), that is, kept them under lock and key, like a choice treasure in her remembrance. Sometimes for conscience. So the apostle speaks of a "condemning and not condemning heart," (1 John 3:20-21). Now God's deputy in point of judicature is conscience; which Nazianzen therefore calls ὀικεῖον δικαςήριον, a domestic tribunal, or a judge within doors. Lastly, Sometimes for the affections. So the prophet Ezekiel says of people, that when they sat hearing the Word, "their heart went after their covetousness;" (Ezek. 33:31), that is, their feats, and hopes, their desires, love and other affections were on shops, ships, land and other commodities, even while they were busied in the worship of God. Each of these faculties called heart in the book of God is liable to its peculiar indisposition and distemper. All put together make up the hard heartedness, of which we are treating; the particular ingredients of which are these that follow.

I. Unteachableness in the understanding. Scripture joins blinding of eyes and hardening of hearts as near a kin. "He has blinded their eyes, and hardened their heart, that they should not see with their eyes, nor understand with their heart, and be converted," (John 12:40). It is proverbially said, *Lapidi loqueris*; one had as good speak to a stone as to an unteachable man: and we are all so by nature. Where that of Paul, "The natural man receiveth not the things of the spirit of

God, for they are foolishness to him; neither can he know them because they are spiritually discerned," (1 Cor. 2:14). Such are often present at sermon, so are the pillars of stone in the church, and they understand both alike.

§2. II. Untractableness in the will. There was reason enough spoken to Sihon by Moses' messengers; but all would not incline him to yield a passage to the army of Israel in an amicable way, because he was hardened. "Sihon king of Heshbon, Moses says, would not let us pass by him, for the Lord thy God hardened his spirit, and made his heart obstinate, *etc.*," (Deut. 2:27-28, 30). So was there enough said and done to Pharaoh but still the burden of his story is this, "He hardened his heart and would not let Israel go." Steep a stone in oil, it continues to still be hard. Pharaoh had various mercies shown him, being delivered from one plague after another on Moses' prayers; but the oil of mercy could not soften him. Beat on a stone with a hammer, it is a difficult thing, and in some cases impossible to make an impression. The hammer of God's word in the mouth of Moses and Aaron, held as it were by the handle of ten notable miracles, gave ten mighty blows at Pharaoh's will; yet could make so little impression, that after the ten plagues, his heart was ten times harder than before.

III. Unfaithfulness in the memory. Pertinent hereunto is that upbraiding passage of our Savior to his disciples, "Have ye your heart yet hardened? do ye not remember?" (Mark 8:17-18) they seemed to have at present forgotten two of Christ's miracles, and are therefore charged with hard-heartedness. Let water fall on flesh it moistened it, on earth it soaks in and renders it fruitful: let it fall on a rock it runs presently off, and leaves no footsteps behind it. Where hardness of heart prevails, (Mk. 8:19-20—as here it did not, and therefore the disciples a little awakened by Christ's interrogations were able to give an account of his miracles) there is commonly no more of a chapter, sermon or pious discourse remaining in the hearer's memory, than there is moisture on a rock after a good shower of rain.

IV. Insensibleness in the conscience. St. Paul speaks of some "past feeling," (Eph. 4:19) and of others "that had their consciences seared with a hot iron," (1 Tim. 4:2) without all sense as a member once cauterized. Smite a stone as long as you will, beat it while you can stand over it, it does not complain: lay a mountain on it; it does not groan. Such are some men's consciences. Let God beat on them with sermon after sermon, cross after cross; let them have worlds of oaths, lies, cheats and other sins to answer for, they feel not the load of these mountains, do not complain of them, fast perhaps with Judas go out from the Sacrament to play the traitor, and with king Ahaz sin yet more in their distress. Although temperance, modesty, and the like dispositions be in some measure quite extinguished, yet if conscience, like Job's messenger, be still left to report the story of this desolation, there is some hope; but if, as David sometime dealt with the Philistines; all are slain, and none left alive to bring the tidings, if not only all ingenuity be banished, but the very mouth of conscience also stopped, the ease is desperate.

V. Unmoveableness in the affections. See an instance of it in king Zedekiah, of whom it is said, "He did that which was evil in the sight of the Lord his God, and humbled not himself before Jeremiah the prophet, speaking from the mouth of the Lord. And he also rebelled against king Nebuchadnezzar, who had made him swear by God: but he stiffened his neck and hardened his heart from turning to the Lord God of Israel," (2 Chron. 36:12-13). Zedekiah's heart was so obdurate, as not to have his affections moved with anything that Jeremiah could say or do.[295] Let a man go about to make an oration to a stone, be it ever so eloquent and pathetical, the stone is not affected with it; no more are many hard hearts with the voice of God's word or rod. Tell them of the beauty of Christ, they are not persuaded to love him; of the ugliness of sin, they are not induced to hate it; of the torments of hell,

[295] Non magis incepto vultus sermone movetur, Quam si dura silex aut Marpesia caut. *Virg.*

they are not moved to fear and shun it. Such is the nature and composition of hard heartedness, which was the first thing to be spoken to.

§3. The second particular is, the sinfulness of that frame, which appears from the expressions, the opposites, and the attendants of it mentioned in holy Scriptures.

I. From the expressions, which are borrowed some from the bodies of men liable to a double πῶρας, others from metals, and others from stones. πῶρος signifies not only the thick brawny skin that grows over the laborer's hand, and traveler's foot, rendering that part insensible: but also among physicians that knottiness which growth on the joints in some diseases as in a long continued gout, by them called *nodosa podagra*, and pronounced incurable by physic, *Tollere nodosam nescit medicina podagram.* Hardness of heart is expressed by this, Mark 3:5. John 12:40.[296] Elsewhere from metals, as in that of Isaiah, "You are obstinate, thy neck is an iron sinew, and thy brow brass," (Isa. 48:4). When men will no more stoop to the precepts of Christ, than a beast would do to the yoke, if his neck were of iron; sinews are instruments of motion, they all go down from the head to the body by the neck; if the neck should be stiff and the sinews of iron, it would not be possible for the head to bow down. Such is the state of obstinate persons. Yes, further, the prophet here ascribes to them a "brow of brass." The brow is that place where shame is accustomed to discover itself; this is said to be of brass, to note their impudence. A hard heart is frequently accompanied with a brazen face. And in other places from stones. (A hard heart is usually called a "heart of stone."—Ezek. 11:19, and chap. 36:26.) Yes, the hardest of all stones, the adamant. "They made their hearts as an adamant stone, lest they should hear the law," *etc.* (Zech. 7:12) stones are drier, and more inflexible than metals themselves. Chemists can distil metals, and alter the shape of them to serve their turn. But Moses could not, without a miracle, fetch water out of a

[296] Πῶρος, durities in artubus, Budæ. *commentar.*

rock. "Well might one of the fathers cry out by occasion of what happened at our Savior's passion, O the hearts of the Jews harder than rocks! the rocks rent, but their hearts were further from rending than before. The earth quacked, but their hardness continued unremoved, almost unmoved."[297] As in Jeroboam's time when the prophet cried, "O altar, altar, thus saith the Lord." It heard and rent; Jeroboam's heart was harder than the very stones and rent not.

§4. II. From the opposites of hard-heartedness; the chief in which is spiritual evangelical tenderness, promised in the covenant of grace, where it is said, "I will give them one heart, and I will put a new spirit within you; and will take the stony heart out of their flesh, and will give them a heart of flesh: (Ezek. 11:19) that is a soft and tender heart. (I do not mean that natural tenderness, caused by constitution or education, of both which it is true, that it softens the manners, and keeps them from fierceness,[298] ascribed to Rehoboam, of whom it was said, "He was young and tender-hearted, and could not withstand the children of Belial." (2 Chron. 13:7)). Such men are fitly compared to ripe plums and apricots, which however soft and smooth on the outside, yet have a hard stone within: like a brick, at first soft when the clay is fashioned, and continues so until the sun have hardened it, yes, by the pouring on of water, softened again; but if once baked in the brick-kiln, no fire will melt it, a whole sea will not moisten it afterwards. So it fares with various men formerly tender-hearted, when once hardened by conversing in the world, and baked, as it were in the kiln of custom.) That which I intend, is spiritual tenderness, ascribed to Josiah, "Because thine heart was tender, and thou didst humble thyself before God: and didst rend thy clothes, and weep before me, I have even heard thee also, saith the Lord God," (2 Chron. 34:27). As metals are melted with the fire

[297] O duriora saxis Judæorum pectora! finduritur petræ, sed horum corda durantur!—Horum immobilis duritia manet orbe concusso. Ambros.
[298] Emollit mores, nec sinit esse feros.

before they are cast in a new mold, so must every heart be melted and softened, before it come to be molded anew. The new creature is always a tame and tender creature. This is that temper which hardness of heart is opposite to, and therefore sinful.

III. From the attendants of it. Diverse have been already mentioned. I shall instance in some few more. "He that hardeneth his heart shall fall into mischief," (Prov. 28:14). Who has hardened himself against God and prospered?" (Job. 9:4). Crying sins are commonly answered with the echo of roaring judgments. Hardness being *in genere culpæ* one of the greatest evils, there must needs be mischief due to it *in genere penæ*. To this may be added stubbornness for when hardness is risen to a high degree, both senses of discipline are obstructed; the ear, "They refused to hearken, and pulled away the shoulder, and stopped their ears, that they should not hear; yes, they made their hearts as an adamant stone," (Zech. 7:11). The eye, "He has blinded their eyes, and hardened their hearts that they should not see with their eyes, and understand with their hearts," (John 12:40). Also "searedness with a hot iron," (1 Tim. 4:2) which is the next door to hanging; such as were formerly burnt in the hand, if they fall again into the hands of justice, are commonly denied their book, and sent to the gallows. Notorious malefactors are stigmatized, so are hardhearted sinners.

Lastly, virulency or bitterness of spirit against the ways and people of God. "When diverse were hardened, and believed not, but spake evil of that way before the multitude."[299] No such bitter enemies to religion as those that after some relentings return to their former frame of hard heartedness: as the worst travelling is when it has freezed after a thaw, so the worst conversing is with men of that spirit,

§5. I am now to show in the third place, that the providence of God is an actor even in this sin, and that both in

---

[299] Acts 19:9. Omnis apostata est osor sui ordinis.

partial hardness, which often befalls the elect of God, according to that, "O Lord, why hast thou made us to err from thy ways? and hardened our heart from thy fear? return for thy servant's sake, the tribes of thine inheritance,"(Isa. 58:17). And from that which is total and final, found in reprobates of whom Paul therefore says, "Whom he will he hardeneth;" (Rom. 9:18) and again, "The election has obtained, but the rest were blinded or hardened," (Rom. 11:7). Now this is done diverse ways.

I. By way of privation. As when the sun departs, darkness follows; yet the sun is no cause of darkness, but the absence of it. So when God departs in that, be it never so little, suppose but restraining grace, hardness follows, yet God is not the efficient of it. (Matt. 13:12). Time was when Pharaoh had restraining grace, while it lasted there were no violent hands laid on Moses and Aaron, by whose ministry all the plagues were brought on him. He is no sooner deprived of that, but his cruelty is let out to the full; Moses threatened with death the last time he saw his face, and all pursued with a bloody intent. Pharaoh's heart had somewhat of softness, and malliableness in it all the while this fire remained, on the removal in which, it returned to its own hardness and coldness, as metal would. As when a man holds a staff in his hand, let him but quit his hold, the staff falls immediately to the ground by its own weight.

II. By way of negation. As when God either refuses to give a people softening means, or denies his blessing on them. So when "Moses called to all Israel, and said to them, Ye have seen all that the Lord did before your eyes in the land of Egypt, to Pharaoh, and to all his servants, and to all his land. The great temptations which thine eyes have seen, the signs and those great miracles: yet the Lord has not given you a heart to perceive, and eyes to see, and ears to hear to this day," (Deut. 29:2-4). In so doing, God himself is said to harden (as St. Augustine has it[300]) when he does not soften, and to blind

[300] Dicitur Deus indurare quando non emollit; excæcare quando non

when he does not enlighten. As the sun freezes and congeals the water, not by imparting coldness to it, but by not imparting heat, and shining on it with fervent beams. So it is (the same father says) in God's hardening, who does not do it by imparting malice, but by not imparting grace. Neither does this denial affix any unlawfulness on him; as the like would do on a good man that had to give, and to spare what his neighbor stood in absolute need of; for it is not the same cause throughout, betwixt God and man: there is a mutual tie of the creatures one to another. All men are made of one blood, (as in the Acts) they are therefore bound by the law of nature to mutual helpfulness. Not so between God and the creature: for the dependence, and consequent, the tie is not mutual. We depend on God, not he on us; therefore for us not to do what he requires, is absolutely sinful, but no law binds him to give whatever is needful for us; therefore not to give, is no sin. If he please to indulge it, it is grace, and not debt; if not, the clay must not contend and find fault with the potter.

§6. III. By way of permission. Hard-heartedness is one of those evils, which God permits, but does not approve, and is accordingly included in that speech, God in time past suffered all nations to walk in their own ways, (Acts 14:16). Therefore the schoolmen on those texts, *Deus non volens iniquitatem, tu es,* (Psa. 5:5) and *Quod non volui elegerunt,* (Isa. 66:4) have founded a notable distinction between *Velle, Nolle,* and *Non velle,* which is not inconsiderable here. God is said to will a thing when he so approves of it, as to effect it. To *Nill* a thing, when he so dislikes it, as to prohibit it; *non velle*, not to will it, when he so dislikes, as not to prohibit, yes, and not to effect it, yet permits it to be for good ends. Of the Lord, it is truly said, That he wills a heart of flesh, and that he *nills* a heart of stone; as for hard-heartedness, although he frequently permit it, yet we must say he is not altogether willing to have

---

illuminat. *De Præd.* c. 1. Non indurat Deus impertiendo malitiam, sed non impertiendo gratiam, Aug. *Epist.* 105.

it, however willing to suffer it. Our temper must be that of Augustine, In a wonderful and unspeakable manner even that which is done against *his* will, is not done without his will; for it would be done, if it were not permitted; neither does he permit it without, but with his will. And again, he is so good as that he would never suffer evil, if he were not so Omnipotent, as to bring good out of evil.[301]

IV. By way of presenting objects of which our corruptions make a bad use. Isaiah's evangelical ministry made the heart of that people fat, (Isa. 6:10) and made their ears heavy, and shut their eyes. The hotter the sun is accustomed to shine, the more the dunghill is accustomed to smell. Men grow hardest under the most gospel ministry; so under mercies of all sorts. He that observes the passages of Pharaoh's story, shall find that his corruptions took many occasions from the carriage of things to harden him yet more and more. After he had been freed from two or three several plagues by Moses' prayer on his hypocritical relentings, he might perhaps begin to think that the God of Israel was such a one as might be deceived with fair shows, and so fear him less. It pleased God not to strike Pharaoh himself with any plague by the hand of Moses;[302] nor to suffer his people to rise up against him and free themselves by main force. This might happily tend to his further hardening, and put him on saying, "If he be so great a God, why doth he not smite me in mine own person, or carry out his people without me? Besides, the same plague was never twice inflicted: he saw that, and might think when one plague was over, that would not come again, and there could not come a worse than that: the God of Israel had surely done his worst already. Come we to the last scene of the tragedy after Israel was departed, things were so carried

[301] Miro et ineffabili modo non fit præter ejus voluntatem quod etiam fit contra ejus voluntatem. Quia non fieret nisi sineret, nec utique nolens sinit, sed volens. Aug. *Enchir*. I. 160. Non sineret bonus fieri male nisi omnipotens etiam de malo posset facere bene. Id. Ibid.

[302] Twiss. *Vind*. part. 2. page 94.

as to cram his corruption, and to make his heart fatter than before. The Hebrews are all found in a place with the sea before them, and great mountains on each side. Their being so pent up, encourages Pharaoh and his host The sea is long divided for Israel; the waves stand as walls on each side, the people pass through as on dry land. Why should not the sea, might he think, make way for me as well as for them? The prey is now in view, let go this one opportunity, they are gone for ever. If the waves stand up but a while longer (as they have done a good while already.) the day is ours. They pass on, and perish.

§7. V. By way of tradition to Satan. Although he has no power of enforcing, yet he has a notable slight of persuading, and by this means of hardening.[303] No doubt but Pharaoh being deluded by the magicians, who were suffered to counterfeit the same miracles which Moses did, was by it hardened through the operation of Satan. We read of an evil Spirit from God troubling Saul, (1 Sam. 16:15) and after that of many hardhearted pranks by him played, such as never were before; and "of the devil's having put into Judas' heart to betray Christ," (John 13:2) after which he was restless until he had done it; as they must needs go, our Proverb says whom the devil drives. It is strange how that man's spirit declined into further, and yet further degrees of hardness; but less strange if we consider that the devil was entered into him. Judas was first a cunning dissembler; the disciples suspected themselves as soon as him, and therefore said, *Master, is it I?* Afterwards a secret thief; for he bare the bag and filched; then a bold traitor, *What will ye give?* and hail Master. In the conclusion, a desperate self-murderer, as the most interpreters judge, in making away with himself.

VI. By way of delivering men up to their own lusts. Hear God of his own people. "My people would not hearken to my voice: and Israel would none of me. So I gave them up to their own heart's lusts; and they walked in their own

[303] Non habet potentiam cogendi, sed astutiam suadendi.

counsels;" (Psa. 71:11-12). How much more is this true of God's enemies? Pharaoh by name, see how these three lusts of his, idolatry, ambition, and covetousness concurred to the making of him so hard-hearted towards God; so hard to be prevailed with by Moses. As an idolater, he was loathe to receive a message from the God of Israel, whom he did not know. "Who is the Lord, said he, that I should obey his voice to let Israel go? I know not the Lord, neither will I let Israel go."[304] As an ambitious prince it went to his heart to have Moses control him in his own dominions, and to admit the commands of any superior Lord, so the Lord says, "Let my people go," was as fire to his bones, and enraged him, who would not hear of any lord over that people but himself. As a covetous man, he was loth to have so fat a collop[305] cut off his flank, to hear of parting with a people by whose pains in making bricks he had such daily comings in.

VII. By way of infliction and penalty. One sin is often made the punishment of another, and hardness the punishment of many sins often reiterated. "When Pharaoh saw that the rain and the hail, and the thunders were ceased, he sinned yet more, and hardened his heart, he and his servants," (Ex. 9:34). The harder they were, the more they sinned, and the more they sinned, the harder they became. Affected hardness is frequently followed with inflicted hardness. Men by customary sinning "make their hearts as an adamant stone," (Zech. 7:12—so the phrase is in Zechariah) of which it is said,

Incidit gemmas sed non inciditur ipse;
Hircino tantum sanguine mollis erit.

That is,

It cuts all stones; itself is cut of none;

---

[304] Vid. Twiss. *vindici.* part 2. Page 94, &c.
[305] Collop: 1. a small portion of food; a slice, *espage* of meat; 2. A roll of fat flesh.

It softened is by blood of goats alone.

Unregenerate persons of hard hearts usually grieve their godly friends, who are cut at the heart to see their obstinacy, as "Christ grieved for the Pharisees' hardness," (Mk. 5:5). *At non inciditur ipse.* But such a one cannot heartily grieve for himself. His heart until it come to be steeped in the blood of Christ, who is that Scape-goat in Leviticus, does not relent, or not to purpose. It were easy to add much more; but I shall now shut up all concerning this proposition, God hardens, with the saying of Hugo de sancto Victore concerning that, "God willeth evil." This is irksome to the ear, and a pious mind does not easily receive it; but the reason is not because what is said is not *well said*, but because what is well enough said is not half *well understood.*"[306]

EXERCITATION IV.

Objections against, and Corollaries from the foregoing propositions. The least things provided for. Luther's admonition to Melancthon. Maximilian's address. Pliny's unbelief. The Psalmist's stumble at the prosperity of the wicked. His recovery by considering it was not full, and was not to be final. The superintendence of Providence over military and civil affairs in particular. The Church's afflictions. Promises cautioned. Duty of casting care on God. He no author of sin. The attestation of this state, and of this writer.

§1. Two things are still remaining, *viz.* Objections against, and corollaries from the forementioned propositions: to which in their order.

Objection against the first. Some think the extending of divine Providence to all created beings, how mean

---

[306] Grave est auditu, et non facile recipit hoc pia mens; non quia quod dicitur non bene dicitur, sed quia quod bene dicitur non bene intelligitur. Hugo de S. Victor. lib. 1. *de sacram.* part. 4. c. page 12.

whatsoever, unsuitable to the perfection of God, whom, they say, it does not become to stoop so low. Epicurus is cited by Lactantius, as speaking to this purpose, and after him Horace.[307]

Answer. They speak like heathens, not knowing the Scripture, nor the power of God. The Psalmist speaks otherwise, "Who is like to the Lord our God, who dwelleth on high? Who humbleth himself to behold the things that are in heaven, and in earth. He raiseth up the poor out of the dust, and lifteth the needy out of the dung-hill. He makes the barren woman to keep house, to be a joyful mother of children," (Psa. 113:5-8). Of his care and providence it is believed and asserted by divines, that it is neither deceived nor tired, and that as the greatest things do not over-burden it, so the least things do not escape it.[308] That assertion of our Savior to his disciples, is most expressed. "Are not five sparrows sold for two farthings, and not one of them is forgotten before God? But even the very hairs of your head are all numbered," (Luke 12:6-7).

Here, by way of *corollary* let God himself alone be acknowledged the preserver and governor of all things. Let no man think by his strength of parts, or extremity of pains to take the work out of his hands, "Melancthon was beyond measure solicitous about church-affairs in that age in which he lived: insomuch that Luther once wrote to his neighbor ministers that they should do well to give him a serious admonition not to attempt the government of this world any longer."[309] That was an honest acknowledgment of Maximilian the emperor, in the time of Pope Julius the second. "*Deus æterne nisi vigilares, quam male esset mundo! quem regimus nos;*

[307] Ex hoc Deus beatus est quia nihil curat, neque habet ipse negotium, neque alteri exhibit. Lactant. *de ira Dei* c. page 4. Credat Judæus Apella. Non ego, namque Deos didici securum agere ævum. Hor.

[308] Providentia Dei nec fallitur, nec fatigatur. Eam nec magna oneerant, nec parva effugiunt. Molin. *Enod. Quæst*. page 23.

[309] Monendus est per vos Philippus ut desinat esse Rector mundi. Wolf. *Memorabil.*

Ego miser venator, et ebriosus ille ac sceleratus Julius!"[310] *O eternal Lord God if thou thyself shouldst not be watchful, how ill would it be with this world which is now governed by me, a miserable hunter, and by this drunken and wicked Pope Julius!*

§2. Against the second proposition it has been objected that there is no such thing as the providence of God superintending human affairs, especially considering the great prosperity which is enjoyed by wicked men. Pliny the great naturalist speaks of it, as a thing to be entertained with laughter rather than belief.[311] And the Psalmist's words are these, "As for me, my feet were almost gone, my steps had well-nigh slipped. For I was envious at the foolish, when I saw the prosperity of the wicked. Behold, these are the ungodly, who prosper in the world; they increase in riches. Verily I have cleansed my heart in vain, and washed my hands in innocency," (Psa. 73:2-3, 12-13).

Answer. That which then satisfied him, should now suffice to answer us. "He went into the sanctuary of God, then understood he their end. Surely thou didst set them in slippery places, thou castedst them down into destruction," (Psa. 73:17-18). Their prosperity was not full, was not to be final. 1st, *Was not full.* The places in which they stood were slippery: their felicity varnished over, but rotten within. That in St. John and only that is perfect prosperity, when the inward and outward man thrive together, "I wish above all things" (he says to Gaius) that thou mayeth prosper, and be in health, even as thy soul prospereth," (3 John 2). With them it is quite otherwise. They have, it may be, fat bodies, but lean souls; full purses, but empty heads and hearts: blest in their estates, "but cursed in their spirits," (Lam. 3:65). Have houses and lands worth many thousands, but hearts little worth, according to that, "The tongue of the just is as choice silver:

---

[310] *Historia Pontificum Romanorum contract*. Per Jacobum Revivum. page 259.

[311] Irridendum est, si quia putet illud, quicquid est summum, agere curam verum humanarum. *Natur. Hist.* l. 6. c. 7.

the heart of the wicked is little worth."[312] Do you call this prosperity? It is in truth nothing less. It is unhappiness rather, and there are those who have not stuck to name it so. *2d*, Was not to be final, "Thou castedst them down into destruction." The world came in fast on them one way; and the wrath of God came as fast another. This fair day of theirs is but a weather breeder; as a calm before an earthquake. "To me belongeth vengeance and recompence," saith the Lord, "their foot shall slide in due time: for the day of their calamity is at hand, and the things that shall come on them make haste," (Deut. 32:35). David expresses it most emphatically, "I have seen the wicked in great power; and spreading himself like a green bay tree," (a tree that retains its virility and freshness even in winter when, fruit bearing trees have cast their leaves) "yet he passed away, and lo, he was not: yes, I sought him, but he could not be found." Let such a one be sought in his counting house, which was accustomed to be the temple, in which he worshipped his God Mammon; he is not there. At court where he was so magnified, and almost adored; he is not to be found in the lodgings there. He that would find him, must seek him in hell. For there he is. This is the end of such worldly prosperity as comes from God, and yet defies him.

§3. The corollary here is, let the superintendence of Divine Providence over all human affairs, in particular over military and civil, be humbly acknowledged. I. Over military. Those Frenchmen were undoubtedly to blame, who in their flattering applauses of Richelieu, did ascribe the reduction of Rochelle solely to him, insomuch, as one of their historians writes, that in the taking of that town, neither the king nor God Almighty had a share in the action, but the cardinal himself.[313] How much safer is it for us to follow the tract of scripture? Which to show how effectual the influence of divine providence is on actions of that nature, is accustomed

---

[312] Prov. 10:20. Nulla verior miseria quam false lætitia. Nihil infelicius felicitate peccantium.

[313] Howel's *lustra Ludov*, page 166.

to compare God to whatever is necessary to secure a city besieged, for example, to weapons, walls, fortifications, watchmen and soldiers. To weapons both offensive and defensive. "Happy art thou, O Israel, who is like to thee, O people, saved by the Lord, the shield of thy help, and who is the sword of thy excellency," (Deut. 33:29). To walls, "I, saith the Lord, will be to her a wall of fire round about, and will be the glory in the midst of her. (Zech. 2:5). To fortifications, "We have a strong city, salvation will God appoint for walls and bulwarks," (Isa. 26:1). If besides bulwarks a city is compassed about with a river, chiefly if with the sea itself, we account it strongly fortified. Hear the same prophet, "The glorious Lord will be to us a place of broad rivers and streams," (Isa. 33:21). To watchmen, "Except the Lord keep the city, the watchmen waketh but in vain," (Psa. 127:1). Lastly, to soldiers, "The Lord is a man of war:" (Ex. 15:3), yes, the Lord is a whole army of men, both front and rear, "the Lord will go before you, and the God of Israel will be your rear-ward," (Isa. 52: 12).

II. Over civil affairs. I have been told that filling the late treaty of a match between the Prince of Wales that then was, and the *Infanta* of Spain, the Earl of Bristol, "then ambassador at Madrid, when things went exceedingly cross to his designs, fell into a deep perplexity, could not test for diverse nights, until a gentleman that lay in his chamber took the boldness to speak to him and said, My lord, I have observed much perplexity, and thereon much restlessness in you, I humbly beseech your lordship to consider that the world was governed five thousand years and more before you was born, and will be so when you are dead. I pray you therefore be not troubled at anything, but refer the issue to God. Whereon he is said to have fallen to rest."[314] Our way to be quiet is to do the like on all occasions; to drive up things to divine providence, and there to rest. Time was when Daniel's head and heart were filled with the visions of God; by which

[314] Report by Mr. Stephen Marshall.

the great changes that were to happen in the government of the world had been newly made known to him: *viz.* the wheeling about of monarchy from the Babylonians (who then were in the height of their power) to the Persians, there to the Grecians, and then to the Romans from a head of gold, to a breast and arms of silver, from them to a belly and thighs of brass, and from them to legs of iron, and to feet part of iron part of clay; yes in the end to a little stone-cut out without hands, which broke the image in pieces. He notwithstanding does not quarrel with providence for intending so notable, so destructive changes to the government then in being; does not go about to demand any account of it from God of such alterations, but takes himself quietly to the praise and admiration of him, by whose wisdom and power they were all in their seasons to be accomplished. "Then Daniel blessed the God of heaven. Daniel answered and said, blessed be the name of God for ever and ever, For wisdom and might are his: and he changeth the times and seasons; he removeth kings, and setteth up kings," (Dan. 2:19-21). We should do well, however things go, to make Augustine's resolution ours;[315] let the world sink or swim, be ruined or prosper, I will bless the Lord who made the world. As for the late wheelings of providence here in this island, and alterations thereon, I for my part say with Anselm once archbishop of Canterbury, "If any be able to understand them, let him give thanks to God:[316] if any are not, let him however bow down his head to worship God; not lift up his horn by way of debate and contention.

§4. An objection against the third proposition, concerning God's special care and providence over the church, and the members of it may be formed in this way. The church of all societies, the saints of all men, are the most in sufferings. Yes some churches, by name those seven in Asia, of which we

---

[315] Felix sit mundus, evertatur mundus: benedicaen Domino, qui fecit mundum. August.

[316] Si quia potest intelligere, Deo gratis agat: si non potest non immitat cornus ad ventilandum, sed submittat caput ad venerandum. Anselmus *Epistola de fide ad Urbanum*, Papage chapter 2.

read in the Revelation, have been extinguished. Where some are apt to infer want of care, and providence rather.

Answer. Be it granted that the militant church is for the most part in a suffering condition, and that Christ our head, being a man of sorrows, typified by the brazen altar on which the fire was continually burning, a wife of pleasures did not become him, nor members used to overmuch delicacy.[317] That every vessel of mercy must expect scouring in order to brightness; and however trees in the wilderness grow without culture, trees in the orchard must be pruned in order to fruitfulness, and corn-bearing fields broken up, when barren heaths are left untouched; yes, that in some particular instances the candlestick has been removed, and the place unchurched, yet the inference is not solid, because first, all afflictions are advantageous to the godly. They often help to make bad men good, always to make good men better. David could say, "It is good for me that I have been afflicted," (Psa. 119:71). Of the godly captives of Judah the Lord says, "He had sent them out of that place into the land of the Chaldeans for their good," (Jer. 24:5). Secondly, because the promises made concerning the church's preservation (such as I insisted on above in the second exercitation of this aphorism) are for the most part, misunderstood, and consequently misimproved. We learn for the future to embrace them with these three cautions.

§5. I. That the promises do in especial manner concern the church catholic, not this or that particular nation or congregation. If that in the beginning of Isaiah twenty-seventh were to be considered as a national church, we all know it has been ruined long since, notwithstanding the promise there made; which must therefore be understood of it as a type of the church universal; that is so watered and kept as to be inexpugnable. Look as by virtue of the covenant made with Noah, that the whole earth should never be again overflowed with a general deluge we may be sure it never

[317] Non oportet membra deliciari sub capite spinis coronato.

shall: yet there have since, and may still be diverse inundations, by which some parts of the earth have been, and may be laid waste; so by virtue of God's promises, we may be confident that the gates of hell shall never prevail against the whole church of Christ; yet may diverse particular churches be ruined (as those in Asia have been.) No man knows how many more may have the same line of desolation, drawn over them, Meanwhile the catholic church, still, not only continues but thrives, because like the sea, it wins in one place, what it loses in another; like the sun, it rises to the antipodes, when it sets to our hemisphere.

II. That a particular church in case it degenerate, cannot challenge such interest in the promises as it might, if it had continued pure. There was to be a time when the vineyard in Isaiah should afford red wine; then it might look for watering every moment, and being kept from all hurt, (Isa. 27:2-3). But there was also a time when it degenerated, and instead of red wine, brought forth wild grapes; when instead of keeping it, the Lord threatened to take away the hedge, and pull down the wall of it; instead of preserving it from hurt, to let it be eaten up, broken down, and laid waste; instead of watering, to command the clouds that they did not rain on it. Who knows but the Lord has said of us in this nation, as concerning the old Jewish church? "Their vine is of the vine of Sodom, and of the fields of Gomorrah: their grapes are grapes of gall, their clusters are bitter. Their wine is the poison of dragons, and the cruel venom of asps," (Deut. 32:32-34). Sure I am, he has already begun to cut our vine until it bleed; and if repentance step not in to turn away wrath, may be provoked to say of England as he once did of Palestine, "I had planted thee a noble vine, wholly a right seed: how then art thou turned into a degenerate plant of a strange vine, to me?" (Jer. 2:21). May the spirit of reformation pass through us all! So shall not iniquity be our ruin, as it otherwise may and will.

III. That the promises use not to be fulfilled all at once, but by certain periods, so as to have their gradual accomplishments. I shall instance in that of Isaiah formerly mentioned. Piscator and Scultetus on the place interpret it of that preservation which God vouchsafed the Jewish church under Ezra, Zerubbabel, and Nehemiah, in a state of peace and purity, notwithstanding the opposition made against it. Others expect a further accomplishment of it, when the Jews shall be called in a glorious manner, and "when the deliverer shall come out of Sion, and turn away ungodliness from Jacob," (Rom. 11:26). So Justus Heurnius in his evangelical embassy to the Indians toward the beginning of the fourth chapter.[318] And the author of an English treatise concerning the calling of the Jews, published by Dr. Gouge; in the year 1621. But the fattest accomplishment of it, is reserved for that period, after which, time shall be no more; when all the Israel of God shall be watered with that pure river of life, clear as crystal, proceeding out of the throne of God, and of the Lamb, spoken of in the last of the Revelation. Of this period, I find the place expounded by popish commentators, by name Sanctius, Cornelius a Lapide, and Tirinus, the last in which understands by the vineyard of red wine, *Ecclesiam beatorum*, the church triumphant: yes, and by some also of our own writers, Oecolampadius in particular, who says the things there spoken of, have respect to the day of judgment.[319]

§6. The corollary here should be that of St. Peter, a serious lesson "of casting all our care on God, for he careth for us," (1 Pet. 5:7). This has been by experience found the only best way of obtaining Christian tranquility of mind: witness that of Wencelaus, king of Bohemia, who after the routing and flight of his army, being himself taken captive by the enemy, and asked how he did, answered, "Never better; for heretofore when I had all my men about me, I could find but little time to think of God. Now being stripped of all them, I think only of him, and betake myself wholly to his providence, who I am

---

[318] Page 139, *etc.*

[319] Hæc ad diem judicii pertinent Gladius quo tunc occidetur Diabolus, est sentential Judicis, *etc.*

sure will hear me when I call on him."[320] That of Bishop Hooper (in a consolatory letter to certain godly Christians) taken in Bow-church-yard at prayer, and laid in the Counter.[321] "Let us (he says) now we are called, commit all other things to him that calls us. He will help the husband, he will comfort the wife, he will guide the servants, he will keep the house, he will preserve the goods." Above all, that of our father Abraham, who when Isaac had said, "Behold the fire and wood, but where is the sacrifice for a burnt offering?" readily answered, "My son, God will provide himself a burnt-offering:" and when he beheld a ram unexpectedly provided, to be offered up in lieu of Isaac, called the name of the place *Jehovah-jireh*, That is, in the mount of the Lord it shall be seen. See we imitate him who is the father of the faithful, in casting all our care on God, both for ourselves, and our posterity.

I. For ourselves. Behold a sure warrant for that from the pen of David, "Cast thy burden on the Lord, and he shall sustain thee: he shall never suffer the righteous to be moved:" (Psa. 55:22). Yes, from the mouth of Christ himself, "The very hairs of your head are all numbered; fear ye not. (Matt. 10:30-31). *Thou* (Augustine says) *that shalt not lose one hair, how comes it to pass that you are afraid of losing thy soul?*[322]

II. By our posterity. There are many that seem to rest on providence for themselves, who do yet macerate their hearts with carking and caring for their children, with thoughts what will become of them when they are gone. As Philip once said, "two hundred pennyworth of bread is not sufficient for them, that every one of them may take a little. And Andrew, there is a lad here who has five barley loaves and two small fishes, but what are they among so many?" (John 6:7, 9). So do these men say in their hearts, what is my small estate divided among so many children? I am not likely to leave enough for everyone to take a little. O fools, and slow of

---

[320] Btyerlink. *Apotheg.* page 20. Ex Ænea Sylvio Nunquam melius, *etc.*

[321] Mr. Fox, *Acts and Mon.* Vol. 3.

[322] Times ne animam perdas qui capillum non perdes? Aug. in Psal. 96.

heart to believe! Have you forgotten what God said to your father Abraham? Read and recall, "I am the Almighty God: walk before me, and be thou perfect. And I will establish my covenant between me and thee, and thy seed after thee in their generations, for an everlasting covenant, to be a God to thee, and to thy seed after thee," (Gen. 17:1, 7). Why may not this God be trusted with thy children too? Sure I am he should. Tell me, who provided for them before they were born? Who put care and tender affections into their mother's heart, milk into their nurse's breasts? Did not God? Is not he, that made provision for them all before they came into the world, and has comfortably maintained them ever since, fit to be trusted with them still, though you are gathered to your fathers, and see corruption? Doubtless he is.

§7. The better to help us in the performance of so important a duty as this, take along with us the following directions.

I. Get and keep assurance of a peculiar interest in the love and favor of God in Christ. We neither trust known enemies nor doubtful friends with what we account precious. They that know God to be their enemy, they that doubt whether he be their friend or not, cannot with confidence cast their whole care on him. "But he that can groundedly say with David, "I am thine, (Psa. 119:84) may go on as he does, "Lord, save me?" He that can say with assurance of faith, "The Lord is my shepherd, (may confidently add,) I shall not want," (Psa. 23:1). The spouse may go "leaning on beloved" with all her weight, when she has first been enabled to say, "My beloved is mine, and I am his. I am my beloved's, and his desire is toward me," (Song of Songs 8:5).

II. Continue in well-doing. Let them that suffer according to the will of God (St. Peter says) commit the keeping of their souls to him in well-doing, as to a faithful Creator. Look how much care a man has to please God, so much confidence may he have to cast all his care on him. While the people of Israel went up to the place of god's public worship, all the males that were of age, thrice in a year, leaving none but women and children at home, giving the enemy fair opportunity for invasion. God undertakes they shall not so much as desire or think of such a thing. "Neither shall any man desire thy land, when thou shalt go up to appear before the Lord thy God, thrice in the year," (Exod. 34:23-24).

III. Treasure up the promises, chiefly such as are made on purpose to assure us of God's caring for us: that in particular, "Let your conversation be without covetousness, and be content with such things as ye have, for he has said, I will never leave thee nor forsake thee."[323] Where there is in the original an accumulation of many negatives to make the assertion as strong as may be, it is as much as if he had said, I will never, in any wise, in any case forsake you. We are accustomed to call the bills and bonds of able men, good security. The promises of God all-sufficient are certainly so.

IV. Reflect on former experiences, and let them be encouragements for time to come. The Psalmist did so when he said, "I have considered the days of old, the years of ancient times—I will remember the years of the right hand of the Most High, I will remember the works of the Lord; surely I will remember thy wonders of old," (Psa. 77:5, 10). Some enquire why David when is asked for a word, and Abimelech told him there was none at hand but that of Goliath, called for it, and said, "There is none like to that:" (1 Sam. 21:6—it is probable he might have found some of better metal, or as good: and some perhaps fitter for his strength, but yet prefers this above all because of his experience.) God had formerly blessed him in the use of that.

§8. Against the fourth and last proposition of Providence's activity even in sin; it may be objected, and usually is, that this tenet cannot be maintained without making God the author of sin, which opinion is an abhorrence to the minds of all sound divines.

I answer, so it is, and ought to be; neither does that assertion lack the attestation of this state. Witness a modern,

[323] Heb. 13:5. Οὐ μή σε ἀνῶ οὐδ οὐ μή σε ἐγκαταλίπω.

but pregnant occurrence, yet not generally known, and therefore inserted here at *in perpetuam rei memoriam.* In the year of our Lord, 1645, there was published in London, an English book, in which God was expressly made the author of his people's sins, though not without some limitations. The assembly of divines then sitting at Westminster, took offence at this, (though some of them being acquainted with the man, whose name it bore, were ready to say of him, as Bucholcerus did of Swenckfeldius, he had a good heart, yet without a well regulated head,[324]) complained of it to both houses of Parliament. They both censured the said book to be burnt by the hand of the common hang-man; and the assembly of divines agreed on a short declaration, *Nemine contradicente*, by way of detestation of that abominable and blasphemous opinion, which was also published under that title, July 17, 1645. and in which we meet with these among other expressions, "That the most vile and blasphemous assertion, by which God is avowed to be the author of sin, hitherto by the general consent of Christian teachers and writers, both ancient and modern, and as well papists as protestants, has been not disclaimed only, but even detested and abhorred.—Our common adversaries, the papists have hitherto only calumniously charged the doctrine of the reformed churches with so odious a crime (in the meantime confessing that we do in words deny it, as well as they themselves) now should this book be tolerated, they might insult over us, and publish to the world, that in the church of England it was openly, and impudently maintained, that God is the author of sin, than which there is not any one point, by which they labor in their sermons and popular oration to cast a greater odium (though most injuriously) on the reformed churches—We are not, for the reverence or estimation of any man's person, to entertain any such opinions as do in the very words of them asperse the honor and holiness of God, and are by all the churches of Christ rejected."

---

[324] Habuit cor bonum, sed non caput regulatum. Scultet. *Annal.* Dec.

This premised, I now assert positively and considerately (yet without obliging myself to make good every phrase that has fallen unadvisedly from the pen of every writer) that what protestant churches say in their public confessions, and allowed protestant writers in their books, concerning God's having a natural influence on the sinful acts of creatures, but without a moral influence on the sinfulness of their acts; his inflicting hardness of heart as a punishment to former sins; his directing and ordering great sins to great good, Joseph's vendition, to the church's preservation, yes, the crucifixion of Christ, to the salvation of the elect, do neither really, nor in due construction amount to the making of God the author of sin. To what has been elsewhere further said of this copious argument, I refer the capable reader to my *Tactica Sacra*[325], lib. 1. cap. 1. §5. et ibidem, cap. 6. §4.

FINIS.

---

[325] Arrowsmith, John, *Tactica sacra, sive, De milite spirituali pugnante, vincente, & triumphante disseratation, tribus ibris comprehensa.* Cantabrigiæ : J. Field, 1657.

www.ingramcontent.com/pod-product-compliance
Lightning Source LLC
LaVergne TN
LVHW010935100826
845153LV00001B/41

* 9 7 8 1 9 3 8 7 2 1 5 1 9 *